Northwestern University
STUDIES IN *Phenomenology &*
Existential Philosophy

On Emotional Presentation

Alexius Meinong

Translated, with an Introduction, by

With a Foreword by

On Emotional Presentation

MARIE-LUISE SCHUBERT KALSI

J. N. FINDLAY

NORTHWESTERN UNIVERSITY PRESS

EVANSTON   1972

Originally published in German under the title "Über
emotionale Präsentation" in the *Sitzungsberichte der
philosophisch-historischen Klasse der Kaiserlichen Aka-
demie der Wissenschaften in Wien,* Volume 183/2 (1917).
Reprinted in *Alexius Meinong: Gesamtausgabe,* Vol. III:
Abhandlungen zur Werttheorie, published by the Akademische Druck- und Verlagsanstalt, Graz, Austria, 1968.

Contents

[ix]

Foreword

ON EMOTIONAL PRESENTATION, published in 1917 toward the end of Meinong's life, is one of the most magnificently thorough of his works and perhaps the only fully lucid and intelligible theory of the possibility of there being values at once given in and through emotion and yet also ontologically independent of emotion or of any subjective attitude. But it is also, like all Meinong's works, of very great difficulty, and this difficulty is augmented a hundredfold in any attempt to translate it or read it in translation. It was therefore with mixed incredulity and delight that I heard of Mrs. Kalsi's brave attempt to render it into English: having been long accustomed to being one of the few Anglo-Saxons who had actually visited Meinong's thought-territory and lived with its Germanic complexity, instead of contenting myself with lying travelers' tales about it, it was strange to think that this territory might perhaps be becoming part of our own Anglo-Saxon domain and that its austere beauty and rigor might at last come to be fully appreciated among so much softer landscape. I have gladly complied with a request that I should recommend and introduce what Mrs. Kalsi has done, and I have also taken it on myself, out of piety toward the memory of Meinong and determination that he should be as well represented in English as possible, to do as much as I could toward improving the faithfulness, the completeness, and the linguistic and philosophical lucidity of Mrs. Kalsi's text. But I have worked within the framework of her sentences, and my editing would not have been possible without her basic labors.

I shall in what follows give a brief section-by-section setting-forth of the main points made in Meinong's remarkable treatise: I may be excused from doing more, since I have expounded and criticized the doctrine of Emotional Presentation in the tenth chapter of my book *Meinong's Theory of Objects and Values* (1963) and more briefly in the second chapter of my *Axiological Ethics* (1970). Those who are perplexed by difficult doctrinal points in the treatise can get what I have to offer there rather than here. My section-by-section summary will, however, be preceded by a brief characterization of Meinong's total enterprise and a comparison and connection of it with the profoundly analogous enterprise of Husserl, both of whom may be said to have expounded one and the same philosophy. But they were deeply similar in their methods and conclusions *not* because they influenced each other—their relation was one of mutual irritation rather than influence—but because both grew out of a soil fertilized by the philosophical genius of Brentano. Both Meinong and Husserl went much further than Brentano, and in somewhat different directions, but in a sense neither of them ever went beyond Brentano's fundamental inspiration.

Meinong tells us in his *Selbstdarstellung* (1923) that, while he cannot offer us a good definition of philosophy, it is undoubtedly a discipline that in some fashion revolves around psychology (not necessarily around empirical psychology): it is a treatment of all that is real or unreal, mind-dependent or mind-independent, from the standpoint of a mind that can be aware of it and that can have other more complex attitudes toward it. This also, of course, is the attitude of Husserl, to whom objects, however important ontologically, are only of consequence to the extent that they are capable of being given to, or set up for, our thinking references. Both philosophers see in intentionality, mental directedness, the power of experience to be *of* anything whatever, without needing to make what it is thus *of* a real part of itself, the central feature of mental life, one which may indeed be elucidated and analyzed but which cannot be reduced to anything radically different or more basic. Such intentionality can be turned outward upon the objects of nature, without thereby absorbing their characters, and it can likewise be turned inward upon itself, which for Meinong and Husserl alike always involves a secondary act which either recalls or directly perceives a primary one. But both philosophers allow intentionality to develop in a third direction, against which the aging Brentano vigorously but vainly inveighed: it is possible for our conscious experience to intend ideal or subsistent objects of various sorts—relations, groups, complexes, states of affairs, truths, propositions, meanings, synsemantic senses, etc.—which are not part of, though they have necessary relations to, the "reality of things." Husserl here built up a formal ontology and a formal apophantics which are precisely parallel to what Meinong calls his object-theory (*Gegenstandstheorie*). But both philosophers also daringly go beyond the domain of the subsistent, Husserl in believing in meanings or thinkables to which no reality can in principle correspond, and Meinong in enriching his object-theory with several genera of incomplete or self-contradictory objects (the square as such or the round square) which must have a definite internal makeup if only in order *not* to exist or *not* to subsist anywhere. Both philosophers further believe in the interesting contrast between certain immediate, not normally considered objects *through* which we refer to other objects (the noemata or thinkables of Husserl and the auxiliary objects of Meinong—what is covered, e.g., in the sense of "the victor of Waterloo") and certain other more ultimate objects (the *Zielgegenstände* of Meinong or the objects proper of Husserl) intended by their means. Husserl has here refinements and exactitudes that we do not find in Meinong: the Kantian stress on the development of intentionality in time through a "synthesis" of many partial references, and the careful clarification and use of the distinction between "fulfilled" or fully intuitive references and those that are "empty" and merely pointing.

Both Meinong and Husserl further work within the tripartite mental classification of Brentano, though they carry out many minor modifications upon it. There are, in the first place, *Vorstellungen*, or ideas, which present objects to us for further mental treatment or response, there are judgments or convinced attitudes, in which we are alive to the distinction between reality and unreality, truth and falsehood, and there are, finally, intentions belonging to the related spheres of feeling and emotion on the one hand, and desire and volition on the other, in which we can be said to take up stances somewhere between wholly favorable acceptance at the one end and wholly unfavorable rejection at the other. Meinong and Husserl likewise draw many parallel distinctions *within* each class of mental intentions. There is for Meinong a Lockean distinction between the basic ideas of simple perception (the *infima* or lowest-order ideas) and the higher-order ideas which project relations, groups, and complexes as higher-order objects (the *superiora*). Husserl has parallel distinctions. If we then turn to the region of judgments, Meinong is deeply interested in the distinction between judgments of being, in which belief has only one object, as it were, and judgments of so-being or predication, in which one thing is believed *of* another. In Husserl there is a not wholly parallel distinction between the one-rayed, nominal reference which seizes an object all in one blow, as it were, and many-rayed references which are built up and build their objects up synthetically. There are likewise parallel distinctions drawn between evident and nonevident belief and between total and partial belief (the latter of which Meinong covers by the term surmise or *Vermutung*) and also a recognition of a class of judgment-like attitudes in which belief is, as it were, suspended. These are Meinong's celebrated class of *Annahmen* or assumptions, to whose analysis he devoted the treatise *Über Annahmen* and whose concept is roughly covered by the Husserlian term "neutrality-modification" (see *Ideas*, §§109–12). From the thetic or doxic sphere of judgments, both philosophers go on to the region of emotional-conative intentionality, but here Meinong draws an interesting distinction, not fully developed by Husserl, between serious experiences (*Ernsterlebnisse*), in which we "really and truly" want or feel about something, and imaginative or counterfeit experiences (*Phantasieerlebnisse*), where it is only *as if* we were doing so. Thus I may experience an imaginary love or hate or desire when I read a story, much as I may also experience imaginary convictions: the *Annahme* or assumption is in fact for Meinong an imaginary judgment. The notion of mental counterfeits of this sort seems true to experience and profoundly illuminating.

In yet another important direction there is a remarkable parallelism between the intentionalism of Meinong and Husserl: both believe in an element *immanent* in experience (something remotely like the "intentional forms" of the Schoolmen) in virtue of which a reference which *transcends* experience is rendered possible. Both derive this doctrine from the Polish philosopher Twardowski, and both make frequent use of his technical term *Inhalt*, content, to stand for the assumed moment *in* experience which renders transcendent reference possible. (It is, e.g., only by experiencing psychological "extensity" as a psychic content that the quite different physical property of extension can be brought into our ken.) Meinong continues to use the term *Inhalt* at all stages of his philosophizing, but in Husserl the concept speedily becomes vestigial. While in the *Logical Investigations* the *Materie* or matter of an intention mediates its objective direction, in the *Ideen* we have only the sensuous matter, or *hylē*, which has to be inspired by an *Auffassung* or conception in order to bring some correlated object before us. The matter-content conception is, however, of central importance for both Meinong and Husserl *at higher levels*, when we consider their remarkable view, based on direct interior evidence, that the *act-element* in an intention, the element of *manner* which represents the *way* in which a state of mind is directed to its object, e.g., believingly, approvingly, can itself act as a quasi-content and can serve to present, to a more loftily ensconced vision, a modified and altered object. Thus the synthesis and the negation which occur in judgments and assumptions, in which a character is predicated or denied of a primary object, can become the vehicle through which a new higher-order *objective* synthesis, positive or negative, a *geurteiltes* or judged, as opposed to a *beurteiltes* or merely judged about, becomes accessible to higher-order contemplation. We become aware of what Husserl called variously states of affairs (*Sachverhalte*) or propositions (*Sätze*), while Meinong coined for them the term "objective" (*Objektiv*), and opposed them to objecta (*Objekte*) or lowest-order objects. And not only can objectives or states of affairs be thus presented to higher-order consideration, but the various judgmental modes of the acts directed upon them, modalities such as inner evidence, partial and suspended conviction, etc., can project new *objective* modalities upon the states of affairs correlated with them, so that we are now faced not merely with facts but with possibilities, necessities, impossibilities, and probabilities of varying grade, concerning which in their turn there can be higher-order judgments and acts of evident knowledge. From, e.g., coming to consider S as P in a peculiar, rationally balanced manner, we may come to apprehend and know the new, higher-order fact that it is to a certain degree probable that S is P. And we must not confuse the objective *Seinshöhe* named by the word "probability" with the inwardly evident surmise and superimposed evident judgment in which this comes through to us. All this is established in Meinong's xvi / ON EMOTIONAL PRESENTATION

monumental *Über Möglichkeit und Wahrscheinlichkeit* (1915), but there is a brief recognition of the possibility of such presentation of objectives by way of subjective modalities in Husserl's *Ideas* (e.g., § 114).

But both philosophers now advance to a crowning recognition: that not only idea-characters and belief-characters project objective lights and shadows on the world, but that this is also true of feeling-characters and wish-characters and will-characters. How we feel toward things and what we demand of things "raises," as even Hume in the Appendix to his well-known *Inquiry* admits, "a new creation"; objects come before us in a new light as precious or base, lovely or unlovely, authentically true or spuriously false, or as simply attractive or unattractive, and a set of corresponding "oughts" or requirements therewith also qualifies the objective scene, so that we can say or see that someone ought to behave thus or thus, that this or that conclusion is to be drawn, that these qualities ought not to be put in the neighborhood of those, or even that foods and drinks, those alleged preserves of purely personal taste, should be compounded in this or that manner. And where there can be this sort of objectivity, there can also be evident knowledge; and we reach the ultimate paradox that love and faith, with their strong element of feeling and wish, may nonetheless be revealers of the nature of things. This doctrine of emotional presentation is the theme of Meinong's treatise that we have before us, but it is equally the theme of Husserl's *Ideen*, §§ 116, 117, 152, and elsewhere. Meinong does not seem to have been influenced in this direction by Husserl, though the *Ideen I* was published in 1913, before *Über emotionale Präsentation* in 1917. A wry, typed commentary of Meinong's on the *Ideen* makes no reference to the passages in question, and Meinong had already taken up his objectivist stance toward values in a paper given at a Bologna Conference, whose contents are detailed in "Für die Psychologie und gegen den Psychologismus in der allgemeinen Werttheorie" (*Logos*, 1912).

Meinong and Husserl are therefore alike in giving us a comprehensive sketch of the logical geography of conscious experience, both as regards its subjective and objective dimensions, and in showing up the necessary interrelations of such dimensions, and in so providing us with a theory of mind of which all analyses in terms of mental contents or mental or bodily behavior give us nothing but the trimmings. Together with Brentano they are *the* philosophers of this region, much as Aristotle was *the* philosopher of medieval times. But there are, of course, profound differences between our two exponents of intentionalism: Meinong was infinitely analytic and argumentative, never coming to a conclusion except after an exhaustive examination of alternatives, whereas Husserl, after an initial phase of exhaustive argument in the *Logical Investigations,* came to rely more and more on intuitive methods, methods which, since his intuitions were good, were also in general profitable, though in some cases not so much so. There was also the conspicuous difference, not so important for our purpose, between the extreme idealism into which Husserl fell in his later work and the extreme realism which became more and more characteristic of Meinong. Husserl progressed in the *Ideen* from a valuable methodological proposal to put belief in the natural world "out of action," in order to cast light on the subjective structures through which this world, and every other possible kind of transcendent world, real or unreal, might come to be given, to a position in which the "brackets" thus put around objects became permanent, and nothing except conscious selves and their conscious references could claim any simple, nonrelative being. In so doing he committed himself to old, refutable confusions of knowing with making, without even the interesting cross-lights provided by Kant's transcendental object or without even the exciting metaphysical mythology of a Berkeley or a Fichte. Meinong, on the other hand, spent his time industriously removing all brackets from the most unacceptable intentional objects, so that not only the golden mountain and the round square but even the Russellian class of all classes not members of themselves acquired some sort of independent status as an object. The moral of all this is perhaps to cry a plague on both houses and to cry for the right blend of the bracketless and the bracketed, of what Ingarden called ontological autonomy and heteronomy, in our theory of mind, fact, and the world.

After this long comparative characterization of Meinong's enterprise, we may proceed to our section-by-section statement of the main points made in the treatise before us. Section 1 of *On Emotional Presentation* introduces the basic notion of "presentation," the bringing of an object before consciousness, which is primarily the function of the idea or *Vorstellung*, the presentation par excellence. (The translation of *Vorstellung* by "idea" has some disadvantages, since *vorstellen*, the corresponding verb, has then to be translated by "having an idea of." It would, however, be impossible to use a traditionalism like "representation," owing to its similarity to "presentation," which would in fact be the more natural word, were it available. The term has the further disadvantage that in English an "idea" is often a *vorgestelltes*, something thought of or imagined, rather than the act or experience of having this present to oneself.) Meinong states his view, argued for in *Über Annahmen* and elsewhere, that it is only at the level of the judgment or judgment-like experiences, in which something is either taken to exist or to be of this or that character, that objects are actually *presented:* there is indeed a more basic form of unanalyzed acquaintance which now goes by the name of an "idea," but full presentation involves the like of judging. Meinong further defends the view that our consciousness of our own mental life involves no Lockean "ideas of reflection": our *having* a certain mental orientation is a sufficient foundation for our becoming conscious of it or making assertions regarding it. (Such assertion is of course the function of a secondary act.) There is therefore such a thing as "self-presentation" in the introspective realm as opposed to the other-presentation (*Fremdpräsentation*) normally exercised by ideas. Other things require ideas to introduce them, but our own experiences introduce themselves. The moral of the section is that "presentation," the bringing of objects before consciousness, is variously effected and by more than one conscious factor.

In Section 2 Meinong deals with objections to the notion of self-presentation raised by his pupil Ernst Mally: the kind of self-presentation objected to is not the presentation of self to some *other* assessing experience but the presentation of self to self in which Brentano believed and against which Mally brings a Russellian charge of senselessness. Meinong discusses various legitimate and illegitimate senses and cases of self-reference and arrives among other things at the view that the objects projected by certain viciously circular references, e.g., certain forms of the Liar paradox, are certainly worse than self-contradictory: they are so ill-formed that they do not even achieve the status of the absurd. Meinong does not, however, hold that it is senseless to talk of them: the class of all classes not members of themselves is not to be compared with an ill-formed structure like *beautiful in truly*. Meinong speaks of defective objects in such a case; and, while we may demur at his allowing such objects to parade the world unbracketed, they certainly enter into the description of the intentions that conceive them and reject them and the logical principles that rule them out. It is not, however, possible in a brief introduction like the present one to argue for the Greek view that one has in a sense to be something in order not to be at all rather than to believe that all this has been finally disposed of by modern analysis.

In Section 3 Meinong luxuriates in drawing distinctions among a great number of different sorts of presentation. Our intellectual experiences of idea and judgment both *present themselves* as *total experiences* to inner observation and therefore furnish us with a case of *self-presentation* which is also a case of *total presentation,* but they are also capable of presenting other things in virtue of that puzzling internal feature which Meinong calls their *content:* such presentation is therefore a case of *other-presentation* (since their objects are other than themselves) which is also a case of *partial presentation* (since their "content" or object-determining feature is not *all* that they are). Meinong now points out that not all cases of other-presentation are also cases of partial presentation, but that there are some cases of *other-presentation* which are also cases of *total presentation.* In all the cases where I am aware of foreign experiences, I make reference to them in virtue of having somewhat similar experiences myself, experiences which, however, normally lack the full seriousness of the foreign experience presented. Thus I manage to refer to the anguished discovery of the dead Romeo by Juliet by counterfeit states of belief and dismay in myself. In such a case we have my *whole* unserious state of mind helping to present *another* whole serious state of mind, and we have therefore a case of *total presentation* which is also a case of *other-presentation.* Partial presentation which is also self-presentation would occur where some element in an experience, e.g., the act or the content, offered itself to abstractive interior examination.

This leads on in Section 4 to the further query whether there may not also be such a thing as partial presentation in the realm of feeling, whether my having a certain sort of feeling toward something may not, in addition to helping to present feelings in myself or in other beings, also serve to add a note to objects which is not a feeling but is projected by a feeling functioning as a sort of content. This anomalous functioning of feeling will be a case of other-presentation which is also a case of partial presentation, as in the case of normal content-presentation; only in this case it will be the *act-aspect* of the feeling (the noesis in Husserl's sense) that will be functioning presentatively. Meinong thinks that there are indubitable cases of such partial presentation, as where an object seems objectively boring or funny. He repudiates the suggestion that in such cases we are conceiving of the object as evoking boredom or amusement in ourselves: nothing need be further from consciousness than the feelings in question. To be ridiculous is as objective a determination "phenomenologically" as being crooked or slow. Section 5 argues for similar partial presentation in the case of desires. Things are given as being such as to have an oughtness-to-be—"oughtness" rather than "obligation" is the inevitable translation of *Sollen* when one is dealing with things rather than agents—and as having an instrumental oughtness-to-be for the sake of something else. In neither case need desires, though effecting presentation, be part of what is presented.

In Section 6 Meinong tries to unravel certain problems concerning act-presentation, i.e., situations where a mental orientation is used as a quasi-content to apprehend similar acts in other real or imaginary persons or oneself in the past. He is puzzled by our capacity to have experiences which counterfeit *both* serious and counterfeit experiences, as when I merely *remember* the contrast between first *perceiving* something and then merely *remembering* it, or as when I remember the changes in conviction regarding some doctrine that I underwent in the past. He dwells also on what is involved in borrowing the object of a presuppositional experience, as when, in thinking of some belief, I obliquely intend the object of that belief. Many modern analysts would refuse to see in all this genuine psychology, but can it be doubted that something comes before us in a queer and different way when we see it as the object of someone else's belief? He then goes on in Section 7 to give a full-scale treatment of the enigmatic notion of "content" which has dominated his thought from the beginning. He attempts to pin down the content of an experience by describing it as the experiential element which connects the experience with an appropriate object, while the act-side of an experience is what is involved in intending an object in a certain manner.

But it remains unclear whether this "element" is something metaphysically postulated or introspectively discerned or merely a way of conceiving of the situation. It seems plain, however, that the second of these three alternatives must be the one he accepts, and that he believes that contents can be prized loose from objects with varying difficulty in different cases and that, when so prized loose, an ideal relation of "adequacy" can be seen to hold between the two independently discernible moments, a relation so far from involving identity that it does not even involve similarity. Thus extensity, as an experienced content, is quite different from extension, the objective feature that it presents, and evident conviction is likewise quite different from the objective "factuality" that it brings to mind; but there is a necessary relation of "adequation" between content and object in the two cases. Meinong emphasizes that presentation by contents is presentation by dissimilars, whereas presentation by acts—as when my own conviction enables me to be aware of yours—is presentation by similars.

Section 8 connects the highly technical concept of a psychological presupposition—the relation of an experience to another experience on which it builds and from which it "borrows" its object—with the equally technical concept of a founded object, i.e., an object which, like a relation or a group, presupposes more basic objects on which it is built and on which it supervenes with ideal necessity. As some cases of psychological presupposition involve no necessity—not all tastes are necessarily connected with their borrowed objects—the notion of psychological presupposition has a wider extension than the notion of founded object. Section 9 deals with a small controversy which I shall not attempt to summarize.

In Section 10 Meinong gives a brilliantly original treatment (inspired in part by the work of his pupil St. Witasek) of the differences among feelings and desires according to the character of the intellectual presuppositions from which they borrow their objects. He points out that what we call aesthetic feelings and desires have as their required presuppositions ideas of thus-and-so-ness and assumptions to the effect that something is thus-and-so, but that they are indifferent to the real being or being-the-case of that which they want or in which they take delight, and that they accordingly do not require to be built upon judgments or other "penetrative" experiences. Aesthetic interest ends with surface appearance: questions of reality which are not questions of seeming reality have no meaning for it. The experiences that we call valuational, on the other hand, are all experiences in which real being or being-the-case is of vital concern: we cannot be said to value anything if our interest ends with mere contemplation. There are, however, other cases of feeling and desire which require a "penetrative" rather than a merely "contemplative" foundation but which yet do not amount to valuations: these are the knowledge-feelings and the knowledge-desires which are marked off by the fact that in them we do not care about the objective content of what is known to be real or the case—its contrary would, if proven real, be equally acceptable. It is in them—the *act* of evident judgment or knowledge—in which we have satisfaction, not the object or content connected with this. This does not, however, mean that knowledge-feelings or knowledge-desires are desires directed upon knowledge as their intentional object: knowledge satisfies them, but "the facts" are their goal. If they were intentionally concerned with knowledge, if they were, e.g., desires *of* knowledge instead of desires *to* know, then they would be simple cases of valuation in which knowledge was the object prized; they would be *Wissenswertgefühle* or *Wissenswertbegehrungen* instead of *Wissensgefühle* and *Wissensbegehrungen*. But those who ask questions or engage in science do not think greedily about knowledge and its excellences: they yearn for "the facts" or the "real structures of things," whatever these facts or real structures may turn out to be. Meinong finally deals with a class of desires and feelings which confine themselves to the experiential act and care nothing for the distanced thus-and-so-ness of objects (as do aesthetic attitudes) or for the reality or factual being of the same (as do scientific and valuational attitudes). We are left, therefore, with four classes of emotional-desiderative experiences: (*a*) those that do not go beyond the act-side of experience—the desires and feelings connected with eating and drinking are a case in point; (*b*) those that are aesthetic and stay within the limits of the content of an idea or an assumption while spurning questions of reality; (*c*) those that are scientific and stay within the limits of the act-side of believing and knowing intentions; (*d*) those that are valuational and involve the content-side of believing and knowing intentions. It is all-important that we should not confuse (*a*), (*b*), and (*c*) with (*d*), as is done when people conceive that sensual

men are invariably out for pleasure, that artists are invariably
out for aesthetic experience, or that scientists always thirst
after knowledge. Meinong's distinctions in this section are subtle but true; and it is worthwhile pondering them, even if this
involves accustoming oneself to barbarisms like "knowledge-
value-feelings" and "judgment-act-desires," etc.

In Section 11 Meinong is now in a position to distinguish
four distinct objects of feeling-presentation: the agreeable (dis-
agreeable), projected by idea-act-feelings, though not involving
feelings as part of their meaning; the beautiful (ugly), projected by idea- and assumption-content-feelings (though themselves involving nothing psychologistic); the true and probably
true (false and doubtful), in a special axiological sense, which
are projected by judgment-act-feelings; and finally the valuable
or good (disvaluable or bad), projected by judgment-content-
feelings. Meinong recognizes that these four objects are objects
of higher order, what Moore called "consequential properties":
they presuppose other properties as their basis, and it must
always be in virtue of being something else as well that something is agreeable, beautiful, true, or good. The agreeable and
the beautiful have, further, an objectum-like character, in
that they attach simply to simple objecta, whereas the "true,"
probably true, and valuable attach most naturally to objectives
and have themselves objective-character. To the four new
classes of object Meinong gives the new name "dignitatives,"
and there are, accordingly, hedonic, aesthetic, logical, and
valuational dignitatives, casting their peculiar lights and
shadows on the more basic objects present in this world. These
lights and shadows are part and parcel of the phenomena,
even though they may have been put there by our feelings
rather than by our mere sensations. But desires also function
presentatively and people the world with a host of objective
demands and requirements, some hedonic ("There ought to
be more pepper in this"), some aesthetic ("That blue ought
to be paler"), some logical ("The same explanation ought to
apply to this fact"), some valuational ("Men ought to practice
generosity"). And there is a curious bifurcation in the desiderative realm between simple *Sollen,* or oughtness, and *Fürsollen*
or *Zweckmässigkeit,* or instrumental oughtness for the sake of
something else. The objective oughts or demands projected by
our desires (but not involving desire as part of their meaning) are called by Meinong "desideratives"; there are therefore

eight basic desideratives corresponding to the four dignitatives. (There is no merely instrumental agreeableness, beauty, truth, or goodness.) Obligation, the notion that leaps to mind when the German word *Sollen* is used, is only a special case of a valuational desiderative. I do not imagine that this will satisfy those Anglo-Saxon moralists who see all excellence in terms of their duty or of what would be their duty if they only had the power.

In Section 12 we pass from emotional presentation to emotional knowledge. Plainly, if our feelings and desires project objective lights and shadows upon the world, there may be cases in which such projections coincide with what is independently there and can be known to be so. We can see that in being thus and thus stirred and moved by objects, and seeing them in corresponding lights, we are also penetrating to what objects most intimately are. We are reaching the point argued by Plato that there are true and false pleasures, and are accepting the view that the modern or Humean diremption of emotive from descriptive meaning represents an impoverishment rather than a disentanglement of reality and truth. Meinong does not, however, indulge in such rhetoric as we are here yielding to, but dwells on the difficulty of finding firm cases of axiological or deontological knowledge, which in the first case he approaches in terms of the notion of justified emotion or justified desire. He finds the most evident cases of such justification in the relative rather than the absolute field: if B justifiably moves us, and A is a necessary precondition of B, then we are justifiably moved by A *for the sake of B*, and such a conditional justification makes no sense unless there is an absolute justification on which it rests (an argument of some weight). In the same way, if A rightly moves us, then the absence of A should move us to the same degree but in an opposite sense (an extremely doubtful example). It is in the realm of the scientific feelings and desires that Meinong finds the least questionable example of unconditional justification. The true and the probable, taken for once in a *non*axiological sense, have plainly a prerogative in this sphere, and it does not make sense to hold that we should be equally justified or unjustified in preferring the improbable or the false. Truth and probability (considered nonaxiologically) therefore have an *objective* dignitative attaching to them, to which the name of "logical dignity" can be given. But in the realm of the ethical or the aesthetic, let alone the hedonic, we have no such plain evidence of the presences of dignities as opposed to dignitatives. Meinong argues, however, that even in the realm of the *a priori* there is a place for rational surmises as well as evident judgments, and that the mere fact that we are disposed to react emotionally or desideratively to some object, and to ascribe a dignitative or a desiderative to it, affords *some* reason for thinking that the dignitative or desiderative in question really attaches to the object. Such evidence for surmise becomes more and more weighty, the more people agree in the reaction and the ascription.

This point of view is further developed in Section 13, where Meinong, after admitting the legitimacy of the concept of what he calls "personal value," defined in terms of the *capacity* of certain objects to arouse emotional and desiderative reactions in certain subjects, also argues for the legitimacy and value of the concept of impersonal values which, though emotionally and desideratively presented, belong *absolutely* to the objects to which they appear to belong and are not merely values *for* this or that person. The scientific development of impersonal value-theory remains a task for the future, as important as the development of personal value-theory, which has so far been so successful.

Section 14 puts forward certain rather disputable theorems regarding desires and desideratives, in which nineteenth-century determinism plays an unacknowledged part: that it is impossible, strictly speaking, to desire the determinately actual or nonactual and that only the "possible" can be desired. But possibility is analyzed by Meinong in terms of the metaphorical involvement (*Implektiertsein*) of certain partially determined objects in the wholly determinate content of what exists or subsists, whether in the future or the past, so that his absolute oughts become in a sense copybook prescriptions incapable of being carried out in the actual world and having practical meaning for us only on account of our restricted view of real objects. *Du kannst, denn du sollst* seems in fact to be an axiom. Such a conclusion is plainly unacceptable, but it is not the place to argue for this here.

In his last section Meinong develops his empiristic approach to the axiological *a priori* more fully. Personal values, the capacities of objects to arouse attitudes in persons, are wholly different from impersonal values which, though presented through attitudes, contain no reference to attitudes in their inner meaning or being. But personal values may nonetheless serve as the empirical grounds for impersonal values, just as measurements of figures may provide inadequate evidence of necessary geometrical relationships. What Meinong is arguing for applies of course to all the cases of emotional and desiderative presentation: in all these fields there may be dignities or objective dignitatives, and desiderata or objective desideratives.

It only remains to summarize some of the main technical terms of the treatise and to connect them with their German originals. The term "idea" translates *Vorstellung* and is to be understood as the experience in which something is put before the mind, whether perceptively or cogitatively, but not necessarily in a fully interpretative, predicative manner: it is *not* to be understood as *what* is put before the mind or as an *image* or likeness of the same. "Having an idea of" translates *vorstellen*. "Content" translates *Inhalt,* the object-presenting side of ideas and other experiences, and this must *not* be identified with the presented object *or with any of its features or aspects.* "Act" translates *Akt,* the side of intentional experience which can vary independently of the object and which corresponds to the *manner* in which the object is intended: *it has nothing whatever to do with activity as opposed to passivity.* "Judgment" and "judgment-like" translate *Urteil* and *urteilsartig,* respectively, while "surmise" or "presumption" translates *Vermutung,* and "assumption" *Annahme.* "Evidence" is used to translate *Evidenz,* though the sense is rather that of "self-evidence" or "inward evidence." "Being" translates *Sein,* and "ontic level" or "level of being" *Seinshöhe* (= degree of possibility or probability). "Exist," "existence" translate *existieren, Existenz;* while "subsist," "subsistence" translate *bestehen, Bestand.* "Factuality" translates *Tatsächlichkeit,* while for *Aussersein,* the status of all objects whatever, regardless of their being or nonbeing, no translation has been attempted. "Being-thus-and-so" translates *Sosein,* the being of a certain sort or the having of certain characters. "Object" translates *Gegenstand,* "objectum" *Objekt,* and "objective" *Objektiv.* "Auxiliary object" translates *Hilfsgegenstand,* and "ultimate object" *Zielgegenstand,* while "incomplete object" translates *unvollständige Gegenstand.* "Serious" experience, judgment, etc., translates *Ernsterlebnis,* etc., while "imaginative experience," etc., and sometimes "counterfeit experience" translate *Phantasieerlebnis*, etc. "Apprehension" translates *Erfassung*, the supreme genus of which, *Wissen*, "knowledge," is a species. "Oughtness" and "ought" and in some contexts "obligation" are used to translate *Sollen*, and "instrumentality" or "purposiveness" translates *Zweckmässigkeit*, while "value" translates *Wert*, "disvalue" *Unwert*, and "valuation" *Werthaltung*. "Presentation" translates *Präsentation*, the key term in the book, while "self-presentation," "other-presentation," "total presentation," "partial presentation," "content-presentation," and "act-presentation" translate *Selbstpräsentation*, *Fremdpräsentation*, *Totalpräsentation*, *Partialpräsentation*, *Inhaltspräsentation*, and *Aktpräsentation*, respectively. "Notion" generally translates *Gedanke* but sometimes *Begriff*. Other technical terms should not puzzle too greatly, though some compound terms will require meditative deciphering.

J. N. FINDLAY

Yale University
May, 1971

Translator's Introduction

GENERAL REMARKS

MEINONG WAS A PHILOSOPHER who developed realism to its extreme limits. He populated his universe immensely. The realism of which he constitutes a radical development can, in a most general outline, be described by the following principles: (1) The universe is a plurality of entities. There are minds, which constitute a subclass of the universe of entities. (2) It is not an essential property of any entity that it be known. In this description it is no accident that the ontological classification of entities is left open.

Chisholm gives a similar formulation of realism, having Meinong in mind. His formulation runs as follows: "The general thesis of all realism [is] that the objects of presentation and belief are ordinarily extra-mental." [1] Chisholm leaves open the independence of the entities upon being known, in the sense that he does not state it explicitly. But it seems to be implicitly contained in his formulation. Proceeding from Chisholm's description, one can state a more developed form of realism thus: while there are many objects which are presented, there are also many which are not presented. And the entities which are objects of presentation are ordinarily extramental. The entities are the preconditions of presenta-

1. R. F. Chisholm, *Realism and the Background of Phenomenology*, 2d ed. (New York: Free Press, 1967), p. 3.

[xxix]

tion; there is no presentation without an entity being presented. This is the kind of realism which was developed by Meinong to its limits. It is a very interesting subject to study because of its radicalism. In fact, it does not fail to leave a deep impression, and this is especially true of the ethical theory which was constructed on the basis of this realism.

It is very difficult to draw a consistent picture of Meinong's philosophy. One must proceed eclectically, for Meinong's is a prolific genius, full of ideas and originality. His imagination captures many possibilities, which are occasionally treated together in one work and not always consistent and clear.

Meinong, together with Brentano, Husserl, Frege, and Russell, stands at the beginning of contemporary analytical philosophy and phenomenology. As Brentano's pupil, he devoted particular attention to what Brentano called "descriptive psychology," which is the empirical investigation and analysis of psychic phenomena.

When Meinong was professor of philosophy at the University of Graz, he developed his own philosophy, in which he postulated, as a result of his psychological-philosophical analysis, a complex and rich universe of entities. It was over this philosophical development in general that the friendship between Meinong and Brentano broke up; all relationships between the two men ceased.

Russell showed great interest in Meinong but was also disturbed by the great multiplicity of entities, which, at that time, was too much, even for Russell.[2] And he missed in Meinong a logical clearness of conception.

Very often, in reading Meinong, one feels reminded of problems dealt with by Gottlob Frege in his theory of *Sinn* and *Bedeutung* and of *Gedanken*, and one wonders how much communication there was between the two men. Frege is mentioned in at least one of the letters which Russell wrote to Meinong,[3] and Meinong himself mentions Frege at least once.[4]

2. See Bertrand Russell, "Meinong's Theory of Complexes and Assumptions," *Mind,* VIII (1904), 204 ff.
3. Rudolf Kindinger, *Philosophenbriefe* (Graz, 1965), p. 152.
4. Meinong, *Über Annahmen,* 2d ed., p. 6. (Full publication data for Meinong's works will be found in the Bibliography at the end of this book.)

But apparently there was no extensive communication or mutual influence. But, if there had been, one wonders how the two philosophers would have affected each other. Under the assumption that they could have open-mindedly communicated, we can barely imagine what their combined thoroughness, inventiveness, intellectual honesty, and endeavor for clarity might have achieved. Be that as it may, Russell, Frege, and Meinong were in many respects dealing with similar problems, which were partly about the meaning and denotation of expressions, partly about that to which presentational experiences refer—called "objects" by Meinong.

On Emotional Presentation is a late work, published in 1917, a few years before Meinong's death. It was written after such gigantic essays as *Über Annahmen* and *Über Möglichkeit und Wahrscheinlichkeit*. It constitutes an aspect of his mature and late philosophy. This late philosophy especially deals with the theory of values and obligations. The theory itself presupposes, first of all, Meinong's theory of knowledge and ontology, which again is based upon the assumption of the dichotomy between the knowing subject and the object known.

In the years previous to the conception of *On Emotional Presentation* Meinong was especially concerned with what he called "intellectual presentation," e.g., ideas (*Vorstellungen*), judgments (*Urteile*), and assumptions (*Annahmen*), all of which are psychic experiences of the subject. In the first part of *On Emotional Presentation* he deals with intellectual presentation. However, the theory, as it is expounded in *On Emotional Presentation,* presupposes so much that it can hardly be understood without references to at least the two works just mentioned, *Über Annahmen* (second edition) and *Über Möglichkeit und Wahrscheinlichkeit.* Proceeding by analogy to his analysis of intellectual presentations, he investigates the so-called emotional presentations, which are the psychic experiences by which values, attributes of pleasantness, aesthetic properties, and obligations are presented. Those entities, in whose being he believed, were discovered by psychological and epistemological analysis. Meinong's argumentation for his philosophical beliefs will be discussed later.

Finally, something must be said about the translation of *On Emotional Presentation* itself. The German text, at first acquaintance, is almost incomprehensible. The sentences are constructed in a complicated manner. The vocabulary and syntax sometimes have a regional flavor. From time to time the syntax breaks down; at one place, for example, Meinong inserts an article which never receives its noun.[5] There are passages in the book which are not clear. But passages which are essentially vague in German should remain vague in the translation in the same sense. For they may be an indication of some intrinsic property of the work which must be noticed so that the interested reader can properly evaluate the book.

A considerable difficulty is presented by the problem of how to translate Meinong's technical vocabulary into English. Many of his terms are traditional philosophical terms. Take, for example, his most general term, "object." This usually suggests something real, some existing individual. However, it is not used in this way by Meinong at all. And this is so with many other terms.

The way in which various concepts are formulated often, by itself, shows the kinship between them. Take, for example, *Soseinsmeinen* and *Seinsmeinen*. I translated *Meinen* with "reference," in the sense of a psychic experience or word or concept referring to something. *Seinsmeinen* should be translated as "a subject's reference to an object's being," and *Soseinsmeinen* as "a subject's reference to an object's being thus-and-so." But, for the sake of brevity, I have omitted "a subject's." Though the two expressions are still awkward, they at least show the similarity or kinship between the two concepts which is contained in the German. The meaning of these two expressions is explained in the introduction following these general remarks.

I would like to acknowledge gratefully the valuable criticism of my interpretation of Meinong's theories which was made by Professor M. G. Yoes and Professor Bredo Johnsen. I am especially indebted to Professor Haywood Shuford for his generous help in understanding the first two chapters of *On Emotional Presentation* and for his suggestions on how to render some of Meinong's technical expressions in English. For valuable criticism and advice in linguistic matters I thank Dr. Erika Nielsen and especially Mr. Bill Wild, who devoted much time to this project.

5. *On Emotional Presentation,* p. 4.

INTELLECTUAL PRESENTATION

Objecta

WE WILL BEGIN our discussion of intellectual presentation with that which is presented, for it is difficult to give a description of presentation without knowing what is being presented, i.e., what the objects of the presentation are.

"Object" and "presentation" in fact are the central notions of the theory with which we are here concerned. Neither of these terms can be defined; they can only be hinted at and indicated. Though Meinong believes that eventually objects can be described without reference to presentation (and this is what actually will be attempted in this Introduction) he arrived at his conception of object only through the analysis of presentation. But what is presentation? Presentation is the presenting of something to a subject or mind. The presenting is an experience of the subject which admits of analysis and which occurs in different forms. Presentation is always the presentation of something. This is not shown but fundamentally assumed in the theory. To each form of presentation there corresponds a different kind of object. The analysis of various forms of presentation will be considered later.

The term "object" expresses another central notion in Meinong's philosophy. This term, also, cannot be defined or otherwise be described. It is the most general of all Meinong's terms. Anything at all is object. For us, or the human mind, "anything at all" means everything that can possibly be thought of or, in Chisholm's words, "anything toward which a psychological act or attitude may be directed." [6] This plainly means everything, anything at all, including presentations, that is, all psychic experiences. For nothing can be indicated, pointed out, or named which is not thought of in some way or other. "All there is," that is, objects, can be subdivided (according to Meinong's theory) into four classes. The subdivision is made according to the kinds of experiences by which the objects are presented.

6. Chisholm, *Realism*, p. 6.

It must be repeated that Meinong holds that it is not an essential property of objects to be presented, though it is an essential property of presentations to have objects.[7] But he arrived at the different sorts of objects by analyzing the presenting experiences. That is, different classes of objects can be characterized according to the kinds of experiences which present them. But, according to Meinong, it should be possible to characterize them without reference to experiences. And we will follow Meinong's proposal in this Introduction: objects will first be described separately from the experiences which present them. Our description is based on Meinong's *Über emotionale Präsentation, Über Annahmen,* and *Über Möglichkeit und Wahrscheinlichkeit.*

The four main classes of objects will merely be named at this point. They are objecta, objectives, dignitatives, and desideratives. Objects are presented by two exclusively different sorts of psychic experiences, intellectual presentation and emotional presentation. The objects of intellectual presentation are called "objecta" and "objectives." The objects of emotional presentation are called "dignitatives" and "desideratives." Our first concern is with the objects of intellectual presentation.

Objecta are the basic objects in the sense that everything is either an objectum or presupposes an objectum or objecta for its own being. Individuals, most relations, and most properties are objecta. For example, the Astrodome, the relations "father of" and "greater than," and the property of being green are objecta. All properties and relations except aesthetic and moral properties and relations (e.g., beautiful, pleasant, good, is-morally-better-than, and their opposites) are objecta. And for the time being let us presuppose that we know what aesthetic and moral properties and relations are. Thus the property of being fat is an objectum; the property of being morally good and the relation of being morally better than are not objecta. Why this is so will be discussed later.

That there are objecta, or objects in general, is shown by the fact that any idea (*Vorstellung*) per se is of something.[8] It must be emphasized at the outset that ideas in Meinong's sense are exclusively experiences of a subject; they are a sort

7. See Chisholm's translation of "The Theory of Objects" in *Realism*, pp. 76 ff.
8. Chisholm, *Realism*, p. 76; *Über Annahmen*, 2d ed., pp. 356 ff.

of presentation. In dealing with Meinong's ideas, one must forget anything which might remind one of concepts or of anything which has to do with meanings or senses. In Meinong's philosophy there is nothing which is even remotely similar to meanings. There are only psychic experiences which present something; that something is an object or objects. Further differentiations are not made. There is nothing else. If objects, or objecta, with which we are at present concerned, were identical with ideas or parts of ideas, then they all would exist or be real. For ideas, when they occur, do exist. For they are experiences.[9] However, one can have ideas of nonexisting objecta, that is, objecta which may subsist; one can thus have ideas of Bismarck, who is dead, or of the Flying Dutchman, or of the *perpetuum mobile*. Since anything of which one can think is an object, of which some are objecta, there are chances that some objecta may not exist. Properties and relations are often agreed not to exist but to subsist (I am using the term "subsist" prematurely). There are also some individual objects, e.g., Zeus, which are objecta and which do not exist. Thus the notion of nonexisting objecta in Meinong's sense should not be too surprising. It must be kept in mind that they are objects, and objects can be anything one can possibly think of.

Now the objecta of which one is having ideas must be different from their ideas. More formally put, the argument runs as follows:

1. Ideas are, by their very nature, of something (of some object).
2. Ideas, when they occur, exist.
3. If ideas were identical with their objects, all their objects would exist whenever someone was having an idea of them.
4. But there are objects which never exist (e.g., the *perpetuum mobile* and Pegasus), yet there are ideas of them.
5. Therefore, ideas are not identical with their objects.

The argument only proves that some ideas are different from the objects which they present. That there are objects at all has already been assumed in the first premise.

9. Cf. J. N. Findlay, *Meinong's Theory of Objects and Values*, 2d ed. (Oxford, 1963), pp. 17 ff.

Another argument for the being of objecta is that they have a definite place in space and time.[10] If they were identified with ideas, we would have the paradoxical result that, for example, Basel would be located inside me on the fifth floor of the Liberal Arts Building of the University of Houston at the same time that it is located in Switzerland.

This argument, put in a more orderly fashion, runs as follows:

1. Any existing object has a definite location in space and and time.
2. In particular, any idea, being a psychic event and being an existing object, has a definite location in space and time.
3. If an idea at location p and time t is of an (existing) object at q and t ($q \neq p$), then the idea and the object in fact are at different locations and cannot be identical.

The argument assumes the being, and even the existence, of some objects. It only proves that ideas of objects which exist simultaneously with the ideas are not identical with these objects. Thus Meinong is merely assuming that objects have being independent of their presentations.

Objecta—which are, as indicated above, special objects— do not have to exist. They are independent of existence.[11] But in some way or other they "are there" and can be presented. Or, because they are presented or because there are ideas of them, they are there. Thus they fall into at least one of the three classes or modes of being, which Meinong calls "existence," "subsistence," and *Aussersein*. The difference between subsistence and existence must be immediately evident. Anything which does not exist, and is not inherently impossible or contradictory, subsists. Thus, the golden mountain, pink elephants, the *perpetuum mobile,* and the perfect circle subsist. However, the round square does not even subsist. But it is an object. So it has merely *Aussersein*. (For objects which have only *Aussersein*, the law of the excluded middle does not hold. Oval triangles are oval and not oval; they surely can be said to be square and circular too, though Meinong does not elaborate

10. *Über Annahmen,* 2d ed., pp. 59 ff., 77; *Über Annahmen,* 1st ed., pp. 256 ff.
11. Chisholm, *Realism,* p. 85.

on these matters.) Now, any objectum has, according to Meinong, at least *Aussersein;* many objecta also subsist; and some objecta exist. But all the existing and subsisting objecta also have *Aussersein.* However, not all objecta with *Aussersein* also have existence or subsistence. That is, anything which can be thought of at least has *Aussersein.*

Aussersein means definitely a mode or class of being. For all objects at least have *Aussersein,* and some of them are also subsistent or existent.

Objectives

Objectives are complex or molecular objects which (if we make the statement "with a grain of salt," as Meinong says) [12] are made up of objecta or other objectives. Thus, that three is smaller than four and is a prime number, or that the boy stole the bread because he was hungry, are objectives constituted of other objectives.

All objectives are analyzable into objecta. Thus, that three is smaller than four and is a prime number is "constituted" of the objecta three, four, prime number, and smaller (than).

Objectives are the being of objecta. For example, Basel's existence, the golden mountain's subsistence, and the round square's *Aussersein* are objectives. Objectives are also objects' having certain properties or objects' standing in certain relationships to other objects. That the number three is prime, that Basel is located in Switzerland, are objectives.

Objectives depend for their being upon the objecta which constitute them. Before there can *be* objectives there must *be* objecta. The "be," when predicated of objecta, is to be understood as at least one of the three alternatives of being. Meinong calls objecta "logical *priora*" or "presuppositional objects" of objectives. He calls objecta also "material" or "constituents" of objectives.[13] The expressions "material" or "constituent" in this connection must probably be taken metaphorically. I say "probably" because in both books (*Über Annahmen* and *On Emotional Presentation*) Meinong uses them in an expressly metaphorical way, but not only metaphorically, for he also

12. *Über Annahmen,* 2d ed., pp. 47, 63 ff.
13. *Ibid.,* pp. 63 ff.

flatly states that objecta *are* constituents of objectives. Apparently these matters are so fundamental and are so little understood that they can only be pointed out, but not clearly explained. In any case, the objective that Romans are round-headed can be said to be constituted of the pair of objecta "Romans" and "roundheaded." This is not to be understood in such a way that the class of Romans is the objectum which is roundheaded but that all objecta which are Romans are round-headed. The class "Romans," of course, is an objectum, but it is not a roundheaded objectum.

The objective that Romans are roundheaded is not simply the pair of objecta "Romans" and "roundheaded" somehow put together; it is rather that the Romans have the property of *being* roundheaded. Thus, a roundheaded Roman is an objectum. The existence of a roundheaded Roman is an objective. The being roundheaded of Romans is also an objective. But they are two different kinds of objectives. The existence of roundheaded Romans, or that there are roundheaded Romans, is what Meinong calls "an objective which is (an object's) being" (*Seinsobjektiv*). But that Romans are round-headed or the Romans' being roundheaded are what Meinong calls "objectives which are (an object's) being thus-and-so" (*Soseinsobjektiv*). That is, the latter objectives are an object's having certain properties or being in a certain state. In objectives of an object's being we have the objective that an object exists, subsists, or has *Aussersein*. In an objective of an object's being thus-and-so we have the objective that an object has certain properties or stands in certain relationships with other objects. The question whether it is true that an object exists, etc., or has certain properties is not asked at this place. However, it may already be said, for example, that "Basel is in Switzerland" and "It is true that Basel is in Switzerland" are two different objectives. In the first case there is the objectum "Basel" being related to the objectum "Switzerland"; in the second case the objective, that Basel is in Switzerland, has a certain property.

Since objectives, as has been mentioned, are dependent upon objects, they are called "objects of higher order." All objects which for their being ("being" referring to all three modes of being) depend upon other objects are objects of higher order. All objects which cannot be unless there are first some other objects are objects of higher order, according to

Meinong. This does not mean that a table cannot be there without its maker or that a child cannot be there without its parents; it means that there can be no children without heads, no tables without legs. Meinong's notion of objects of higher order cannot be made precise. In a negative manner it can be said that they are not individuals. And, at the most, they subsist.

Meinong does not give an explicit argument for the independent being of objectives. But this would not be necessary, since objectives are special objects, and their presentation is a special kind of presentation. If the argument, which is about objects and their presentation in general (see p. xxxvi, above) should prove—though in fact it does not prove—that all objects have being independent of the subjects to which they are presented, then the same argument would prove that all objectives have being independent of the subjects to which they are presented. Objectives are a subclass of objects, and their special form of presentation are a subclass of all forms of presentation.

Objectives are presented by psychic experiences which are called by Meinong "judgments" and "assumptions." (These sorts of experiences will be discussed in greater detail in the following sections.) Judgments and assumptions, as psychic experiences, exist when they occur, according to Meinong's theory. They are objecta. Objectives never exist; at the most, they subsist. All objects of higher order at the most can subsist.

Objectives subsist when they are facts or when they are true—which means the same thing. For objectives are called true if and only if they are facts.[14] That the sum of the angles in a triangle amounts to 180 degrees, that New York is the most populous city in the United States, that pink elephants are pink, that Hector is Priam's son, that the circular square is circular, are all facts and subsistent objectives. It does not make any difference into what classes of being the constituent objects fall. New York and the United States exist; triangles, Hector, Priam, and pink elephants subsist; but circular squares have merely *Aussersein*. That some triangles are circular is not a fact and thus not a subsistent objective. For Meinong tells us that only factual (or true) objectives subsist. What sort

14. Findlay, *Meinong's Theory of Objects and Values,* pp. 83 ff.

of being does he attribute to unfactual objectives? Objectives are a subclass of objects. All objects have *Aussersein;* some objects exist; many subsist. All objects must belong to at least one of the three classes of being. We have already learned that objectives never exist but that all factual objectives subsist. Since unfactual objectives are a certain kind of objective and are therefore objects, and since unfactual objectives do neither subsist nor exist, they can at most and must at least have *Aussersein.*

According to Meinong,[15] for each objectum there is a pair of objectives, that is, one objective of its being and one of its nonbeing, e.g., that Hector exists and that Hector does not exist, or that the oval triangle subsists and that it does not subsist. One of these objectives is a fact and therefore subsistent. The other one, then, has only *Aussersein.* All false or unfactual objectives have only *Aussersein.*

But take, for example, "The oval triangle is circular" and "The oval triangle is not circular." Which of these sentences would stand for a subsistent objective? The objectum "oval triangle," about which the objective is, has only *Aussersein;* therefore, the law of the excluded middle does not hold for it. That is, of objects with *Aussersein* it cannot be said that either they have a certain property or they do not have that property. Thus Meinong cannot and does not seem to claim that for *all* objects there are pairs of objectives, namely, objectives of the object's being thus-and-so and of the object's not being thus-and-so and that only one member of each pair subsists or is factual and that the other member has only *Aussersein* and is not factual. For such a claim, if it were made, would at least break down in respect to objects which have merely *Aussersein.*

However, in respect to subsistent individual objects, like Pegasus and Dr. Faustus, the objectives which are their having certain properties are factual if they are at least consistent with, implied by, or even mentioned in the poetry which deals with those objects.[16] Their truth depends upon previous conventions. We may venture to complete Meinong by saying that of any existent or subsistent objects there are pairs of objectives (indefinitely many) which are the objects' having

15. Chisholm, *Realism,* p. 85.
16. *On Emotional Presentation,* §§ 1 and 9.

certain properties (or standing in certain relationships) or the objects' not having these properties (or not standing in those relationships). And one member of each pair is a factual objective, though the means for determining which one it is are not always given. For obviously, the law of the excluded middle holds for all existing objects. In order to be consistent with Meinong, we must say that, for many subsisting objects, some conventions must first be adopted, conventions of the kind we have just mentioned.

We have said that objectives which are factual are also true. However, in order to discuss the theory of truth in Meinong's works, we need to introduce additional entities; for example, pseudo-existent objects.[17] Since the distinction between the truth of objectives and their factuality is not of primary relevance here, it is preferable for our purposes to leave the question of truth out of consideration, and we will concern ourselves only with factuality.

Presentation of Objecta. Ideas

In Meinong's theory any object is a potential object of presentation. The presentation is a subject's experience, which belongs exclusively to the subject. Thus we have the object on one side and the presenting experience on the other side. We will not even ask by what mechanism, according to Meinong, the connection between the object and its presentation is established; that can be considered a psychological or physiological question with which we are not concerned. But still, there are no "vehicles" or "mediations" of reference of any other kind—like meanings, senses, intentions, concepts, or whatever one wants to call them. Whatever entity would be comparable to a meaning in someone else's theory is, for Meinong, part of the psychic event itself, which is the presentation and which is located within the subject. It is part of an event—likewise an object in Meinong's sense—which occurs and ceases to exist; it is not some linguistic or Platonic entity.

To give adequate expression to this presenting event, which is of objecta and which Meinong calls *Vorstellung*, we have used the word "idea" in our translation. This word must express here that something happens on the part of and by the subject; it

17. See Findlay, pp. 83 ff.

must express an event. Idea is precisely an event. Meinong seems to hold that in certain ways ideas are comparable to individuals, for they are said to exist.[18]

Meinong analyzes all presenting experiences into two aspects, act and content. There is no explicit definition of either aspect but only more or less vague indications of what they are. The reason for this may be either that the terms "act" and "content" are provisional terms for theoretical entities which stand for something as yet not empirically shown and/or that they are primitive terms in Meinong's philosophy which cannot be defined but serve to explain other terms. I cannot say whether both of the reasons apply or which of the two reasons applies; but probably the former does, for Meinong spends much time and effort on making precise the concept of content.

Each sort of experience corresponds to a separate sort of object. Ideas (*Vorstellungen*) are experiences which present objecta. Judgments and assumptions are experiences which present objectives; they will be dealt with in the following section.

For Meinong ideas are passive experiences,[19] almost in the way that a surgical operation is a passive experience. Still, the subject is involved in it. Ideas do not happen to the subject in quite the same way that an operation would. They happen in the subject; their nature is confined to, limited by, and dependent upon the subject's makeup. Two subjects can have ideas of the same thing but in their own individual way. What the subjects contribute to the experience Meinong calls "act," though it is a passive experience which happens to the subject and is not produced by it. The subject receives something; the reception depends upon the subject's attitude and character.

Thus, in spite of their passive character, Meinong subdivides ideas into act and content.[20] The result of the differentiation is almost impossible to describe—as we have just seen—because we do not really know the entities into which ideas are differentiated. In respect to ideas, the act is a quite indescribable, hypothetical thing. Meinong himself, however, attempts a descrip-

18. See Chisholm, *Realism*, p. 105.

19. *On Emotional Presentation*, § 1; Findlay, Chap. VIII.

20. For the following, see *On Emotional Presentation*, pp. 48 ff.; Findlay, Chap. VIII.

tion as follows: the act of an idea is that part of the idea-experience which remains constant (in the subject) when the objects of the idea-experience vary; or, the act of an idea is that which all ideas (in a subject) have in common.[21] What they all have in common, of course, is that they are objecta. This is a circular statement, since objecta can be described only as those objects which are presented by ideas. But we are speaking of the most basic concepts in Meinong's philosophy; and, in speaking of things which are most fundamental, circularity cannot be avoided if anything is to be said about them at all. Moreover, there are ideas which somehow and somewhat differ from one another, but not in respect to their content. There are, among others, perceptual ideas of some objectum and our imagination of that objectum. Meinong gives as an example the tone C as it is presented in perception and the same tone C as it is presented in imagination.[22] The idea in the first case he calls the "serious idea" of C; the idea in the latter case he calls the "counterfeit idea" of C. The two ideas are the same in respect to the content: both of them are of the tone C; but they differ, according to Meinong, in respect to the act. This still does not say what, then, the act is like. But at least one can say: if two ideas which have the same objects differ in some way, they differ in respect to the act.

The content of an idea is that which varies when the objects of the idea vary.[23] Contents correspond directly to what they are about. If the idea is of blue, the content directly corresponds to blue (note that it is not said that it is blue!); if the idea is of number, the content corresponds directly to the objectum number. What the content in this case is cannot be said—at least, not with the information that is at our disposal. Contents are not further analyzed by Meinong, at least epistemologically.[24] Contents are not contributed by the subject in the way that acts are. In having an idea of the tone C, whether by perceiving or by imagining it, we have the same content, namely, that part of the presenting experience which corresponds to the tone C. In perceiving the tone C and in perceiving the tone A, we have experiences in which the contents differ, be-

21. *On Emotional Presentation*, pp. 50 ff.
22. *Ibid.*, pp. 51 ff.
23. *Ibid.*
24. *Über Möglichkeit und Wahrscheinlichkeit*, p. 330.

cause different objects are presented, but in which the acts are alike: both ideas are perceptual ideas of a tone.

The presentations we have just described, which are experiences of ideas, are also called "unmediated" or "immediate presentations" (*unmittelbare Präsentationen*). In immediate presentation the content of the idea-experience corresponds directly to the objectum which is presented. For example, an idea of the content "red apple" corresponds directly to the presented objectum "red apple."

The justification for attributing "immediacy" to a certain kind of presentation is given by the fact that in Meinong's philosophy there is also mediate, or mediated, presentation (*mittelbare Präsentation*),[25] which differs clearly from that kind of presentation which is called "immediate." This notion of mediate presentation is very hard to explain. The bare facts of mediated presentation are as follows: if there is an idea, then there is an objectum which is presented by the idea-experience. The content of the idea can, on certain occasions, be one thing and the presented objectum quite another. That is, the above-mentioned direct correspondence between objectum and presentation is not established. The content, in some special case, could be "that aquatic creature"; its mediate objectum, however, could be "this mermaid." Of course, the content "that aquatic creature" corresponds directly to the objectum "that aquatic creature"; nevertheless, the really ultimate objectum (*Zielgegenstand*), in this particular case, is "this mermaid." In such a case, the objectum, "that aquatic creature," takes on an "auxiliary" function in the presentation of "this mermaid," and "that aquatic creature," in such a function, is called by Meinong an "auxiliary object" (*Hilfsgegenstand*). How exactly objecta can aid in presenting another objectum in this way is not explained. It might be of some help to call to mind some experience like the following: there may be an occasion where one thinks of a central European, but the (ultimate) object which one really intends is a German. According to Meinong's theory, the mere idea of a central European guarantees that there is the objectum, a central European, which is immediately presented by the idea. This objectum serves as auxiliary object when it is used as a detour on the way to presenting mediately the objectum, a German.

25. See *Über Annahmen*, 2d ed., pp. 132, 180, 240 ff., 256, 286, 356; *Über Möglichkeit und Wahrscheinlichkeit*, § 33.

Presentation of Objectives. Judgments and Assumptions

Objectives are presented by two kinds of experiences, which are called "judgments" and "assumptions." These two expressions do not denote anything like linguistic expressions. They denote psychic experiences which present something to the subject. Like ideas, they are presenting experiences. However, they present other kinds of objects than ideas do. Judgments and assumptions present objectives.

Like ideas, judgments and assumptions are happenings completely within, and confined to, the subject.[26] The presentations which have so far been discussed concern two objects, or perhaps two groups of objects, which are mutually exclusive: the presenting experiences within the subject and the presented object or objects outside the subject. "Outside the subject" is to be understood in such a way that the object which is outside the subject is, in its being, independent of the subject (see above) and that it is not part of the presenting experience. These presentations are called by Meinong "other-presentation" (*Fremdpräsentation*).

To repeat: the experiences which present objectives are of two kinds: judgments and assumptions. Judgments are emphatic experiences; they accept objectives as facts, regardless of whether they are facts or not.[27] Judgments are the subject's assent that something is the case, that an object has certain properties, stands in certain relationships to other objects, or has a certain mode of being. The judgment that an object has a certain mode of being is a judgment of (an object's) being. Judgments that something is the case, that an object has certain properties, or stands in certain relationships to other objects, are judgments of (an object's) being thus-and-so. If a judgment presents an objective which is not factual, then it is a false judgment. False judgments present unfactual objectives or objectives which have merely *Aussersein*.

Assumptions present objectives without special emphasis on their factuality or unfactuality. Assumptions are, so to

---

26. See Findlay, Chap. VIII.
27. See Findlay, pp. 60 ff., 100 ff.; *Über Annahmen*, 2d ed., pp. 18, 47, 87 ff., 101 ff., 139 ff., 252 ff., 341 ff., 352; *On Emotional Presentation*, pp. 3 ff., 23 ff.

speak, acts of entertaining presentations. However, they are also either true or false. They are true if they present factual objectives; they are false if they present unfactual objectives. They also present either objectives of (an object's) being or objectives of (an object's) being thus-and-so.

The same objectives can be presented by both judgments and assumptions. The two presentations differ only in the emphasis with which the objective is presented. They are comparable with perceptual or serious ideas and counterfeit ideas. The serious ideas correspond to judgments; counterfeit ideas correspond to assumptions.

Objectives themselves are indifferent to whether and how they are presented, that is, whether they are presented at all and whether they are accepted or assumed. Objectives have their being, i.e., either subsistence or *Aussersein,* independent of any judgments or assumptions which present them.

Like ideas, the two kinds of presenting experiences of objectives, i.e., judgments and assumptions, are subdivided by Meinong into act and content. Again, neither act nor content is explicitly described in so many words. They seem to be basic entities which can be characterized only by circumlocution. Thus we are not told what content is, but we are told that the content is that part of the experience which corresponds directly to the objective which is presented. The corresponding content remains otherwise undescribed. However, the correspondence between objectives and contents is one-to-one. That is, for one presented objective there is exactly one content and vice versa.

Of course, as we said before, objectives are, figuratively speaking, "constructed" out of objecta or other objectives. It is left entirely open whether objectives are actually thus constructed or not. Since the information about objectives in respect to their construction is vague, it is not of much use to try to relate their supposed constituents to other supposed constituents in the presenting experiences.[28] This means that, since Meinong gives us no analysis of the constituents of objectives, there is no sense in relating them to (the contents of the) presenting experiences by coordinating the constituents of objectives with constituents of contents. Thus we must

28. See Chisholm, *Realism,* pp. 75 ff.

content ourselves with the information that the content of experiences which present objectives is that part of the experiences which directly corresponds to the objectives.

There is, however, one property which both objectives, and judgments and assumptions, have in common. They cannot be unless other things are there first. Thus, as objectives depend upon the objecta which "constitute" them (see above), so judgments and assumptions depend upon ideas, which are the raw material which make experiences such as judgments and assumptions possible. For example, without previous ideas of Phoenix, teacher, and Achilles, the objective that Phoenix was the teacher of Achilles cannot be presented. Objecta are called "object-presuppositions" for judgments. Ideas are called "psychological presuppositions" for judgments and assumptions.[29]

Judgments and assumptions can be of the same content. In other words, judgments and assumptions can present the same objective. But they differ in respect to their act. The differentiation which was made above between judgments and assumptions is a differentiation which concerns only their act. So the act-aspect of judgments is the emphatic acceptance of objectives. Objectives are actively apprehended and accepted by the experience. The act-aspect of assumptions is a mere entertaining of an objective without any acceptance. Both of these experiences are active experiences in the sense that through them the subject gets hold of objectives at will. The reader will recall that ideas happen to the subject and that they are not, in that sense, active. In order to indicate this difference between ideas and judgments and assumptions, Meinong calls ideas "content-presentations," and he calls judgments and assumptions "act-presentations." He uses still another expression, namely, "partial presentations," for presentations like, for example, ideas (there are more kinds of partial presentations than ideas) because there only the content is predominantly involved; he uses the expression "total presentations" for all kinds of presentations in which both act and content are equally involved.[30] Thus, judgments and assumptions are also called "total presentations."

29. *On Emotional Presentation,* § 8.
30. *Ibid.,* § 1.

Self-Presentation

We have already talked about other-presentation. Other-presentation involves two mutually exclusive groups of objects: (1) the presenting experiences and (2) the presented objects, which are independent of the presenting experiences.

However, according to Meinong's theory, there is another kind of presentation, which is called "self-presentation." This sort of presentation does not involve the two mutually exclusive groups (presenting experiences and presented objects). It involves only the presenting experience. The presenting experience presents itself to the subject. The presenting experience (which by itself is of an object) is, simultaneously with its occurrence, presented to the subject as precisely the experience. We will see that the notion of self-presentation is very difficult to understand. Meinong deals with it in all of the following books: *Über emotionale Präsentation, Über Möglichkeit und Wahrscheinlichkeit,* and *Über Annahmen.* However, none of them is helpful for an understanding of these matters. It is quite possible that Meinong's earlier psychological writings prove more useful in this respect. As for the information which the aforementioned books give, we will see that the notion of self-presentation and the notion of some kinds of presenting experiences cannot be reconciled. That is, given one, the other cannot be as Meinong wants it to be.

Before the notion of self-presentation is explicated, a word should be said about Meinong's reasons for introducing the notion of self-presentation. The purpose of the notion of self-presentation is to avoid a multiplicity of presenting experiences where this can be avoided. Such a multiplicity is unavoidable if for the presentation of a presenting experience a new and different presenting experience is required, and so on. According to Meinong, there is no reason not to assume that the presenting experiences can do that presenting job for themselves—if their presentation occurs simultaneously with them.[31] As an example he mentions a toothache: one knows exactly *when* one has it. The pain (which is a perception) is something the subject knows *when* it occurs. This is the only argument in favor of the notion of self-presentation

31. *Ibid.,* p. 8.

which I could find in Meinong's books. In fact, Meinong's theory receives some support from common experience; there are presentations of which one is aware while they are occurring, as, for example, perceptions and other judgments.[32] "Awareness of a presenting experience while it is occurring" seems to be the only way to paraphrase "self-presentation." The expression "awareness of" cannot be further explicated; it must be accepted as it is and must be recommended to generous common sense.

According to Meinong's theory,[33] in a self-presentation the whole presenting experience is presented, that is, its act and its content. However, mainly the act of the presenting experience is emphasized. Though both act and content are presented in self-presentation, the act receives preferred treatment. According to Meinong's nomenclature, self-presentation is therefore called "act-presentation" and "total presentation." [34]

What we have said in the preceding paragraphs is all the explanation that Meinong gives of self-presentation in *On Emotional Presentation, Über Annahmen,* and *Über Möglichkeit und Wahrscheinlichkeit.* Evidently it is not enough; for we need to know under what circumstances presenting experiences become self-presenting experiences and how it is possible that the same presenting experiences do not differ from one another when they are self-presentations and when they are not self-presentations. There is no objective criterion. The only criterion there is is awareness. But whether Meinong would say that awareness increases with an increase of the intensity of the experience cannot be answered here. Meinong does not use the term "awareness," and "intensity" is not related by him to self-presentation.

Though the content of an experience is presented in self-presentation, the act of that same experience plays the most important role in a twofold manner: it is the main aspect of the experience which is presented, and it also is the aspect which does the presenting in self-presentation. Self-presentation is an active experience. It does not happen to the subject but is evoked by the subject. It is like judgments

32. According to Meinong, perceptions are judgments of existence, that is, they are of objectives.
33. *On Emotional Presentation,* p. 23.
34. *Ibid.,* § 3.

or, specifically, perceptual judgments. This makes it an active experience, a "total presentation" or "act-presentation," according to Meinong.

It must be remembered that all presenting experiences can present themselves. How, when, and under what conditions they do so, Meinong does not tell us. He tells us that self-presentations are active experiences like judgments and that they are identical with the experiences which they present. All this may be acceptable in respect to judgments in two ways: (1) according to Meinong's theory and (2) according to common experience. In the first case: judgments are total or act-presentations where the act plays the predominant role. In the second case: one can safely say that most of the time one is aware of one's own judgments, at least of the ones which are sufficiently articulated and explicitly formulated. However, the situation is different in respect to ideas.

According to Meinong's theory, ideas are passive experiences with an "inactive" act-aspect. They happen to the subject. Their acts can be only negatively indicated by saying what they are not and that they are the whole experience of having an idea minus the content.[35] And they are called "content-presentations." Now, self-presentations are "act-presentations"; their act is the main presenting ingredient of the experience. They are "total presentations" like judgments. An experience *simpliciter* and the same experience as self-presentation are one and the same thing, with the one difference that the subject, in the latter case, is aware of the experience.

So, clearly, ideas and self-presentations which are ideas are incompatible. If we take ideas and self-presentation as they are given in Meinong's theory, then the togetherness of an idea and a simultaneous awareness (as self-presentation) of it is impossible. For according to Meinong it should then be required that the same idea must be passive and active in the same respects at the same time and that the same idea must be both partial presentation and total presentation at the same time,[36] which are altogether incompatible.

35. See *Über Möglichkeit und Wahrscheinlichkeit*, § 33; *Über Annahmen*, 2d ed., pp. 13, 44 ff., 57, 85, 105, 138 f., 237, 254, 328 f., 341; *On Emotional Presentation*, pp. 51 ff.
36. *On Emotional Presentation*, §§ 1, 3.

In fact, Meinong never gives an example of the self-presentation of ideas. The only example he gives is the presentation of a perception (perceptions are called by him "judgments of existence"). In *On Emotional Presentation* he gives exactly two examples (page 8)—namely, that of a headache and that of a toothache—which are sensations and of which one is aware while one has them. Aches are sensations or perceptions of something.

Beyond the Meinongian context, the question must be asked now whether one can be aware of ideas at all. Naturally, it must first be determined what sort of things ideas are. I would propose that ideas are understood to be Meinongian entities, namely, presenting experiences. We shall not analyze them, for present purposes, into act and content. They remain unanalyzed. However, we take them to be presenting experiences of the same things which Meinong calls "objecta," namely, individuals, properties, and relations.

The reader is asked to catch himself having an idea of an individual, property, or relation. He will find that, in the case of such an awareness, not only the experience which is an idea is present, but another experience, in which the idea occurs as, so to speak, a mentioning. For example, pick any noun or adjective, e.g., "brown" or "horse" or "Hercules." The awareness of experiences presenting just those objects which are named by "brown," "horse," and "Hercules" is always more like a judgment: e.g., "Now I'm thinking of brown," or "Now I am imagining Hercules," or "Now I am aware of having an idea of an object called 'horse.'"

In those cases, the idea-experience and the awareness of it are different things. The awareness is a judgment; it is, moreover, a perceptual judgment about the idea. The idea is not caught independent of any context whatsoever. It is caught as the object of a judgment. It is, so to speak, embedded in another experience.

Any decision concerning the awareness of ideas must be made by any subject for himself, for it is an empirical matter of introspection. But it seems that ideas are elements of psychic experiences which function as foundations of other experiences. They are so elementary that they can almost be considered as hypothetical entities.

EMOTIONAL PRESENTATION

The Problem

OVER THE DECADES, Meinong revised many of his old views. This holds in particular for his meta-ethical and meta-aesthetic theories. *On Emotional Presentation* is his last and most mature monograph on these matters. In order to give as coherent a picture as possible, we will mainly refer to this book in our outline of his theory.

The questions with which Meinong was concerned can be formulated thus: We have expressions for moral and aesthetic attributes; we have expressions for obligations and for rules of moral behavior. We use these expressions frequently and with a positive attitude of conviction. Do these expressions denote anything, do they refer to any object? What sort of objects would they be, and how are they presented? How can we know that statements attributing an aesthetic or moral property to something are true? What is the whole situation of knowledge—if there is such a situation at all—in moral and aesthetic matters? Meinong fully realizes the precariousness of the situation, especially since the value-theory of his time took a very psychologistic, relativistic attitude, to which he himself occasionally refers.[37] He does not intend to overthrow it or completely antagonize it, but he intends to find a reconciliation between that theory and what he believes to be the general convictions of common sense.

The only way for Meinong to get to moral and aesthetic objects, if there are any, is by the investigation of experiences that seem to be relevant. The relevant experiences are sorted out, that is, all experiences which pertain in some way or other to moral and aesthetic matters. Of some of those experiences it is clear to him that they present something, and it is by way of these experiences that Meinong arrives at moral and aesthetic objects.[38] We will come back to this question a little later.

37. *Ibid.*, footnotes to pp. 111, 112, 131, 134.
38. *Ibid.*, pp. 98 f., 150 f.

Once Meinong has got hold of the objects, he naturally considers them to be independent of their presenting experiences, and he classifies and describes them.[39] In all this, the previously achieved results in the theory of objecta and objectives and their presenting experiences serve as a guideline by analogy to which he formulates his theory of moral and aesthetic objects.

The last two sections of the book are mainly concerned with the problem of knowledge in the domain of values and obligations. Meinong is not deceived by his wishful thinking concerning the (*a priori*) knowledge of objects but points out clearly the difficulties involved, which, as he believes, lie in the knowing subject and not in the objects known.

I shall not trace the roundabout investigations which led Meinong to his final results but shall proceed as I did in the first part of this Introduction and describe the objects in queston first. The presentation of the objects will then be considered, and finally I shall give a short account of Meinong's view of the problems of knowledge concerning moral and aesthetic matters.

Dignitatives

We are now dealing with the realm of values and obligations, i.e., moral and aesthetic properties and obligations. All these are objects, too. However, they are not objecta and objectives, though their features are similar to those of objecta and objectives. The relationships between moral and aesthetic properties and obligations are similar to the relationships holding between objecta and objectives. That is, as objecta are related to objectives, so moral and aesthetic properties are related to obligations. We shall return to this shortly.

The justification for their being (independent) objects is founded on the fact that there are experiences presenting them. We must wait until we have talked about this kind of presentation, which is emotional presentation, before we can consider the justification. For the time being it must be taken for granted that they are objects, and we ask now what sort of objects they are.

39. *Ibid.*, p. 99.

Meinong also calls the class of moral and aesthetic properties "values," if the term is taken in its broadest sense. The values are any properties belonging to the basic classes of the beautiful, good, true, and pleasant.[40] In *On Emotional Presentation* Meinong concentrates on aesthetic properties. In respect to the moral properties, he mainly stresses their impersonal character. "Value" is not used as a proper technical term; Meinong uses, for a technical term, the expression "dignitative," which means roughly the same thing as "value," or a "dignity" possessed by someone or something. One of the reasons for Meinong's choosing new and often strange-sounding words is that the traditional terms already have so many connotations that they are not as manageable as Meinong would like them to be.

The dignitatives are not objecta. Drawing on Findlay's interpretation, I shall try to explain why Meinong believes that they are not objecta. Objecta can consist of all sorts of congruous and incongruous combinations of objecta, the most extreme of which are the impossible objecta, of which the square circle and the oval triangle are examples. Another example of an incongruous combination is the objectum "multicolored golden-winged aquatic night." No such combinations are feasible among dignitatives; there are not enough different sorts of dignitatives for that; there is no such variety or heteronomy among dignitatives as among objecta.[41] Dignitatives are only the four basic properties: beautiful, good, true, pleasant, and their contraries. All these can be combined as one wishes. Something can be true and good, good and unpleasant and ugly, beautiful and unpleasant, and so forth. But the number of combinations is limited by reason of the limited number of basic properties.

Dignitatives are also not objectives. For clearly they are properties and not an object's being or an object's being thus-and-so.[42] They are in a class by themselves, but they more resemble objecta than objectives.

40. From the text it is not clear whether only actions are good or also persons and circumstances. I shall not attempt an explanation of this term.

41. Findlay, *Meinong's Theory of Objects and Values*, p. 314; *On Emotional Presentation*, pp. 95 f.

42. *On Emotional Presentation*, pp. 95 f.

Dignitatives are *superiora,* or objects of higher order. We recall that anything which needs for its being some other object, that is, a presuppositional object, is an object of higher order. Thus objectives are objects of higher order because they need for their being objecta as presuppositional objects. Objectives are the being, or being thus-and-so, of objecta. Or, objectives need for their being other objectives of a lower order. In that case, objectives of lower order constitute objectives of higher order. Some objecta are objects of higher order; an example is difference, which needs at least two presuppositional objects which are different. Similarity is also an object of higher order. In short, all relations are objects of higher order because they need for their being objects between which they hold. The dignitatives are not relations, but they need for their being other properties, i.e., objecta, to which, as Meinong says, they attach themselves.[43] As an example, let me quote a passage from *On Emotional Presentation:*

> The property "beautiful," like the property "red," not only requires something of which it is a property, but it requires another property or complex of properties as its basis, which is as much a necessary condition for its occurrence as a red thing is for the property red.[44]

This does not mean that "beautiful" is a property of properties; it means that "beautiful" needs other properties in order to occur. In order for an object to be beautiful, it must first have other properties in virtue of which it is beautiful.[45]

Meinong is deeply concerned with the question of what he calls "personal" and "impersonal" values or "relative" and "relation-free" values. According to this division, values are either dependent on a subject for whom they are a value or they are independent of any subject.[46] In the former case, the value rises or perishes with the subject or the subject's interest, as happens with some stray pieces of objects to which children become attached. But most dignitatives, like those of

43. *Ibid.,* pp. 92, 94 ff.
44. *Ibid.,* p. 92.
45. *Ibid.,* p. 6.
46. For the following see *ibid.,* pp. 127, 129 f., 131, 133, 135 f.

the classes beautiful, good, and true, are relation-free or impersonal. There is, according to Meinong, as yet no definite proof of this statement, but there are indications of its correctness. Predicates like "beautiful," "true," and "good" name properties of objects in the same way as "blue" or "prime number" do. These predicates have no characteristic by which it is indicated that the properties which they name are relational. Another argument in favor of impersonal values is, for Meinong, the attitude of public opinion. To be sure, people disagree in what they call beautiful, true, or good. But anyone who calls an object good or beautiful, etc., is utterly convinced that he is right in attributing this property. Another argument in favor of impersonal values is found by Meinong in timelessly beautiful examples of art, as in Greek sculpture and German poetry and music.[47] They are beautiful and have been accepted as beautiful through the ages, through all changes of taste and aesthetic theories.

Impersonal values are independent of any subject's acknowledging them; this they have in common with objecta and objectives. Personal values occur only in connection with a subject and a subject's acknowledgment.

The presuppositional objects of impersonal values do not have to exist. It is not of primary relevance into what class of being they fall. The value, especially of aesthetic dignitatives, depends upon the properties which the presuppositional object has. In Meinong's words:

> The impersonal value is not then attached to the being of the objectum but to the being thus-and-so of the objectum in question. I believe therefore that, as regards impersonal value, the so-called true value, one is justified in denying that the being of its object is relevant.[48]

Thus a fictional person in a novel may be good, a poem never written or said may be beautiful, and objectives never presented may be true.

An object's having a certain value or having a property which is a dignitative is naturally an objective. We will return to this later.

47. *Ibid.*, p. 149; Findlay, p. 319.
48. *On Emotional Presentation*, p. 141.

Desideratives

In the preceding section Meinong's theory of values was considered. Values in a broad sense, i.e., dignitatives, are comparable to objecta. However, they are exclusively of higher order. These dignitatives serve as presuppositional objects to another class of objects, namely, obligations, or, as Meinong calls them, desideratives.

First, some general remarks concerning obligations. For Meinong an obligation is always an obligation for something to be,[49] that is, for something to be realized or to be done. Obligations usually find expression in commands and commandments and other expressions of similar order. Obligations cannot be unless there is something good, worthwhile, praiseworthy, beautiful, true—in short, anything of value about which they are. Thus, in the obligation that one must honor one's father and mother, it is one's father and mother who have a certain value. In the obligation that great pieces of art must be preserved, it is the great pieces of art which have beauty. The values must be there first before there can be any obligation. However, for Meinong, obligations do not concern values directly, though values are the presuppositional objects of obligations. Obligations concern objectives.[50] This means that they concern objectives of which objects which have value are "constituents." Take, for example, parents, and assume that parents have value. Then there is some objective that parents are honored. This is an objective with which the obligation, namely, that one must honor one's father and mother, is concerned.

There is one restriction in respect to objectives with which obligations are concerned, that is, they must be possible.[51] I cannot enter into a discussion of Meinong's theory of possibility. But I can say what possible objectives are not, according to Meinong.[52] They are not something that has happened, like the assassination of royalty in 1914; they are not present changes of things which at present are (or are not) the case, as, e.g., somebody in prison is free right now; they are not

49. *Ibid.*, p. 142.
50. *Ibid.*, p. 141.
51. *Ibid.*, pp. 142 ff.
52. *Ibid.*

anything which definitely will or will not be the case, as that it will be winter in five months (when it is now July). Accordingly, there cannot be the following obligations: the assassination of royalty in 1914 must not have happened; the prisoner must be free right now; it must be winter in five months (when it is now July). Thus, obligations must concern objectives which are not the case but which can be realized though they are not necessarily realized; and, according to Meinong, what must be can be.

There are two kinds of obligations, "obligations simple" and obligations for a certain purpose, "obligations of means." [53] Simple obligations always concern objects which have unconditional value and not value in respect to something else. Thus parents have such value, and Michelangelo's *Pietà* is, simply, beautiful. But there are objects which obtain value for a certain purpose or aim. For example, someone wants to be a competent physician. For this it is worthwhile to be well trained in some of the natural sciences. Thus, in respect to the goal of becoming a competent physician, being well trained in some of the natural sciences is worthwhile or good; and there is an objective, namely, one's being trained in some of the natural sciences, with which an obligation is concerned. And this obligation is an obligation of means.

Although desideratives are not objectives (why they are not will be explained soon), they have some similarities to objectives, of which the just-mentioned division of desideratives into obligations simple and obligations of means is one. Meinong says that obligations simple correspond to objectives of (an object's) being,[54] which, as we remember, are an object's existence or subsistence or *Aussersein;* and obligations of means correspond to objectives (of an object's) being thus-and-so. That is, that characteristic of an obligation of means which corresponds to the thus-and-so is its being an obligation for a certain purpose.

Desideratives are objects of higher order in respect to dignitatives because the dignitatives are their presuppositional objects. Their need for presuppositional objects is another feature which they have in common with objectives. In virtue of this feature they naturally are not objecta. But they also

53. *Ibid.,* pp. 98 f.
54. *Ibid.*

are not objectives. Meinong gives the following reason: when an objective is denied, the result of the denial is an objective contradictory to the given one.[55] This is not the case with desideratives. When they are denied, the result is usually a desiderative contrary to the given one. To illustrate this, the following example is given: If "You must honor your father and mother" is denied, the result is "You must not honor your father and mother," which is precisely the opposite order to the one given. In virtue of this feature, Meinong believes that desideratives cannot be objectives. Since they are not objecta and also not dignitatives, they form a class of objects by themselves.

Thus we have described briefly all classes of objects. But Meinong says that it is by no means certain that these four classes really exhaust all the classes of objects.[56] There may be more; and it depends on future investigations to uncover all possibilities.

Presentation of Dignitatives.   Feelings

In the description of dignitatives and desideratives we have presumed that there are such objects. Meinong does not give a proof of their independent being, but he infers their being from the existence of certain experiences, and he believes that he has shown, as we remember, that, whenever something is presented, that something has being, independent of the presentation. But it needs to be shown that, since dignitatives are not presented by ideas and since there are certain emotions, emotions can present. First, there is self-presentation; then, we are aware of emotional experiences because they present themselves. Thus we know that emotional experiences are presentations; they consist of act and content, both of which are prerequisite for self-presentation.[57] Since they are presentatives, they are also presentatives of something other than themselves.[58] Long before Meinong wrote

55. *Ibid.*, pp. 96 f., 102 f.
56. *Ibid.*, p. 100.
57. *Ibid.*, p. 132.
58. *Psychologisch-ethische Untersuchungen zur Werttheorie*, p. 29; "Für die Psychologie und gegen den Psychologismus"; *On Emotional Presentation*, p. 99.

On Emotional Presentation, he had come to the conclusion that the main kinds of presenting emotions are feelings and desires. What sort of objects they present has been our main concern in the previous two sections. His arriving at those objects is explained in the following way: because of the duality of objecta and objectives which corresponds to the duality of their presenting experiences, Meinong says that he is prejudiced in favor of a duality in all additional classes of objects, especially since he has already discovered the pair of experiences, feelings and desires. Following his prejudice, he takes the duality as a heuristic principle.[59] Therefore, he assumes that there are objects of feeling and objects of desire, of which the first is probably idea-like and the second objective-like.

Then, investigating feelings, i.e., experiences concerning dignitatives, Meinong writes,

> When I say, "The sky is blue," and then say "The sky is beautiful," a property is attributed to the sky in either case. In the second case a feeling participates in the apprehension of the property, as, in the first case, an idea does. And it is natural to let the feeling be the presentative factor in the second case, as an idea is always taken to be in the first case.[60]

In this example an idea presents the property "blue" and a feeling presents the property "beautiful." Thus feelings can be significant for the characterization of objects. They present properties which objects actually have.[61] In analogy to ideas, feelings function as "content-presentatives of objects." In the same way as ideas are called content-presentations or partial presentations and passive experiences, so feelings are called content-presentations, partial presentations, and passive experiences. And just as ideas by themselves, outside the context of a judgment or assumption, do not properly apprehend anything, so also feelings need to be supplemented by judgments and assumptions if a dignitative is to be apprehended as the property of some object.[62]

59. *On Emotional Presentation,* pp. 112 f.
60. *Ibid.,* p. 28.
61. *Ibid.,* pp. 28, 29.
62. *Ibid.,* pp. 105 ff.

Dignitatives are also "constituents" of objectives [63] which are either true or false. How to determine whether a value-statement is the statement of a true or false objective is quite a problematical question, to which we will return in the final section of this Introduction. It belongs to the whole problem of knowing in the sphere of emotional presentation.

For any value-experience there is a psychological presupposition.[64] That psychological presupposition (or also psychological object-presupposition) is the idea of an object or the assumption or judgment of an objective which has the value. There must first be objecta which are beautiful or good, objectives which are true, objecta or objectives which are pleasant. The content of the psychological presupposition is the presuppositional content for the value-feeling. The value-feeling, of course, has its own content, which corresponds to the value presented, e.g., beauty, ugliness, truth, goodness, etc.

Thus, whenever a value-feeling occurs, it presupposes the idea of some objectum or an assumption or a judgment. Just as dignitatives for their being presuppose some object (existing, subsisting, or with *Aussersein*), so the presentations of dignitatives, namely, feelings, presuppose for their occurrence presentations of those objects which are presuppositional in respect to dignitatives. However, the psychological presupposition may occur without the occurrence of the value-feeling. One may have an idea of Michelangelo's *Pietà*, or one may perceive his *Pietà* without experiencing or feeling its beauty. But the *Pietà*'s beauty cannot be felt without one's having an idea of the *Pietà*.

Presentation of Desideratives. Desires

Obligations are not objectives or objecta, according to Meinong. Therefore they cannot be presented by intellectual

---

63. Judgments present objectives. Here, objectives evidently sometimes have dignitatives as "constituents." However, Meinong's earlier theory named only objecta and objectives as "constituents" of objectives. With the development of his meta-ethical theory Meinong should have made amendments to his original theory of objectives, which he apparently did not do.

64. *On Emotional Presentation*, § 8.

presentation. Thus they are emotionally presented. Since they resemble objectives, they are presented by emotions which resemble judgments. Feelings do not come into consideration, for feelings resemble ideas, and they present values. For Meinong, then, desires are the presentatives of obligations. This, he admits himself, seems to be odd at first sight. For one easily finds examples of cases where something which we would call undesirable is desired.[65] The actual occurrence of desires is not such that obligations could be explained from the point of view of the subject who has the desires. Something, for example, may be desired which is for us unobjectionable but does not seem to be an obligation. *On Emotional Presentation* does not explicitly deal with this question. Its problem is not primarily whether all unobjectionable desires present actual obligations but how obligations are presented by desires. Whenever an obligation is presented, it is, according to Meinong, presented by a desire. These are results which he obtained in his psychological investigations of previous years and which are already more or less presupposed in *On Emotional Presentation.*[66]

We remember that obligations for their being need presuppositional objects which are dignitatives. Dignitatives, for their being, need presuppositional objects which are either objecta or objectives. The presentation of dignitatives has psychological presuppositions which are either ideas or judgments or assumptions. Now desires which present obligations have, as their psychological presuppositions, feelings, or value-experiences, and therefore depend on all the presuppositions pertaining to feelings. Like all presentatives, they consist of act and content. The content corresponds to that which is desired. The content also determines the strength of the desires.[67] This is understandable when we realize that the valuable is desired; and, the more valuable something is, the more it is desired. Thus the intensity of a feeling or desire is the presentative of the intensity of value or obligation which is the proper object of the feelings or desires.[68]

65. *Ibid.,* p. 141.
66. See his earlier writings: "Für die Psychologie und gegen den Psychologismus"; *Über Annahmen,* 2d ed., Chaps. XXIV, XXV; and *Psychologisch-ethische Untersuchungen* (not available to me).
67. *On Emotional Presentation,* p. 102.
68. *Ibid.,* p. 100.

Just as not every valuable object when it is thought of or perceived needs to occasion a feeling of value, so not every value, when it is presented, needs to occasion a desire. Depending upon whether a value is personal or impersonal, the desire is personal or impersonal. That is, impersonal desires present impersonal obligations; personal desires present personal obligations. Obligations are personal or impersonal depending upon whether their presuppositional objects are personal or impersonal values. However, in the same way as a valuable object may not occasion a desire, so it may also occasion a misapplied desire. For example, the impersonal beauty of an El Greco should in all propriety be only the presuppositional object for obligations which concern its preservation and public benefit. It should not occasion the desire to steal it in order to own it, though that might very well happen. But this desire would be an error or a misguided desire, comparable with errors in judgments.[69] Such errors naturally are possible only if there are certain standards by which the justification of desires can, at least in principle, be measured. The standards are supplied by the theory of values; for only the being of something of value should be desired.

That there are impersonal values and corresponding impersonal obligations is not doubted by Meinong. But he knows that in particular cases there is no method *as yet* for deciding whether a certain object really has the value which is being felt and whether a certain desire presents an actual obligation. Meinong compares our knowledge of values with our relationship to the external world. He says, "Under favorable conditions there is very good evidence that there is such a world but very bad evidence as to what its character may be."[70]

Meinong believes that obligations and objectives have some features in common but that they are presented by two different classes of experiences. However, even desires and judgments have features in common, of which one is that they both depend on psychological presuppositions. As judgments are divided according to their presenting either an objective of (an object's) being or an objective of (an object's)

69. *Ibid.*, p. 108.
70. *Ibid.*, p. 138.

being thus-and-so, desires are divided according to their presenting either an obligation simple or an obligation for a certain purpose.[71] But desires are not true or false. And, like feelings, desires "cannot know and cannot apprehend completely." [72] At this point their similarity to judgments breaks down. This, if I understand it rightly, can only mean that to be aware of an obligation is to experience a judgment. But an obligation is presented by a desire whenever a command is given or a commandment is formulated. Then the command and commandment are expressive of desire.

Justification of Feelings and Desires

The question of the justification of value-judgments and of desires is naturally very difficult. Meinong is fully aware of the difficulty.[73] Obligations and values are objects of higher order. Any knowledge of them, if there is any, must be *a priori*.[74] Anything that seems to be perceptual in connection with them is comparable to empiricism in mathematics. But, before dealing at all with any *a priori* knowledge, we must first state that, according to Meinong, desires and feelings are neither true nor false, but justified or unjustified. Obligations are not factual, as some objectives are.[75] It makes no sense to ask for the factuality of obligations. This question can be asked only in respect to objectives. The justification of feelings and desires depends upon the justification of judgments of value and judgments concerning obligations.[76] The question now is: are such judgments decidable? Obviously, at present they are not. Meinong reduces the question thus: Is there a remote chance that they might be decidable? Let us now see what he has to say in that respect.

Let us take an example which Meinong uses. A father commands his son, "Come here!" This command expresses a desire. The desire concerns the son's obligation to come. Now the desire is justified if the judgment, "It is a son's obligation

71. *Ibid.*, pp. 98 f.
72. *Ibid.*, p. 106.
73. For the following see *ibid.*, §§ 12 and 13.
74. *Ibid.*, p. 117.
75. *Ibid.*
76. See footnote 63, above, p. lxi.

to come when the father calls him," is true. The judgment is true under some conditions. There must be values in virtue of which the son's coming to his father or following his father's command is an obligation. In order to determine whether there are such values, value-judgments must be decidable. Before Meinong speaks about errors in desires, he focuses his attention on value-errors. There are two kinds of errors involved. First is the error in the presupposition of values, which is an intellectual error. Meinong says, by way of example, "Anybody is also simply intellectually wrong who values a sugar pill for its healing power." [77]

The other kind of error concerns the valuation proper. There is some similarity between this and intellectual experiences which concern evidence. We have not talked at all about evidence in this Introduction, for the problem of evidence is not a major topic of *On Emotional Presentation,* and it is treated at length in Meinong's earlier works. For our purpose it will suffice to accept the term as it is, undefined, and to use it only to divide valuations into two groups, namely, those which are directly evident and those which are not. Some judgments of value, according to Meinong, are directly evident. Thus, "justice, gratitude, benevolence carry the guarantee of their worth in themselves." [78] The same thing is true of great pieces of art.

But what about cases of valuations about which there are differences of opinion? First of all, whoever believes something believes that he is right in his belief. Beliefs are contagious; that is, someone else who originally had no opinion may become inclined to adopt the same belief, "at least to the extent that for him the fact of that belief means either a strong or weak presumption in favor of the truth of that which is believed." [79] Whenever a presuppositional object and a value are simultaneously given, there is "presumptive" evidence that the object has the value.[80] The lack of verification is, according to Meinong, no greater than in judgments of external perception. There are, in principle, means of knowing whether a given object has a dignitative or not (we mostly

77. For the "logic" of valuation see Findlay, Chap. IX; *On Emotional Presentation,* p. 108.
78. *On Emotional Presentation,* p. 109.
79. *Ibid.,* p. 120.
80. *Ibid.,* pp. 121 f., 152.

lxvi / ON EMOTIONAL PRESENTATION

do in fact know it, if the dignitative in question is truth or falsehood), but thus far only "divinatory approaches" can be made. Though any possible knowledge must be *a priori*, we must start from our actual valuations and experiences.[81] When there is a general strong feeling about the value of a certain object, a public consensus, it may be assumed that the object actually has the value as a property. The facts of tolerance and intolerance in respect to certain issues must also be considered. Any value-experience can in principle be considered to be as reliable as a perceptual experience. However, for this sort of intuition one must have a certain talent, which obviously is quite rare, especially in respect to moral values. In comparison with morals, aesthetic intuition is quite unproblematical.

In summary, Meinong says that "emotions are justified if the judgments which attribute their proper objects to their presuppositional objects are justified." [82] This is apparently to be understood thus: if we are "normal," then we have the experience of a dignitative when we are confronted with it. However, the experience is not perception, because dignitatives are not perceptible. A judgment like "This objectum is, in virtue of certain perceptible properties, beautiful" is *a priori*. This does not mean that taste, for example, cannot be trained. All knowledge of dignitatives and relevant desideratives is compared with mathematics, which first developed from quite empirical statements and methods.[83] As the properties of ideal triangles can be shown in actual triangles, so ideal states of affairs of dignitatives are concomitant with real states of affairs, and any lawful connection between them becomes empirically apparent.[84] Which real states of affairs are connected with dignitatives can be empirically stated by singling out those intellectual experiences which arouse emotions. Of course, the occurrence of the emotions is no proof of the subsistence of a specific dignitative, but it gives a reason in favor of the presumption that there is a specific dignitative.

This theory of knowledge concerning dignitatives and desideratives in reality depends upon Meinong's belief that

81. *Ibid.*, § 13.
82. *Ibid.*, p. 140.
83. *Ibid.*, pp. 149 f.
84. *Ibid.*

there are values independent of the subject's experiencing them. That there are such values is known by our experiencing them. This is circular, of course. But surely Meinong was aware of that. Taking into consideration the character of this topic, one cannot hold it against him.

MARIE-LUISE SCHUBERT KALSI

Houston
January, 1972

On Emotional Presentation

1 / Self-Presentation and Other-Presentation

ELSEWHERE [1] I HAVE ATTEMPTED to explicate the notion of presentation and its application beyond the intellectual domain.[2] The primary aim of the following discussion is to provide a detailed clarification of the concept of presentation and to illustrate its application. But first some general remarks must be made.

The notion of presentation has its origin in the fact that there are experiences in virtue of which the apprehension of the specific character of an object is rendered possible even though the apprehension may be incomplete. This is shown most clearly in the case of ideas (*Vorstellungen*), which,

1. See "Über die Erfahrungsgrundlagen unseres Wissens," No. VI of *Abhandlungen zur Didaktik u. Philos. d. Naturwissenschaft* (Berlin, 1906), pp. 72 ff.; *Über Annahmen*, 2d ed. (Leipzig: Barth, 1910; 1st ed., 1902) [unless otherwise indicated, all citations of *Über Annahmen* are to the second edition]; *Über Möglichkeit und Wahrscheinlichkeit* (Leipzig, 1915), § 33; see also "Für die Psychologie und gegen den Psychologismus in der allgemeinen Werttheorie," *Logos*, III (1912), 10 ff.

2. In the present discussion, "intellectual" is opposed to "emotional" in the same sense as *Geistesleben* and *Gemütsleben* are opposed in the psychological discussions by A. Höfler or St. Witasek. Accordingly, feelings in particular are paradigm cases of the emotional, in connection with which one easily thinks of *Gemütsbewegungen* (cf. E. Becher's terminological proposal in "Gefühlsbegriff und Lust-Unlustelemente," *Ztschr. f. Psychol.*, LXXIV [1915], 150), so that in the following discussion we concentrate on them and on desires as the primary elementary experiences characterizing the field of the emotional.

though they have an object, do not enable us adequately to grasp this object since they lack the active character requisite for such apprehension.

Thus one might feel tempted simply to identify the presentation of an object with having an idea of it. This would be in agreement with the meaning of the word "presentation" in the Romance languages and in English, and it would make it unnecessary to distinguish between the notion of having an idea and the notion of presentation. But if the results of recent investigations concerning these matters are reliable, there are objects, i.e., *objectives,* which can be apprehended even though we cannot have ideas of them. However, the experiences apprehending such objectives, that is, the experiences that might more precisely be called "thoughts," exhibit a characteristic which varies directly with the characteristic exemplified by the apprehended objectives. One can talk of the contents of thoughts just as one can talk of a characteristic part of ideas, namely, their content, which is the means by which their objects are apprehended. Naturally, there can be no experienced content of thought apart from an act of thinking. However, on account of the intimate relationship between the content of a thought and the object of that thought, it makes good sense to say that the content presents the object to thought. Thus, it appears that the notion of presentation has an actual use in this connection.

In the light of these considerations, there is presentation without any having of ideas. The introduction of the concept of thinking into the explication of the notion of presentation immediately effects a change in our analysis of ideas. If in thinking it is mainly the content which does the presenting, and it is the content which might technically be called the "presentative," it may be reasonably presumed that in the having of ideas (*bei der Vorstellung*) the content alone performs a similar function. It does not follow, however, that thinking and having ideas are indistinguishable. The distinction is justified by the fact that in the having of ideas there is presentation without any "completed" (*fertige*) apprehension, whereas in thinking the presentation is simultaneously combined through the thought-content (*Denkinhalt*) with the total thought-experience (*Denkerlebnis*), and so with the completed (*fertige*) apprehension of the objective. In comparison with the original paradigm of all presentation offered us by the having of ideas, the presentation which exhibits itself in thinking is, to some extent, more closely connected with active apprehension. There is a kind of analogue to this: if circumstances other than those covered by the paradigm previously referred to obtain, something like a separation of the characteristic elements of presentation can be noted.

This is the case where "mediate"[3] presentation, or rather, presentation mediated by a reference by way of being-thus-and-so (*Soseinsmeinen*), takes the place of "immediate" presentation. When, for example, the object "something black" (*Schwarzes*) is to be apprehended instead of the object "black" (*Schwarz*), the black-content doubtless functions as a presentative, but not this content alone, since the content of the thought-experience also participates in the presentation. Through this content access is gained to that special case of being-thus-and-so (*Sosein*) which is that of being black (*das Schwarzsein*). The situation here is consequently so different from our original paradigm that one might hesitate to subsume a reference to "something black" under the general heading of "presentation" at all. It is likewise doubtful whether a reference by way of being-thus-and-so is not quite as much a case of complete apprehension as is a reference by way of being (*Seinsmeinen*). That the two cannot thus be equated seems to be clear insofar as "something black" (*Schwarzes*) and "black" (*Schwarz*) would then be quite on a level, inasmuch as for the apprehension of "something black" (*ein Schwarzes*) a judgment or at least an assumption of being is quite as necessary as in the apprehension of "black." Apparently a reference to an object as being thus-and-so achieves no more here than an idea achieves in our paradigm. Reference to an object as being thus-and-so must therefore be considered as a case of presentation even though there are important differences.

But presentations mediated by a reference to an object as being thus-and-so, which are called by me "mediate presentations," lie a little beyond the main scope of the present discussion. Here we are concerned with the whole domain in which presentation is to be found, and immediate as well as mediate presentation. First appearances had identified being presented with being the object of an idea, but the whole field was widened when objectives entered the scene and the man-

3. *Über Möglichkeit und Wahrscheinlichkeit*, pp. 194 ff.

ner in which objectives were apprehended. It is above all important to realize at this point that the enlargement effected by admitting objectives has not taken us beyond the realm of the intellect, but that such an extension is required; for the domain must also include our emotional experiences, our feelings, and our desires.

This is made clear by the facts of internal perception. Each perception is a judgment of existence (*Daseinsurteil*).[4] Each judgment is a nonindependent experience which depends on another experience as its "psychological presupposition."[5] It has traditionally been taken for granted that ideas are in the exceptional position of being the indispensable presuppositions for all other psychic events. I have, however, tried to show that in perceiving inner experiences there is no reason to believe that the relation between apprehension and what is apprehended is mediated by an idea of the latter.[6] Such a mediation is necessary whenever something external to the judging subject is to be apprehended through a judgment. But why should a judgment not directly turn toward an internal event without the mediation of ideas, which, after all, are internal to the subject too? So far the idea of a simultaneously occurring inner experience has never been empirically shown to exist separately and apart from this experience itself, so that it can be assumed that, in the perception of an internal event, the perceptual judgment immediately directs itself to this event. And so we might say that this event supplies the material for the judgment which, under different circumstances, is provided in respect to physical (outer) events by the content of an idea. Since the function of an idea's content is called "presentation," we were justified in using the same term to apply to the same thing in the case of internal perception. It must, however, be remembered that that which presents is at the same time the presented, so that the expression "self-presentation" is appropriate. Such self-presentation is to be contrasted with other-presentation (*Fremdpräsentation*), where the content of the idea functions as the presentative.

When these expressions were first used as technical terms,[7]

4. Cf. "Über die Erfahrungsgrundlagen unseres Wissens," p. 16.
5. Cf. *Psychologisch-ethische Untersuchungen zur Werttheorie* (Graz, 1894), pp. 33 ff.; see also below, pp. 26 f., 59 ff.
6. "Über die Erfahrungsgrundlagen unseres Wissens," pp. 72 ff.
7. *Über Annahmen,* pp. 138 ff.

H. Bergmann remarked that "Brentano had in his *Psychologie* already used the notion of self-presentation." [8] This is borne out by the following pronouncement of Brentano: "In the same psychical phenomenon in which a sound is presented we apprehend simultaneously the psychic phenomenon itself in its double aspect: insofar as its content is the sound and insofar as it is present to itself as content." [9] The following statement, however, makes it clear that I cannot unreservedly accept Brentano's view, since he says that "there never is a psychic phenomenon in us of which we have no idea." [10] However, in view of what was said above, to be "conscious" of a feeling does not require an "idea of a feeling" (*Gefühlsvorstellung*), to say nothing of unconscious feelings. In fact, Bergmann says that

> even Meinong must admit that when a judgment about an internal state or event is joined to a self-presenting idea of, say, a sound, not only an attitude characteristic of judgment is added—were this the case it would only be a judging of the sound and not of the hearing of it—but there is also an added reference to a new object, namely, the hearing of the sound. In other words: if I have an idea of *a* and a judgment is conjoined with this idea, I cannot understand why this judgment is about my idea instead of being about the *a*. If the judgment is to be about my idea, a new object-relationship must emerge; and if Meinong refuses to call the relationship "having an idea," we have a terminological, not a real, disagreement.[11]

This is yet another proof that Bergmann's attempt at agreement fails: our differences, however, are more distinctly contrasted, as we shall see below. It is of minor importance that I surely must "refuse" to call a relationship, albeit an "object-relationship," "having an idea," in that I always mean by "having an idea" an experience. It is more important that the "disagreement" in question is not merely terminological, as becomes evident when interest shifts from the domain of having ideas, into which "hearing" falls, to some other domain, e.g., that of emotional experiences. For it is clear that, in respect to hearing, that is, generally in respect to ideas, the presentation, even the self-presentation, is carried out by the having of an idea. But it is also evident that, in a self-presentation of feeling, the feeling

8. *Zeitschr. f. Philos. u. philos. Kritik*, CXLIII (1911), 112.
9. F. Brentano, *Psychologie*, I, 167.
10. *Ibid.*, p. 180.
11. *Ztschr. f. Philos. u. philos. Kritik*, CXLIII, 113.

takes the place of an idea, and that, in a self-presentation of desire, the desire takes the place of the idea. However, it is not terminologically permissible to call a feeling an "idea" merely because it presents something.

Quite often the opinion is expressed that an internal experience cannot be apprehended at the very time of its occurrence.[12] It can only be remembered later, and so not perceived (at least not in the strictest sense of the word). This obviously does not agree with what I have just said about self-presentation. But as far as I know, no one has yet shown something that prevents the apprehension of an experience from occurring at the same time as the experience. It is a commonplace experience that when I have a sufficiently bad headache or toothache I know about it only too well at the same time. Under favorable conditions, I can also simultaneously direct my knowledge to what I am now experiencing as visual, aural, or other sensation, etc. But the tendency to look for greater complications in what seems so simple surely has its main source in those exaggerated developments of self-perception which are spoken of as "self-observations." These without doubt demand a great deal of the observer's intentions and attention, and they may demand almost too much in some experiences, as, for example, in strong affects. All attempts to overcome such difficulties may disturb, i.e., modify, the total psychic state and the experiences under observation. The attempts may render the reliability of the observations questionable, even if the observations can be obtained at all. But there is, however, no reason to assume that such disturbances must occur in every case of self-observation.[13] And there is still less reason to assume that this, though it may be true for self-observation, must also be true for the much less exacting case of self-perception.

It is wrong to believe that my statements regarding self-presentation threaten the exceptional position that traditional thought has assigned to ideas in preference to other elementary psychic experiences (*psychische Elementarerlebnisse*). But it is correct to hold that, if a feeling presents itself immediately to perception, the perceptual judgment does not need a special idea as its basis. This does not alter the fact that all thinking requires an object which is thought about, all feelings require an

12. See, e.g., H. Driesch, *Ordnungslehre* (Jena, 1912), p. 14.
13. Cf. "Über die Erfahrungsgrundlagen unseres Wissens," p. 53.

object which pleases or displeases, and all desires require an object toward (or against) whose being or nonbeing they are directed. This object (we shall refer [14] to it under the label of "presuppositional object" [*Voraussetzungsgegenstand*]) does not have to be apprehended by way of an idea; the facts of self-presentation seem to have established this. But even then the object must be apprehended by means of a psychic experience which somewhat indirectly presupposes an idea, though it itself is not one. We conclude that all psychic experiences are in fact "founded" on ideas and that self-presentations can claim no exceptional status.

14. See below, pp. 26 f., 59 ff.

2 / On the Paradox of Russell and Mally: Defective Objects

ONE SHOULD NOT, however, make use of the notion of self-presentation without first considering a difficulty which arises in connection with certain traditionally famous paradoxes that have again aroused much attention in recent years. Their significance for object-theory and, more especially, for the theory of apprehension has been very recently emphasized by E. Mally.[1] His object of concern was the relatively special case of a thought as a self-presenting experience. What he undertook was somewhat analogous to what had been done by B. Russell and A. N. Whitehead. For Mally's primary concern is to demonstrate the thesis that the notion of a thought which refers to itself (*sich selbst trifft*), and the notion of a thought that does not refer to itself, are alike "meaningless" (*sinnleer*) notions.[2] A judgment (and also an assumption) which presents itself seems to suffer from the same defect.

The first question naturally has to do with the validity of Mally's argument. Doubt arises not only in connection with the notion of self-presentation as characterized above. (This difficulty might be mitigated by the novelty of this notion.) But even such commonplace, familiar statements as that each judgment has an object, or that each judgment is either affirmative or negative in "quality," and so on, are not compatible with the thesis in question. For nobody would wish to hold that what is asserted of judgments in general is not asserted of the

1. "Über die Unabhängigkeit der Gegenstände vom Denken," *Ztschr. f. Philos. u. philos. Kritik*, CLX (1914), 37 ff.
2. *Ibid.*, § 1.

asserting judgment in question. The impression that in such cases one is confronted with something "meaningless," in whatever sense this word may be understood, is not in accord with direct experience (*Empirie*). It is altogether evident that, in general, thoughts do not concern themselves. If I think that, in the case of isosceles triangles, equal sides subtend equal angles, or that, during the events of the war in 1915, the Axis powers proved the match of their numerically superior enemy, it is difficult to see how these thoughts should be affected, as things meant or referred to, by these very thoughts themselves. Whoever denies this makes no meaningless claim, but a claim which is trivially true. But how can there be any resolution of the unmistakably paradoxical situation with which we are here confronted?

It would not conform to our general demand for simplicity to carry out an inquiry into a problem in apprehension-theory within the limits of set-theory, within which F. Burali Forti's and B. Russell's paradoxes have been almost exclusively discussed during recent years. Nevertheless, it might initially help to clarify the situation to consider first the so-called Russellian paradox, which is exclusively concerned with sets.[3] This treats of the set of sets that do not contain themselves as elements, and the question is whether such a set contains itself as an element or not. If it does not contain itself as an element, then it has precisely the characteristic feature of its elements; it must, in consequence, be an element of itself. If it contains itself as an element, it must have the characteristic feature of its elements, that is, it must not contain itself as an element. Thus there seems no way out of the conflict.

There is one striking presupposition on which the preceding considerations are founded. Is it possible for a set to contain itself as an element? As far as I can see, this is no more possible than for a whole to contain itself as a part or for a difference to be its own object of reference or its own foundation (*Fundament*). An object of higher order can never be its own subordinate.[4] The above seeming dilemma could easily be resolved. We

3. Cf. A. Rüstow, *Der Lügner*, Erlanger Dissertation (Leipzig, 1910), p. 3.
4. Cf. my discussion in "Über Gegenstände höherer Ordnung und deren Verhältnis zur inneren Wahrnehmung," *Ztschr. f. Psychol. und Physiol. d. Sinnesorgane*, XXI (1899), 189 f. (*Gesammelte Abhandlungen*, II, 385 ff.).

have to admit that in this way we can cut the knot, which, however, for the sake of theoretical interest, should be disentangled. The set that contains itself as an element is after all conceivable, and we must seek to determine in what follows what could possibly be meant by such a set.

As already stated, no collective can contain itself as a part. But there are circumstances in which it is natural to form a new collective out of the collective itself and its parts, which we will provisionally call a "derivative collective."

The sort of circumstances which might motivate the formation of a derivative collective is shown in the following example: all tables or chairs in a house, all houses in a town, are simple collectives. Also, the totality of all existing tables, chairs, or houses are natural collectives, and no one would think of including the set of chairs as an element in itself, though it is an object. But imagine that, instead of chairs, tables, houses, etc., one is concerned with the set of houses, set of chairs, and so on, in connection with which the set of these sets might also be considered; then it is in no way perverse to form a collective that contains both these sets and the set of these sets. This notion of set (*Mengengedanke*) is of course not identical with the notion of the set of the sets of tables, chairs, etc. It is clearly a derivative set, but also a natural as opposed to an unnatural set, even if for (or against) the formation of the latter there are no prohibitions whatever, since everything can in the end be collated (or put together) with everything. The alternative to Russell's paradox concerns derivative sets, that is, natural derivative sets. The principle of naturalness is then a relationship of similarity between the original (non-derivative) set and its elements.

What does this alternative come to on the interpretation given? The alternative is now concerned with the question as to whether a set of sets which do not have any natural derivative sets can itself constitute a natural derivative set. If the answer is in the negative, that our set does not point to a natural derivative set, or, more briefly, to a derivation, then no doubt it is similar in this respect to the sets which are its elements and which likewise cannot be included as components in natural derivative sets. If the answer is yes, then our set is not similar to its constituents. In the first case the dissimilarity of our set with its constituent sets lays the foundation of a new similarity; in the second case its similarity lays the foundation for a new dissimilarity. Thus we note that here too the similarity permits in the one case the formation of a new derivation, i.e., set, whereas dissimilarity in the other case does not permit this. No doubt we have here some complicated and perhaps some-what subtle states of affairs, but is there anything self-contradictory in them? All that it means, in the end, is that two objects may be similar in one respect and dissimilar in others. Black and white are different from each other; neither of them can be predicated of red or blue; in this respect they are similar. If similar things can form a collective, but dis-similar things cannot, then two objects considered in one way can form a collective, while considered in another way they cannot. The paradox, therefore, is easily resolved if a rigorous interpretation of the situation is given.

Let us return to E. Mally's argument. The problem is to de-termine whether a thought (D') about a thought (D) (*Den-ken*) which is not about itself (*sich selbst nicht trifft*) is about itself. If D' is not about itself, then it (D') is subsumable under the concept "thoughts not about themselves." Thus D' is about itself. If D' is about itself, then it (D') is not about itself since it is subsumable under the concept "thought which is about itself." The meaninglessness (*Sinnleerheit*) of the thought and its contrary is supposed to consist in just this. Here the analogy with what was said about sets is easily recognizable. An ex-perience is about an object insofar as it is a sufficiently ade-quate means of knowing the object (*Erkenntnismittel*). As pointed out elsewhere,[5] adequacy is not necessarily an exact or a partial likeness, but it conforms sufficiently to such a re-lationship for us to apply the aforementioned considerations to it.

First of all, it is clear, as mentioned above, that there are many thoughts, such as the thought of a triangle or of the war year 1915, etc., which certainly are not about themselves. Hence, it may well be asked in the case of a specific thought (D'), i.e., the thought of a thought (D) (*Denken*) that is not about itself, if it is about itself. If there is reason to deny this, thought (D) is a member of the class which is its own object. The thought itself falls under the domain of what the thought is about. In this respect it is about itself. If there is reason to give an affirmative answer to the question whether

5. *Über Annahmen*, pp. 263 f.

it is about itself, then the thought does not agree with its object and hence so far does not refer to itself. A thought which is at once about itself and not about itself is indeed peculiar. But these two adequacy-relationships (*Adäquatheitsverhältnisse*), i.e., the thought being at once about itself and not about itself, can coexist as long as they relate to different foundations (*sich auf verschiedene Grundlagen beziehen*). There is no more incompatibility here than in the analogous coexistence of exact likeness and unlikeness (as obtained in the case of colors) (*Gleichheit und Ungleichheit*). The appearance of a certain strangeness is accentuated in this case in that the two contrasting relations not only coexist but seem to be built on each other. Similarly, we can conceive of sameness and difference being analogous in this sense. Red differs from green to a certain extent, green from red to the same extent. If red and green are combined in a binary (*zweigliedrig*) complex, then the members of this complex differ from each other, but they are also like each other in virtue of the property of being different from the respective other member of the complex, and in being different from it to this definite extent.

However, there are circumstances which might prevent us from allowing this kind of tolerance, and which would make the charge of "meaninglessness" plausible and significant. There is scarcely doubt that these particular circumstances provided the characteristic grounds on which E. Mally and his predecessors based their positions.

The now famous example of the Cretan who says that all Cretans lie is not so much a case of these peculiar circumstances as is the simpler version of the statement (*Behauptung*) "What I say now is a lie or false." One can see at once that the two contradictory constituents are not compatible. Consider the sentence "If I lie, then I do not lie; if I do not lie, then I lie." This again would present no difficulty if someone were to say, "In saying that A is B, I lie." If the speaker is telling the truth, then he lies in respect to A and B, and A is not B. If he lies in saying "I lie," then A is B. The situation is different when there is, so to speak, no logical space available for the contradictory constituents, as, for example, when somebody simply says, "I lie," no more and no less. It is not relevant in such a case to bring in the linguistic expression and the intention to deceive; it suffices to say, "What I think or what I apprehend is false," if my thought points to nothing beyond this falsity. In the case of such an incomplete expression, as in the analogous incomplete expression "What I apprehend is correct," one is confronted with a peculiar defectiveness in the object of thought, which always becomes evident when an apprehending experience tries to refer to itself as immediate object. This point of view is clearly different from Mally's position, which we rejected above, in that he is opposed to any apprehension that is about itself, no matter what the circumstances may be. It might, nonetheless, be asked why the difference between an immediate and a remote object is of such importance in this connection.

First, let us examine more closely the peculiar state of affairs (*Sachlage*) that is involved (*beim*) in the apprehension of immediate objects. As far as I can see, its peculiarity is attributable to the circumstance that the immediate object of an apprehension (for which the object is never absent) is the apprehension's logical *prius*.[6] (Though, as is well known, there are fundamental epistemological assumptions held by some contemporaries which would instead make the apprehension the logical *prius* of the object.) However, my claim may be so evident to most readers that they might be inclined to extend it to hold for all objects instead of restricting it merely to immediate objects. Whether such a generalization is warranted will presently be determined. I am not in a position to establish my restricted claim, but I believe that its truth will be immediately evident to whoever gives careful consideration to the subject matter before us. If an immediate object is to be apprehended, this object, either as existent, as subsistent, or at least as having *Aussersein*,[7] must be given as a precondition for the experience. It is understood by this that the object is nowise dependent on the apprehension, but that the apprehension rather depends upon the object. Consequently, under our presuppositions, the experience of apprehension cannot possibly be identified with the object apprehended by it. The logical *prius* cannot coincide with the logical *posterius* if one wants to avoid an absurdity similar to that involved in the old *causa sui*, where, incidentally, the meaning of the word *causa* was understood in a sense that has little to do with what we

6. The notion of logical *prius* will again be dealt with further below (p. 62).

7. See below, pp. 19 ff.

mean by "cause." It must be concluded that I cannot lie in saying that I lie, and also that I cannot think that I think, without there being something else beyond my single act of thinking.

Moreover, the invalidity of the claim (that a thought and its object coincide) can, if the claim were made, be made clear in another way. Consider the case in which a person A thinks of the thought of B, which in its turn may be concerned with the thought of C. This could go on indefinitely, but if it should become too complicated for A to follow, he might decide to stop at, e.g., the thought of B [8] and only to note *in abstracto* that B thinks, but not what he thinks. However, that does not alter the fact that the objective series on hand must have an end and that the end must consist in an object that is not itself an apprehension. This is no less evident than the, curiously enough, often misunderstood [9] fact that no relations can be based exclusively on relations as *inferiora*. The thinking of which A thinks must in any case be the thinking of something, and this something cannot consist in thoughts *ad infinitum*.

What would the situation be like if the thought that is to be apprehended by A is not the thought of B or C, but A's very own apprehending thought? In the first place it is clear that it is impossible for a thought which is its own immediate object (*nächster Gegenstand*) to have an immediate object other than itself. For, if the thought of which I am thinking is identical with my thinking, then this thought cannot have an object distinct from the thinking of it. Thus the object is in this case identical with the thinking. Now, if I think of my thinking, this thinking itself is the thinking of my thinking, and so forth *ad infinitum*. This series does not stop at some independent object, i.e., an object that does not in turn refer to something else. It is questionable whether this infinite complexity is at all mitigated by the fact that the infinitely many links of the series coincide on account of their identity, an identity in virtue of which all members of the series collapse, so to speak, into one. In this case it is all the more obvious that this residual member is a thought which is not directed to its own object.

8. ["D" in the original text, obviously an error.—Translator.]
9. Cf. the acute discussion by O. Hazay, *Die Struktur des logischen Gegenstandes* (Berlin, 1915).

If the difficulties connected with the identification of apprehension and the object of apprehension under the condition stipulated (namely, that the apprehension is of an immediate [*nächster*] object) show themselves in so sharp a light, it may seem even more dubious whether these difficulties can be eliminated by removing the restrictive conditions. We have already seen that under certain circumstances an apprehension can be directed to itself. In principle this was illustrated by the Cartesian Cogito, whose domain most certainly includes the respective "cogitatio." Empirically one can easily learn that this only occurs with more remote objects. It is not at all necessary to refer the Cartesian Cogito to the act of thinking which apprehends the Cogito. However, if one wants to refer the Cogito to the act of thinking which apprehends it, one cannot use the experience of internal perception to do this. Instead, the "cogitare" must first be apprehended *in abstracto,* in which case the present thought-experience can be included in its range of application. Consequently, for the present, the above-mentioned restriction to immediate objects is justified on purely empirical grounds. One can better understand these matters by considering that the mode of apprehending immediate objects is primarily an immediate reference to the object's being, whereas the mode of apprehending more remote objects is primarily a reference to an object's being thus-and-so.[10] In principle, any immediate object can be apprehended by reference to the object's being thus-and-so, but there is seldom occasion to resort to this approach. On the other hand, immediate reference to the object's being is possible only in the case of immediate (*nächste*) objects, whereas any reference to an object as being thus-and-so has no limitations in this respect. Thus it is apparent at once that an immediate reference to an object's being, and a reference to an object as being thus-and-so, involve grasping the object by two entirely different modes of apprehension. It is thus not surprising that the identity-restriction is essential for one mode of apprehension, but not so far for the other. One can go a step further and say: in order to belong to the collective of intended objects (*Zielgegenstände*), to which in a way some auxiliary object refers as being thus-and-so, and which constitute the range of this auxiliary object,[11] a certain

10. Cf. *Über Annahmen*, p. 277.
11. Cf. *Über Möglichkeit und Wahrscheinlichkeit*, § 27.

similarity with this auxiliary object is a prerequisite. Exact likeness is the maximum degree of such similarity. In many cases [12] it can be considered as the exact likeness of an object to itself.

Let us once more return to the thinking which is about itself and to its analogues, the objects which do not satisfy the requirements stipulated for the identity-restriction in regard to immediate objects. It is a striking feature of these cases that they are experiences which do not have objects in the way other experiences do, which in a sense lack objects altogether. The objects of such experiences might well be called "incomplete objects" (*unvollständige Gegenstände*) if this expression had not already been used in the sense of "incompletely defined objects" (*unvollständig bestimmte Gegenstände*).[13] Perhaps we might call each of these defectively incomplete objects a "defective object" (*defekter Gegenstand*). E. Mally's expression "meaningless" (*sinnleer*) may appropriately apply to such defective objects, so that it might be presumed, as previously noted, that E. Mally's and his predecessors' attention to these defective objects was well placed.

Someone might say that the significance of such defective objects is excluded by the fact that similar difficulties arise where we clearly are not concerned with defective objects. This can be seen in the traditional form of the paradox of the Liar. For when a Cretan says that all Cretans lie, the object in question is obviously incomplete. But universals (however one wants to interpret them) are by no means defective objects. The same result would follow if someone were to say: "All that I am saying," or, if he were writing, "All that I am writing is a lie or false," or something similar. In respect to objects it would in no way be different if someone said: "All that I am saying is true," or "All that I am apprehending is an object"; and no difficulties would arise, even if the experience of apprehension is expressly included. Such inclusions do not need to result in absurdities. Where such absurdities do arise, they depend upon states of affairs (*Sachlagen*) which allow incompatibilities to occupy, as it were, the same place. This is a condition for

---

12. It can be seen in a simple example that this is not always the case: the man who agrees with me as regards his father and mother is, no doubt, my brother, but only if I am not meant by it myself.

13. Cf. *Über Möglichkeit und Wahrscheinlichkeit*, p. 181.

which the defective nature of the objects is not responsible. In reality, what we have in the paradox of the Liar is by no means so very enigmatic. Each judgment involves the belief that what it judges is true. If someone judges that all his judgments are false, he asserts, if he includes this judgment in its own scope, both truth and falsehood as regards the same objective. That absurd consequences result from this is not at all surprising. One might object to the Liar that his judgment is quite as false as if someone should find the same line at once straight and bent. The fact that one ordinarily lets judgments of the kind in question pass unnoticed, and is then amazed to discover the resultant absurdities, focuses our attention on the fact that it seems unnatural to include a judgment itself in the range of objects to which it is directed. It is, in fact, so unnatural that even one who thinks naïvely avoids making such a mistake. However, it has not thereby been shown that the inclusion of a judgment in the range of its own objects is in all circumstances impossible. In the same way, what was previously said of defective objects is not rendered invalid by the fact that whatever happens in the case of defective objects could also happen in the case of other objects.

In respect to defective objects, let me point in passing to a circumstance that may assure them a special object-theoretic interest. As is well known, there "are" many objects that do not exist, and many which do not even subsist. But because they "are" anyway, though they cannot be said to be in a sense which warrants applying the traditional word "being" to them, I believed, and still believe, that I am justified in attributing to them something being-like (*seinsartiges*) by predicating "extra-being," or *Aussersein,* of them.[14] Such *Aussersein* seems clearly to be predictable of all objects. This involves a consequence which is somewhat strange: that there can be no negative or contradictory opposite to *Aussersein* as there is to existence or subsistence. This in itself should make the notion less acceptable. But defective objects now shed (at least for myself) a completely unexpected light on this notion. May one say of objects which possess *Aussersein* that they "are"? This

14. See my discussion "Über Gegenstandstheorie" in *Untersuchungen zur Gegenstandstheorie und Psychologie,* edited by me (Leipzig, 1904), p. 12 (*Gesammelte Abhandlungen,* II, 493 f.); see also *Über Annahmen,* pp. 79 f.

without doubt is true: that when I say, "I think that I think,"
or "I write that I write," and other similar things, these words
say that I think "something," and something which differs in
each case. Here again the object cannot be absent. The question remains whether the defective object is itself apprehended
and not some nondefective object, namely, the incomplete
object which is the subject of the corresponding general judgment, and concerning which one has to say on closer consideration that it ought not itself to be an object intended. If
the former is the case, then one is confronted with defective
objects which lack even *Aussersein,* though this expression is
indeed peculiar. In this case one is not really confronted with
an object, and experiences of apprehension in this instance
lack a proper object.

Obviously one can argue against this claim by mentioning
"impossible objects" whose givenness, i.e., *Aussersein,* I felt
obliged to emphasize.[15] If *Aussersein* cannot be denied to the
round square, how can it be denied to defective objects, which
in some respects pose fewer difficulties? Doubts repeatedly expressed [16] regarding the truth of my assertions on this matter
have not provided me with sufficient ground to revise my
claims. But it would not be surprising if further research in this
peculiar, unfamiliar field of objects should produce unexpected
results; and it might be a mark in favor of a future resolution
of present controversies if the objection to the theory of defective objects just set forth should be shown to have something right about it which has been erroneously taken to be an
argument against the *Aussersein* of impossible objects. Consider the statement that the round square is round (or the
statement that it has corners). It has been claimed that I cannot make this statement. This claim is not justified if "round"
is construed as a *constituent* of the concept "round square"; but
the claim *is* justified if "round" is treated as something *conse-*

15. See *Über die Stellung der Gegenstandstheorie im System der
Wissenschaften* (Leipzig, 1907), pp. 14 ff. (also in *Ztschr. f. Philos.
u. philos. Kritik,* CXXIX [1906], 60 ff.).

16. See H. Driesch, *Ordnungslehre,* pp. 48 ff. By the fact that
elsewhere (p. 74) the impossible object can expressly be "excluded,"
it seems to be apparent that with this author, too, these objects must
be "something"—not least through the possibility that the "square
circle" (p. 66) can be used in a syllogism.

quent upon being a round square, even if it is so only in a limiting case (*Grenzkonsekutivum*).[17] Certain reservations are likewise necessary in respect to the *Aussersein* of impossible objects. It has often been pointed out [18] that an intuitively (*anschaulich*) apprehensible object can also be apprehended nonintuitively. The objective plays a different role in intuitive and nonintuitive apprehension; [19] in spite of the identity of that which is intuitively and nonintuitively apprehended, the immediate auxiliary objects [20] which help us to apprehend our object are not identical, and these immediate objects should be especially labeled according to their typical differences. In the case of intuitive apprehension, the traditional expression *concretum* naturally suggests itself, and the etymological picture of coalescence exhibits the characteristic difference between intuitive apprehension and the mere patchwork of the nonintuitive. The term *disconcretum* might fittingly be applied to the latter (this term used analogously to "discontinuum" and other similar expressions). Using these expressions, one can simply say that for the apprehension of impossible objects one always has available a *disconcretum* but never a *concretum*. It is wrong to say that I cannot apprehend the round square at all but that the intuitive apprehension of it is by its very nature excluded. It can also be said that though a round square neither exists nor subsists, the round square has *Aussersein* as a *disconcretum;* but it does not and cannot have *Aussersein* as a *concretum*. Here we have a typical case of something which lacks *Aussersein,* and in this respect our defective objects are not alone.

Let us summarize the result of our special inquiries by saying that E. Mally has not proved that thinking cannot under any circumstances apply to itself. The difficulties which he has pointed out are traceable to the special nature of defective objects and to the fact that the domain of what can rationally be believed is to some extent restricted by factors involved in every judgment. The emerging peculiarity of defective objects is not, however, only of object-theoretic interest, but is also

17. Cf. *Über Möglichkeit und Wahrscheinlichkeit*, pp. 277 f., 287 ff.

18. Also by me; see *Über Annahmen*, p. 247.

19. See *ibid.*, p. 281.

20. *Über Möglichkeit und Wahrscheinlichkeit*, pp. 195 f.

valuable as marking off a typical case in which self-reference is denied to an intellectual experience, since this would unavoidably amount to the apprehension of a defective object.

I cannot tell to what extent these matters influenced A. Phalén's notion of "*Subjektobjektivität*" and his opposition to the claim that there is this kind of subject-objectivity.[21] But clearly, E. Mally's opposition to Idealism,[22] which is based on his argument regarding the defective series, does not lose its force as a result of any critical remarks above.

In the light of the main theme of our inquiry, one must ask whether the result of our present considerations supports self-presentation or not. For in internal perception, which is most important in this context, immediate reference to an object's *being* holds first place, and the objects to which it relates are immediate objects. It looks as though what we above called the identity-restriction is especially required in the case of self-presentation. But, on the other hand, one cannot ignore the fact that self-presentation, as embodied in internal perception, does not involve the peculiar situation met with in the case of defective objects. This is easy to understand if one remembers some of our recent cases, as, for example, the notorious case of a thinking about thinking. If I experience a thinking (D), and apprehend it by an internal perception (D'), to which D presents itself, this involves no restriction on the possible objects of D. It is obvious that there would be an illicit identification only if D and D' were to coincide. It thus becomes apparent that what we previously called "incomplete apprehension" [23] is only in a qualified sense a kind of apprehension, since it is only a precondition for "complete apprehension," and since only with the addition of a judgment or an assumption does it become a complete apprehension. Perhaps it is an unnoticed misunderstanding of the expression "self-presentation" which is responsible for the seeming difficulties. That which presents itself can at first glance be taken as *quod praesentat se ipsum sibi ipsi*. The *sibi ipsi* must have led to a defective object, while the mere *se ipsum* does not. But self-presentation certainly does occur in such cases and is immune from criticism, as far as I can see.

21. Cf. my mention *ibid.*, especially pp. 418 ff.
22. *Ztschr. f. Philos. u. philos. Kritik*, CLX (1914), § 6.
23. See p. 3, above.

3 / Emotional and Intellectual Presentation

IN THE PRECEDING PASSAGES we spent more time on self-presentation and its object-theoretic and epistemological significance than might be justified by the choice of our topic alone. Therefore, it is now time to remember what was previously said, namely, that in internal perception not only intellectual but also emotional experiences function as presentative factors, so that *emotional* presentation can be set side by side with *intellectual* presentation. This is made immediately clear by the fact that not only intellectual experiences but also emotional experiences, e.g., feelings and desires, are internally perceived. If this fact leads us back to self-presentation, then these feelings or desires, that is, the emotional experiences, must be presentative factors.

They are to be contrasted with the cases of intellectual presentation from which we started above and which are cases of other-presentation. It is, however, evident that there must also be *intellectual self-presentation*, since intellectual experiences are not excluded from the domain of internal perception. The two resulting types of intellectual presentation are also clearly different in respect to the role assumed in each by the content of the intellectual experiences in question. As we saw, the content alone takes part in intellectual other-presentation, to the extent that we have so far been acquainted with it, so that we can speak in this connection of a *content-presentation*, and can feel inclined to characterize intellectual self-presentation, by contrast, as being also *act-presentation*. This characterization, however, needs further qualification. Even if

[23]

the act plays a role in intellectual self-presentation which it does not, as indicated, play in other-presentation, it is not usually, so far as we know, the only presentative factor in the case. Content must also be taken into account in intellectual self-presentation, since internal perception, for example, not only informs one that one has an idea but also what the idea is of.[1] The obvious contrast between self- and other-presentation might therefore more adequately be labeled that of "partial and total presentation." [2]

Whether the contrast between partial presentation and total presentation thus pointed out in the intellectual domain also holds in the emotional domain will become evident when we investigate the contrast between self- and other-presentation in the case of emotional experiences. In the beginning such presentations seemed only to show us cases of self-presentation, but the quest for other-presentation soon proves fruitful. If one does not need an idea of feeling (*Gefühlsvorstellung*) to be conscious of a present feeling, then the question can well be put whether remembrance of a past feeling has more need of an idea of that feeling. In respect to past feelings, the situation has changed characteristically, and has become similar to the situation involved in external perception, insofar as the object that is to be apprehended in remembering does not belong to the present psychic life of the remembering subject. The question must, on the other hand, be raised as to where memory would acquire the idea of the (past) feeling if there were no trace of such an idea at the time most favorable for its emergence, that is, the time when the feeling was experienced.

We know that perceptual ideas and serious ideas (*Ernstvorstellungen*) leave dispositional traces which make possible imaginative ideas of the same objects (*gegenstandsgleiche Phantasievorstellungen*). Imaginative acts of thought are surely dependent in an analogous manner upon serious acts of thinking (*Ernstgedanken*), taking assumptions to be imaginative thoughts, and judgments to be serious thoughts. The fact that this dependence does not seem (empirically speaking) to limit the freedom of making assumptions is accounted for by the relatively great uniformity of thought-objects, a uniformity

1. Cf. "Über die Erfahrungsgrundlagen unseres Wissens," pp. 55 ff.
2. *Über Möglichkeit und Wahrscheinlichkeit*, p. 251.

which means that the lack of the requisite dispositional traces will not readily be apparent. On the other hand, such traces are quite common in the sphere of emotional life. It is generally known that in order to enter into a certain peculiar affect one must at least have experienced something similar. From now on I shall say, instead of "think oneself into" (*hineindenken*), "feel oneself into" (*hineinfühlen*) or "empathize" (*einfühlen*); and I shall mean, by the term, imaginative feelings (or, imaginative desires), since normally these are not serious feelings (or serious desires). In such imaginative experiences the means are clearly given by which to apprehend in memory past emotional experiences, without having to depend upon presenting ideas.[3] This is also a case of emotional presentation, which is, however, naturally not self-presentation but other-presentation. This kind of presentation can naturally also be expected to take place where emotional experiences are not being remembered, but in some other way judged or only assumed.

These cases of emotional other-presentation show how wrong it would be to think that self-presentation and total presentation, on the one hand, and other-presentation and partial presentation, on the other hand, are necessarily connected. For we have just encountered an other-presentation which is, at the same time, total presentation. And that this is not peculiar to emotional experiences is shown by the fact that in the intellectual domain total presentation of this kind is also found whenever we remember or otherwise apprehend intellectual experiences that are not present at the time. Here, therefore, we have two different kinds of other-presentation, of which the one is partial presentation and the other total presentation. We are, however, led on by the analogy between the emotional and the intellectual to take one step further, and to ask whether in emotional experiences, besides the other-presentations which are total presentations, there are not also partial presentations, in whose case the content of the experiences in question alone has presentative functions.

3. Cf. "Über die Erfahrungsgrundlagen unseres Wissens," pp. 75 ff.

4 / Partial Presentation in the Case of Feeling

WE MUST NOW ANSWER the preliminary question as to whether, in respect to feelings and desires, act and content can be differentiated as is done in respect to ideas. As is well known, there is quite often mention of the content of feelings or desires. I, myself, once wrote about the "content of value-feelings." [1] According to my later use of the expression,[2] this is not, however, quite exact, for, at a closer look, talk in this connection is of objects and not of contents. In the same way, one should rather speak of "objects of desire" whenever one speaks of contents of desires, the things, that is, toward whose existence or nonexistence the desire is directed (*Begehrungsgegenstände*). Nevertheless, and in general, contents will correspond to such objects, so that the just-mentioned objects of desires and feelings seem at the same time to guarantee that there are contents of such feelings and desires. It will, however, be clear, in the first place, that these contents are not part of the feelings and desires in question, but of their psychological presuppositions. Whenever someone likes a color or sound, his feeling is concerned with an object, and that by way of a content. But this content is an integral part of the idea of the color or sound and is, therefore, not in the same

---

1. In *Psychologisch-ethische Untersuchungen zur Werttheorie*, pp. 39 f. and *passim*.
2. In "Über Gegenstände höherer Ordnung . . . ," *Ztschr. f. Psych. and Physiol. d. Sinnesorgane*, XXI (1899), 185 ff. (also *Gesammelte Abhandlungen*, II, 381 ff.).

sense a content of feeling as it is the content of an idea. It is really not the content of the feeling but the content of the experience which constitutes the psychological presupposition of the feeling. It can accordingly be called the "presuppositional content of the feeling," to which, clearly, a presuppositional content of desire will correspond, since one may talk in the same way of the presuppositional objects of feelings and desires. This is quite the same as in the case of objects which are judged and assumed and of the contents prerequisite for their apprehension: in that case, too, we are concerned with presuppositional objects or presuppositional contents of thought.

Between the presuppositional objects and the experience with whose presupposition we are dealing, there is, we may admit, *another* objective relationship in virtue of this presuppositional relationship (*Voraussetzungsverhältnis*). When the smell of a flower pleases me, when I am rejoiced by the German and Austrian victories of 1915, and when, at the same time, my wishes are directed to the return of peace among civilized nations, this certainly does not merely mean that certain ideas and thoughts, to which certain objects correspond, have been made the presuppositions of my feelings or desires. It means also that, in virtue of these presuppositions, certain feelings and desires are directed to certain objects and that these objects may accordingly be called the objects of the feelings and desires in question. Wherever objects (that is, objecta or objectives) are emotionally approached,[3] objects are thus connected with the approaching experiences. These probably were connections considered when objectivity (*Gegenständlichkeit*) was attributed, not only to ideas, but to all other experience, and was classed as a characteristic common to everything psychic.[4]

One might try to read this interpretation into the locution "the experience has a presuppositional object," implying thereby that its presuppositional object is also simply its object. Such a use of words is arbitrary and blurred, as can most simply be seen from the fact that, in respect to an experience, one can talk of its presuppositional content in just the same way as in regard to its presuppositional object. It is not, however, possible to maintain that the content of the presupposition is at the

3. *Über Annahmen*, pp. 144 ff., 160 ff.
4. Cf. F. Brentano, *Psychologie*, I, 115 ff.

same time *the* content, or even *a* content, of the experience. The content of the idea- or thought-experience which underlies, e.g., a value-feeling, can in no way be regarded as the content of this feeling. Any legitimate mention of the content of a feeling or a desire would therefore seem to be eliminated.

The fact, however, that there is this danger of mistaking something for a content of a feeling which really is only the presuppositional content of that feeling does not mean that the feeling may not have a content of its own. An analogy with thinking will be of considerable help at this point. It was seen that thought-experiences have—in addition to their possible basis in ideas—a constituent which performs an apprehending or immediately presentational role in especial coordination with objectives, and which accordingly has content-character.[5] This, therefore, is properly called thought-content. It becomes apparent at first in the contrast between affirmation and negation: to such thought-content the contrast between liking and dislike, or between desire and repugnance, is a clear and often used analogue. Without a doubt we have in such a case to do with something content-like, or rather, with the contents of feelings or desires, which, like the contents of judgments, are not merely the contents of their psychological presuppositions. If, therefore, there are proper contents of feelings and desires, then the preconditions for a partial presentation which is a content-presentation are also given in the case of emotional experiences.

That these are more than mere possibilities is shown by some everyday attributions, as when people talk about a refreshing bath, fresh air, oppressive heat, disturbing noise, beautiful color, funny or sad, boring or entertaining, stories, sublime works of art, valuable people, good resolutions, etc. There is no question as to the close relationship of such attributes to our feelings. And there is no question that these attributes are fully analogous to other properties which are familiarly presented by ideas. When I say, "The sky is blue," and then say, "The sky is beautiful," a property is attributed to the sky in either case. In the second case a feeling participates in the apprehension of the property, as, in the first case, an idea does. And it is natural to let the feeling be the presentative

5. *Über Annahmen,* p. 341.

factor in the second case, as an idea is always taken to be in the first case.

Neither traditional thought nor common prejudice is, however, in favor of this theory, as may become clearer in regard to the aforementioned casually assembled attributes. Perhaps it will be directly objected that "beautiful," "pleasing," "boring," and "troublesome" express feelings and that feelings cannot be ascribed as properties to things and events. However, as stated in this form, the objection certainly does not prove anything. If "pleasing" means a feeling, then "blue" means an idea (or perhaps, immediately, only a sensation). But the statement about the blue sky does not intend to make an idea a property of the sky. Naturally, it is quite important to see that feelings are more subjective than ideas, so that feelings cannot at all readily be expected to characterize things or events as regards their objective properties, unless, indeed, one holds the general opinion that there is only an intellectual apprehension of such properties and that feelings do not extend beyond the boundaries of our inner life. The feelings in question may, however, be admitted to have some significance for the characterization of objects. It is only essential to find the right interpretation for the corresponding adjectives. A seemingly viable mode of interpretation has long been in use. Everything is correctly called "pleasing" which excites a feeling of pleasure, "beautiful" which excites a liking, etc.

In the face of all this, the question cannot be avoided: What can the obvious analogy between "The sky is beautiful" and "The sky is blue" really tell us? Once in a while the opinion is voiced that when someone, looking at the sky, says that it is blue, he "really" wants to say that he is having a blue sensation caused by the sky. Ordinarily, however, a judgment based on perception or a purely perceptual judgment is not taken to be about an experience of the judging person or about a causal nexus, but about the sky and its property of being blue. If this is undoubtedly right, then the statement "The sky is beautiful" is not to be understood as related to our experience in a different way. Here, too, there is no indication of a reflection upon a feeling or of the apprehension of a causal nexus. Nevertheless, the latter could not have remained unnoticed by anyone who was trying to give an attentive account of his experiences. Parity is easily established if, in the case of a feeling, a thought of causality and of internal experience is *not* interpolated, a thought contrary to direct experience, and if the relation between the feeling of liking and the object sky is assimilated to that generally held to hold between the idea of blue and the sky. In the sense of such parity, it is to be expected that under favorable circumstances the feeling should function as a content presentative of objects.

The previously mentioned doubts are not of great importance here. This is most obvious in the objection which goes furthest in denying that feelings can function as a means of apprehension. Whoever persistently argues that only ideas can function as presentatives will be refuted by what we previously said regarding the presentative functions of the thought-experiences. And whoever believes that the very nature of emotional experiences does not allow them to be presentations would have to give up his prejudice in the face of the facts cited in what was said above regarding emotional self- and other-presentations.

But the matter is different if one only points to the extreme subjectivity of our feeling-experiences and regards this subjectivity as an impediment in presentation. It may indeed be suspected—and we shall return to the point [6]—that feeling, which is so often alien or even hostile in its relation to knowledge, fulfills the task of intellectual apprehension quite insufficiently, whenever, that is, it is forced to assume that function. One should not, on the other hand, demand too much in this respect, since any subjectivity, even that of ideas, e.g., sensations, will impede their use in knowing.[7] It nevertheless is conceivable that, even if feelings were considered to be inferior to the most subjective of our ideas, they might still, even under these unfavorable circumstances, present objects. These objects would remain inaccessible to apprehension if presentation were exclusively confined to the intellect.[8]

6. See below, pp. 105, 132.
7. Cf. "Über die Erfahrungsgrundlagen unseres Wissens," Sections II and IV.
8. The following definition goes much farther: "That part of our active soul . . . which perceives values, is called feeling" (Glasenapp, "Der Wert der Wahrheit," *Ztschr. f. Philos. u. philos. Kritik,* CXXIII [1901], 189). However, it is dubious whether the author wants to be taken literally.

Perhaps it might suffice to clear up such misunderstandings if we pointed out that certain highly respectable thinkers have in fact tried directly to include a whole class of *sensuous* (*sinnlich*) feelings in the class of sensations.[9] But they did not succeed in their attempt on account, I think, of the utter disparity between feelings and all intellectual experiences. Whenever "*Lebenswärme*" has occasionally been attributed to feelings,[10] it is surely to be taken metaphorically. Direct experience is more precise: it does not attribute any such things to sensations, if feelings are left out of consideration in their case. This also holds for nonsensuous or, as they are often called, higher feelings, even if they are not complex enough to be simply called "emotional disturbances," and it does not merely apply to them externally so as to justify talk of a concomitance of "feeling-sensations" (*Gefühlsempfindungen*). When we take such direct aspects into consideration, the second- or third-order arguments which were collected by C. Stumpf (with his usual sagacity) carry little weight, so that, in the main, I can assent only to E. Becher's position,[11] despite Stumpf's recent "Apology."[12] But I think that we can yet draw from this position the conclusion that feelings, despite all their peculiarities, have an affinity with intellectual experiences. One need not, on grounds of their total disparity, deny them a quasi-intellectual functioning *a limine*.[13]

It is evident that such presentation will take on the character of content-presentation or partial presentation as much in the case of feelings as of ideas. Whoever wants to make a guess as to the frequency of such feeling-presentations should expressly consider another point. To make the fact of content-presentations of feeling more acceptable, a paradigm verbal case such as that of "beautiful" works much better than a

9. Cf. C. Stumpf, "Über Gefühlsempfindungen," *Ztschr. f. Psychol.*, XLIV (1907).

10. Quoted by E. Becher in *Ztschr. f. Psychol.*, LXXIV (1915), 151.

11. *Ibid.*, p. 153.

12. "Apologie der Gefühlsempfindungen," *Ztschr. f. Psychol.*, LXXV (1916), 1 ff.

13. H. Driesch's explanation of pleasure and displeasure as "eine Gruppe bedeutungsmässiger reiner Solchheit" may be understood as recognition of this; see his *Ordnungslehre* (Jena, 1912), p. 86.

paradigm like "pleasing," since the meaning of the word "pleasing" refers expressly to the feeling-experience of "pleasure," which again suggests that previously refuted casual conception which is not suggested by the expression "beautiful." If, in exceptionally clear cases, we are certain of this presentational conception, then it is clear that this conception is at least a possible one even in cases where causality is etymologically suggested. This is especially clear where the etymology of the word lightly indicates causality, without forcing it on our linguistic instinct. "Ugly" (*hässlich*) is the contrary of "beautiful," and etymologically (in German) it means much the same as "worthy of hate," something, that is, that excites our hatred or at least our displeasure. Anyone, however, knows from his own experience that, in using or hearing the word "ugly," he normally does not think of his own emotions (his hatred, or the like) but rather thinks exclusively of a property of the object, as he does in the case of "beautiful."

The situation becomes, in general, less difficult to understand if, as explained elsewhere,[14] one draws a distinction between what a word or statement expresses and what it means, its meaning. In this sense, what is expressed is an experience, while what is meant is an object. When one is asked what connects a word with the object that it means, the answer is simple where the word expresses an idea: since an idea has the function of assisting the apprehension of an object through its content, the word that expresses the idea will be connected with the object apprehended by means of the idea, which is also the meaning of the word. We may explain that such words as "pleasure" and "pain," which express experiences which cannot simply be considered as aids to intellectual operations, nonetheless have their meaning: this is due to the fact that they are total presentatives in cases of self- and other-presentations, where, however, the expression and meaning of a word may very well coincide. If an experience thus expressed can, under certain conditions, function as a partial presentative, it is understandable that such a word will not get a new meaning in each such case. The lack of a fixed meaning does not therefore mean that such an experience could not act as a partial presentative. All the above-mentioned expressions of feeling,[15] and many

14. *Über Annahmen,* § 4.
15. See above, pp. 27 f.

others, can accordingly be interpreted as involving cases of feeling-presentation wherever other appearances render an application of causality or a reflection upon internal experiences improbable.

5 / Partial Presentation in the Case of Desire

IN OUR PRESENT ATTEMPT to show that there are partial presentations in the emotional domain it was natural to begin by studying feelings. This makes it easy to interpret desires in the same sense by recurring to what was said about linguistic structures. This permits us to interpret the following expressions as standing for partial presentations: "desirable," "worthy of effort" (*erstrebenswürdig*), "detestable," and also "awful," and once again "ugly" (*hässlich*), insofar as the hate that is expressed in "*hässlich*" can be interpreted as a case of negative desire, though the meanings of the words themselves (*Wortbedeutungen*) suggest a reflection upon the desire-experiences in question. A word like "end" (*Zweck*), on the other hand, does not attract such an interpretation; in the use of this word, partial presentation plays an exceptionally important role.

The traditional way of analyzing the notion of purpose,[1] so energetically undertaken, has never failed to recognize how closely purpose, end (*Zweck*), is related to desires. However, the role undertaken by desires in purposes (*Zweck*) was thought to have been rightly understood in a manner analogous to the role undertaken by feeling in the notion of beauty, these roles corresponding to the previously refuted view in terms of causality. If A is the cause or the condition of B, and if B is desired, so that the desire for B entails the desire for A, then A

1. See especially the thorough studies of R. Eisler in *Der Zweck: Seine Bedeutung für Natur und Geist* (Berlin, 1914).

[34]

is also said to be the *means* toward the end B. One speaks similarly in cases that are only treated *as if* someone desired A for the sake of B. But whenever the notion of an end is properly thought out, the notion of an object of desire as such becomes unavoidable. (This object is naturally one of the objects which will consequently be called "borrowed objects").[2] Thus one cannot avoid including the notion of desire in those considerations. This is frequently not at variance with experience. If someone says: "I want to devote myself to psychological research and am acquiring for this end all prerequisite physical and physiological knowledge," it seems believable enough that it is in express regard to the proposal that he has adopted that the psychological research is said to be his "end" (*Zweck*).

When I simply say, "I am opening my umbrella in order not to get wet," there is no doubt that a desire not to get wet is present. But that the desire is thought of, and that the teleological construction with "in order to" is used to express a reference to this desire, is not clear from the natural sense of these words. They are about the umbrella and the rain but not about a desire. Nevertheless, the relation stated between the opening of the umbrella and the not-getting-wet is not merely a causal one. It is easy to find an analogy to what we previously said about feelings. As, e.g., beauty in the former case, as compared to purposiveness (*Zweckmässigkeit*) in the present case, is not constituted by a relation to an experience but is an object in its own right, for whose apprehension the feeling and the desire function as presentatives in either case, or better, as partial presentatives. For it is the content of the desire in the strict sense and not the presuppositional content which does the presenting. The content is that aspect of the desire which is quite as evident in the contrast between desire proper and reluctance, as is, in feeling, the aspect evident in the contrast between pleasure and displeasure, or as is, in thinking, the aspect evident in the contrast between affirmation and negation.

It becomes even clearer that there is no thought of a desire when someone says that a switch-button device on a typewriter serves the purpose of saving key levers. This thought is nonetheless quite different from the causally oriented thought that

2. Cf. below, p. 48.

the switch button effects a saving. Whenever such a purpose is thought of, an actual desire does not have to be experienced; an imaginative desire is quite sufficient. But even when a seriously experienced desire functions as means of apprehension, the notion of purpose presupposed by this conception appears to be independent, as regards its object, of wishes or desires, a fact which supports the tendency to treat the notion of purpose nonsubjectively.

Oughtness (*Sollen*) has the same degree of significance, but in a more transparent way. Its close relationship to desire [3] has rarely been doubted, and occasionally it has even been believed to be constituted by a pair of desires.[4] This can be explained by the fact that, if one sticks to language, obligation is often attributed to subjects in the form of a "Thou shalt" or in similar forms, and the subjects are expected to take account of their obligations through their desires. But this second desire is hardly essential, for which the following expressions may serve as examples: "It ought not to have been" (*Es hat nicht sollen sein*), "Sword on my left, what should thy friendly gleam portend?" (*Du Schwert an meiner Linken, was soll dein freundlich Blinken?*), and so forth. The following consideration might be even more convincing: that in "Thou shalt honor thy father and mother," the obligation in no way primarily relates, if one may so put it, to a "thou." This is similar to the "may" in "You may yet experience a lot of things." The possibility stated here is, like any possibility, a matter concerned with an objective,[5] which does not exclude a certain "inhesivity" in the subject of the objective.[6] In the same manner, the "shalt" is primarily a determination of the objective "to honor father and mother," and only by way of this, as it were, can the "shalt" be attributed to the subject of the objective. Just as with "may," the obligation is also, in the first place, a specification of being, even if the "shalt" is simultaneously addressed to a person and his desires. So this possibly quite unimportant desire can be left out of consideration when the nature of obligation (*Sollen*)

3. Cf., e.g., *Psychologisch-ethische Untersuchungen zur Werttheorie*, p. 184.
4. See Christian v. Ehrenfels, *System der Werttheorie* (Leipzig, 1898), II, 195 ff.
5. Cf. *Über Möglichkeit und Wahrscheinlichkeit*, pp. 87 ff.
6. *Ibid.*, p. 143.

has to be determined, and it is only the other, "first" desire whose relationship to the notion of obligation urgently requires clarification.

It might, however, appear plausible, as in the case of "beautiful," to say of an objective that it *ought to be* when it either is or could be desired. But when a father tells his son through a third party that he ought to come, the father normally does not think about his wishing, ordering, or desiring, but would *have* to think of these were the "ought," of which he talks, constituted by a relationship to his desires. Perhaps he only thinks of what he desires, so that, were the son close enough, the father's experience would have been best expressed by the exclamation "Come!" In that case the expressive rather than the meaning-function [7] would be in question. Nevertheless, the sentence "He ought to come" may also, for itself, be understood as the expression of an ordinary categorical judgment, the form of which would break with all analogy if "He ought" has some reference to the desire of the speaker. Therefore, it is better to take this "ought" as a determination of the objective "that he come" (*dass er komme*), which is peculiarly modified by the "ought" in the same way that an objective in "He can come" is specified by "can." Still, not all relationship between the objective and the desire must be discarded, but one must not see in this relationship a part of the object of the statement. This relationship would be analogous to that between a sense-experience and an object of sense, or between a feeling and the object which we call "beautiful." In short, all difficulties disappear if we admit that an object is apprehended by a desire, which, as the object's presentative, does all that can be asked of a means of apprehension.

The result of the analysis becomes only slightly different when the desire essential for the obligation is not the desire of the speaking person. When one speaks of one of the Ten Commandments, such as "Thou shalt not kill," the pronouncement of the commandment need not be accompanied by an appropriate serious desire. If, however, there is no serious desire, a possibility that might very well arise, then we are dealing with an imaginative desire, which, if not introverted but extroverted, could as readily promote a partial presentation

7. Cf. above, pp. 31 f.

as do imaginative experiences belonging to other experience-classes. So we can forget about all seeming "reductions" in respect to obligation and can grant it an objectivity of its own which is accessible through presentation by desire (*Begehrungspräsentation*).[8]

Later we shall say more regarding the objects which confront us in the thought of purposiveness and obligation.[9] Here we have only attempted to show that, in respect to these objects, it is not enough to regard desires as total presentatives, any more than it is enough to make a similar claim for feelings in the case of the objects "good" and "beautiful." Desires, like feelings, must be held capable of partial presentation.

8. For final clarity in these matters I am deeply indebted to the discussion of my young colleague, Dr. Franz Weber, with which he won the Wartinger Prize awarded by the Philosophical Faculty of the University of Graz in May, 1916. Since the author will have to wait for the publication of his book until the end of the war, I think I may now make use of his stimulating remarks.

9. See below, p. 98.

6 / Content, Act, and Object from the Point of View of Presentation

IT HAS PREVIOUSLY been pointed out that partial and total presentation cannot be characterized as content- or act-presentation.[1] It may, therefore, help to get a clear picture of the manifold facts of presentation when they are expressly surveyed from the point of view of the content and act of the presenting experiences.

Let us start with the content. The presentation in that case is in the main partial presentation, which has always been acknowledged to be the main achievement of the experienced having of ideas (*Vorstellungserlebnis*), but which, as we say, is also encountered in thought-experiences and no less in emotional experiences. This may be called "presentation proper" (*eigentlich*) to distinguish it from "inauthentic presentation," which we encounter in all cases of total presentation. Of course, the content also takes part in an inauthentic presentation; and while it cannot by some process of abstraction be separated from the act, it can, in relation to the act, be, as it were, pushed into the foreground. Then, the presentation is either self-presentation, that is, presentation of the subject's own simultaneous experience, or, like partial presentation, a case of other-presentation in which the subject's own but nonsimultaneous experiences, or some experience other than that of the subject or some nonexistent experience, is presented. When the content is thus isolated from the act, it is not easy, as

1. See above, p. 23.

[39]

pointed out elsewhere,[2] to concentrate on this content and not, instead, on the object which belongs to this content. These difficulties seem especially great in the case of ideas. It is evident that it is easier to differentiate the content from the object (i.e., the objective) in the case of thought-experiences, since the contrast which concerns the objective is called that of "positive" and "negative," whereas the contrast which concerns the thought-content is called that of "affirmative" and "negative," which is, at least in regard to its first member, a partial linguistic differentiation. In the case of feelings and desires, language primarily refers to the contents "pleasure" and "displeasure," "desire" and "repugnance"; but it refers, at the same time, to the acts of feeling and desiring. It is one of the main goals of the present discussion to point out the corresponding objects of these contents, or to supplement earlier remarks concerning this question

When the act is the presentative element, its functions are strictly confined to total presentation, whereby the original presentation, which under favorable circumstances may accompany the content, ceases to be present. To emphasize the act within the whole of total presentation is of course a matter of abstraction. It may be easier to effect than an emphasis on the content, because the danger of putting a properly presented object in the place of the presenting content is here eliminated, since such an object is absent. For the rest, any sort of abstraction, including that of the act, is far from easy.[3]

Regardless whether such an abstraction of the act is or is not successful, we here encounter, in connection with act-presentation, i.e., total presentation (if it is not a case of self- but of other-presentation), a peculiar difficulty, which must be mentioned since it might reveal a weakness in our presentation-theory and thereby lead to a modification of the same. It is, in general, quite easy to differentiate in memory between serious and imaginative experiences. For I know very well that the night before last I saw a bright light on the front of a streetcar, whereas yesterday afternoon I only thought of the light without seeing it. Now, the difference between serious and imaginative ideas is a difference in act.[4] But, on the other

2. "Über die Erfahrungsgrundlagen unseres Wissens," pp. 58 ff.
3. Cf. "Über Gegenstände höherer Ordnung . . . ," p. 240 (*Gesammelte Abhandlungen*, II, 436).
4. Cf. *Über Annahmen*, p. 342.

hand, in order to apprehend a past experience, I do not need, as said before,[5] to have an idea of this event but a fitting presentative element in the form of an experience as similar to it as possible. Since we have to apprehend something past and not present, we have under normal circumstances an appropriate imaginative experience at our disposal. If I want to remember either the perceiving or the remembrance of that bright light, I do not see the light but have to make use of an imaginative idea of that light. The perceptual idea and also the imaginative idea of the bright light are therefore presented to me through an imaginative idea. How, then, is it possible that I remember, at one and the same time, both the perceptual idea and the imaginative idea, and that I am able to tell the difference between the two?

I cannot, at present, give a complete answer to this question. But there are two points of view which may be the beginnings of an answer and which will not entail a change of the main theses of my theory of presentation. In particular, in the example of the light, direct experience seems to show that the idea by means of which the light is apprehended is not in both cases equally in the center of our immediate remembrance. On one occasion I think directly of the light and its existence, whereas on the other occasion I think of the idea of the light and of the existence of this idea. When we remember in the first case that we saw the light, as our example requires, the idea of the light (through its content) not only functions in a partial but also in a total presentation, which, like the partial presentation, forms the basis for an affirmative judgment of existence. In the second case, on the other hand, though we have a total presentation and the affirmative judgment coordinated with it, the partial presentation is the foundation, not of an affirmative judgment, but at most of an affirmative assumption or perhaps even of a negative judgment. For I remember having "only" thought of the light, i.e., having thought of it though it did not exist at the time. Perhaps I even remember circumstances which exclude such an existence. In our example, I may know that I remembered the light about noon—at a time, therefore, when streetcar lights are not lit. Anyhow, the ideas of the light in the two cases of remembering occur in contexts sufficiently different, which contexts are by themselves sufficient criteria

5. See above, pp. 24 f.

for differentiating the two ideas. To look for the difference in the act itself would presuppose a great deal of psychological knowledge, and such a difference does not make itself particularly evident to direct analysis.

No doubt this thought introduces considerable complication into facts which would otherwise look quite simple. Another example may make this even clearer. Imagine that someone who has grown up in the thoughts and beliefs of a certain creed becomes convinced that A is B. After he has achieved some independence in critical thought, he stops believing that "A is B" out of reasons that later seem to him insufficient, so that, from then on, his old belief is reinstated. Nevertheless, the belief is then again given up for a different, more lastingly effective reason. It is then easy for the henceforth unbelieving person to remember the different stages of his changing convictions concerning the statement "A is B." But presentatives for all these intellectual experiences are only assumptions, since he does not believe the statement any longer. By what means will he then remember his earlier convictions? The apparatus of all indirect criteria here appears to be disproportionately cumbersome. Rather, everything seems to work so simply that it may be suspected that a special presentative is needed in each case, once for the apprehension of the judgment, once for the apprehension of the mere assumption, as it is also requisite for judging the falsity of a statement.

The need which thus becomes apparent seems to encounter empirical fulfillment, and that very clearly in the domain of the thought-experiences. Granted that I did not make too high an appraisal of the role played by assumptions in these experiences,[6] it must also be granted that there is so great a difference between various kinds of assumptions (e.g., "explicit assumptions,"[7] on the one hand, and references by way of being and being-thus-and-so,[8] on the other) that it is hard to believe that we are dealing with the same species of assumptions. Primarily there seem to be two types of assumptions, which may be indicated, perhaps quite superficially, by saying that in one case the assumption-experience quite clearly differentiates itself from its psychic surroundings, whereas in the

6. See *Über Annahmen,* especially the summary, §§ 61 ff.
7. *Ibid.,* § 15.
8. *Ibid.,* §§ 45 ff.

other case it can easily fail to be noticed as a special sort of experience and, therefore, has to be exhibited by a more or less indirect analysis. The first type clearly stands in a much closer relationship to judgments than the second type. Perhaps as provisional labels the following expressions might do: "judgment-like assumptions" for the first type, "shadowy assumptions" for the second type (*urteilsartig* and *schattenhaft*).

Here we have a duality that has already been pointed out by E. Mally in a quite different connection.[9] As is well known, objectives can be expressed in two very different manners: through the statement, e.g., "*A* exists," and through a noun which often is a verbal noun, "*A*'s being there" or "the existence of *A*." In obvious contrast to the fact of the wide-ranging equivalence of the preceding expressions, the following expressions are not equivalent: one can readily say "It is true (or false) that *A* exists" but not "The existence of *A* is true (or false)." E. Mally tried to explain this by supposing it to be possible that

> we not only think [an objective] but we at times also "judge it in imagination," to put the matter concisely. In such an assumption, that is, we not only reproduce the judgment-like apprehension of the objective by means of its content, but we also imitate or imaginatively copy it in respect of its act of judgment, its moment of conviction; we act as if we were judging it. Besides assumptions of this kind, which are imaginative judgments, there seem to be other assumptions which merely reproduce the content of (possible) judgments and which consist in the "mere thinking" of the objective, i.e., a statement of the objective in which the moment of conviction is not reproduced. It is only as far as their content is concerned that these assumptions enter relevantly into further intellectual processes.

If, as I have tried to show,[10] truth (in contrast to factuality) is a matter which concerns objectives of apprehension (*Erfassungs-objektive*), then it is indeed natural that objectives, apprehended by assumptions of the first kind, should more readily be called "true" (or "false") than objectives apprehended by assumptions of the second kind.

9. "Gegenstandstheoretische Grundlagen der Logik und Logistik," Supplement, *Zeitschr. f. Philosophie u. philosophische Kritik*, CXLVIII (1912), 62, footnote.
10. See *Über Möglichkeit und Wahrscheinlichkeit*, pp. 39 f.

For our present concern, a description of the two kinds of assumptions is more important, which might be reformulated by making use of a characterization of the relationship of judgment to assumptions which I have given elsewhere.[11] According to this characterization, judgments may be considered as assumptions to which the moment of belief (in one of its degrees) has been added. It is then possible that an assumption should itself exhibit a moment which is indeed not that of belief or conviction—the assumption, therefore, does not cease to be an assumption—but which is sufficiently belief-like to make the assumption appear judgment-like, as is not the case in regard to a different kind of assumption which consists merely in thinking something. Whether in the "mere thinking" of an objective the moment in question is completely absent, or whether it is so qualified that the assumption to which this moment is attached so to speak withdraws from the possibility of being a judgment, must remain undecided at present. The expression "imaginative judgment" cannot be recommended for use in the case of judgment-like assumptions if it is to be used in a manner similar to "imaginative feeling" or "imaginative idea." [12] But the expression "judgment-like assumption" is more appropriate. The expression "shadowy assumption" (schattenhafte Annahme) is formally independent of the first expression; so that we still may refrain from deciding whether there is another type of assumption besides these two.

The expression "shadowy" (schattenhafte) has nonetheless not been selected without an intention of showing, not only in the case of assumptions but in the case of all imaginative experiences, that this duality of types, in the widest sense of the word,[13] is to be found. In the case of the understanding of words or statements, one has long been made aware of the fugitive character [14] of our perception of such understanding, because of which the experiences which aid us in apprehending the meaning of such words and statements so easily elude our notice that we even come to doubt their presence and take refuge in nominalistic conceptions. Such conceptions are, how-

11. *Über Annahmen*, p. 340.
12. Cf. *ibid.*, p. 383.
13. Cf. *ibid.*, § 65.
14. See "Über Gegenstände höherer Ordnung," pp. 237 ff. (*Gesammelte Abhandlungen*, II, 434 ff.).

ever, excluded by the very fact that our intellectual apparatus functions so reliably in most cases that a complete replacement of thing-ideas by word-ideas is out of the question. But the contrast is then all the more distinct between ideas which are mainly notional (*begrifflich*) and which are not absent in this case, and intuitive ideas which under different circumstances would be quite unmistakable. These intuitive ideas may indeed belong to the domain of imagination, but this does not obliterate their affinity to perceptual or serious ideas. It can readily be seen that the situation does not differ in the case of feelings and desires. Whoever, for example, blamed himself during the latest war-events for his indifference to, and incapacity to comprehend the extent of, the misery and the immense sorrow which men had brought on one another only shows the great difference between what is so misleadingly called "merely intellectual apprehension" of a feeling and the sympathetic entry into the feeling-situation of others, or "empathy" in the strictest sense of the word. In either case, we have to do with imaginative feelings. Some of these are such that they might conveniently be called "shadowy," just as their counterpart in the intellectual domain is called so. But their opposite in the domain of feeling cannot be called "judgment-like" but would have to be called "serious-feeling-like" (*ernstgefühlartig*), as it would have to be called "serious-idea-like" in the domain of ideas. If we can afford to neglect to differentiate the main experience-classes within our class of shadowy experiences, we may do the same in regard to the second type of imaginative experiences: we might call them "serious-experience-like" or, more briefly, "serious-like" or "quasi-serious"; and we might summarize the result of our discussions thus: imaginative experiences occur in at least two clearly distinct types, that of the shadowy and that of the quasi-serious experiences.

We can easily apply our result to the problem from which our investigations started. If imaginative experiences, whether in their totality or especially in regard to their act-side, can function other-presentatively, then the quasi-serious imaginative experiences are to be regarded as aiding the presentation of serious experiences, while for the presentation of imaginative experiences the shadowy imaginative experiences will suffice. It is evident, for the rest, that for self-presentation the quasi-serious imaginative experiences are more favorably placed than the shadowy experiences, which primarily play their role in partial other-presentation, and not in self-presentation or total other-presentation.

It may not be pointless to emphasize that total presentation, and its so-to-say derivative form act-presentation, are normally accomplished by imaginative experiences. But there are exceptions. Naturally, no one is better capable of feeling for the pain of another than one who suffers the same pain. The expression "feeling for" does not mean a sympathetic value-feeling [15] but merely a self-submersion in someone else's feelings. In a similar manner, someone's state of belief can be apprehended most faithfully by somebody who holds the same belief. The serious experience seems to be a better presentative than the imaginative experience, which, however, has the advantage of being a more manageable and more accessible means of apprehension than the former.

We must also include the presented objects in our survey of the main facts of presentation. First of all, it is obvious that an experience, to the extent that it can present something in different manners, is also correlated with different objects. By means of the same idea I can apprehend blue color and this idea itself; by means of it, I can also apprehend a nonpresent idea of blue which is either my own or someone else's and which is undetermined as regards existence (*Dasein*) or nonexistence and is therefore existence-free (*daseinsfrei*). The latter case, that of existence-freedom, does not presuppose a special mode of presentation but is subsumable under the standpoint of total other-presentation. One circumstance with which we briefly dealt before [16] deserves special notice, namely, that the description of the multiplicity of presentational manners does not exhaust the multiplicity of the objects correlated with an experience, if mediate presentations, which we said we would ignore,[17] are included in our description. It must be remembered that dependent psychic events are quite tightly knit to the objects of their psychological presuppositions. The judgment which judges its objective, perhaps even presents itself or presents other judgments, also judges the subject matters of the objective (*Objektivmaterial*) which are appre-

15. Cf. *Psychologisch-ethische Untersuchungen zur Werttheorie*, p. 46.
16. See above, pp. 25 ff.
17. See above, p. 4.

hended by ideas. Whatever is judged about has a claim to be taken as an object of the judgment. In the same way, when some ornament pleases me, not only its beauty is an object of my feelings but also the ornament itself. And when we are proud of the victories of the German and Austrian armies, not only the value of these victories is an object of our feeling of pride, but likewise the existence of those victories and the victories themselves. These presuppositional objects—though they are more than merely presuppositional objects—are in no way presented by the dependent experiences in question: they are their objects but not objects of their presentation. If we should want a special name for them, we might call them "borrowed objects." Thus we might differentiate them from the objects of presentation or these experiences' *own* objects. It must, however, be admitted that in the emotional domain the borrowed objects have traditionally been mistaken for the proper or "own" objects of our emotions.

7 / An Attempt to Make the Notion of Content More Precise

OUR NOTIONS CHANGE and adjust themselves as we progress in knowledge. It should, therefore, not surprise us if anything new which has turned up in our discussion should provide us with an incentive to further elaboration of the notions of the apprehension of objects which we have here been applying. This holds especially for the notion of content which has rendered good service in my inquiries over the past twenty years, and which could also be made the basis of the foregoing discussions without, I hope, doing harm. It seems therefore appropriate to confront this notion with our recent results. But first we shall try to alleviate certain misunderstandings, for which the manner in which this notion was once introduced by myself bears considerable responsibility.

The fundamentally metaphorical character of the expression "content" and its (in consequence) widely differing applications blur the notion so much that it has become almost useless. It must, therefore, be explicitly defined before it can become appropriate to the needs of the strict work of science. These demands must be satisfied, and so definition becomes unavoidable. Nevertheless, all things considered, I was not well led by my individual linguistic instinct when, for the first time in 1896, without giving much account of my procedure, I opposed the expressions "content" and "object" in a quite definite manner,[1] and in 1899 characterized their meaning quite

1. "Über die Bedeutung des Weberschen Gesetzes," *Zeitschr. f. Psychol. u. Physiol. d. Sinnesorgane,* Vol. XI (1896) (*Gesammelte Abhandlungen,* II).

briefly as being something altogether acceptable and unproblematic.[2] The problems, however, which were to be solved by making a contrast between content and object more precise have not been essentially changed since K. Twardowski's work. And it pleases me that my book, written in 1899, was published just at a time which marked the beginning of acute concern with such problems.

This is shown by the attention which E. Husserl gave to it as early as 1900,[3] and also by Th. Lipps's various publications since 1902, in which he repeatedly takes up this theme, which has not since disappeared from the literature. Though Lipps has remained close to my intentions in drawing my distinction,[4] Husserl, e.g., in his attempt to detect multiple meanings (*Bedeutungen*) of words, has differentiated at least five meanings of the expression "content" and actually uses the word in those senses. Other authors may disagree even more as to the usage of the word, and it is impossible to avoid the misunderstandings which have underlain quite a few polemical arguments against my original object-theoretic position. Under these circumstances it seems advisable, above all, to explain once more, and perhaps more fully, my thoughts of the year 1899 concerning the notion of content. At the same time I will give the reasons why I decided to use the word in this special sense and why I still recommend an agreement in its favor, though it is now definitely in need of a terminological pinning-down.

At this place I need not emphasize a point that had to be emphasized in 1899: no one any more will be inclined to identify object and content. We also need not spend time in showing that the object is different from the experience which apprehends it, or which is suited for such apprehension. That which I called "content" at that time is part of such an experience, and it seems to be the best procedure to start by taking into consideration the coordination of the experience to "its" objection in order to isolate the part to be emphasized as content from the whole of the experience.

Let us consider those experiences, first of all, to which no

2. "Über Gegenstände höherer Ordnung und ihr Verhältnis zur inneren Wahrnehmung," § 2.

3. In Volume II of his book, *Logische Untersuchungen*.

4. If I understand rightly, the main difference is made by the tendency to think of an object only in relation to the apprehending subject.

one would deny the capacity to apprehend objects under favorable conditions. I am thinking of ideas, in the broadest sense of the word; one is not limited to imaginative ideas. The name is not very important for what follows, but it is important for our immediate concern, which is to differentiate between two cases of relevant experiences, each of which apprehends a different object. When I observe the blue of the sky or the green of a meadow, the two objects blue and green are naturally not apprehended by two utterly similar experiences, though they are similar in some respects, especially in the circumstance that they are both ideas, or perhaps even perceptual ideas. Now, that in which the two ideas must differ in order to be such as to apprehend different objects I called the "content" of these ideas.

There is a complement to this notion of an idea's content which consists in pinning down that part of the idea which is unaffected by changes, however wide, in the object which is to be apprehended by the idea and so represents the idea's relatively constant element. The ideas of color, sound, taste, number, etc., have this in common, that in each of these cases we have an idea of something; and it seems to be most natural to contrast that which these cases of ideas have in common, that is, the idea as act, with the idea's content.[5] Right away two possible misunderstandings must be eliminated. One concerns language, the other concerns its subject matter. The word "act" is, above all, not meant to indicate activity. The contrast between active and passive, which seems to me, despite objection from various sides, to be of fundamental importance, holds in fact only within the confines of what is entitled to be called an "act." Ideas especially, whose act-aspect we are now discussing, are passive experiences, like feelings; whereas judgments and assumptions, whose act-aspect we shall soon discuss, are active experiences, like desires. A misunderstanding concerning our subject matter would, however, be to mistake the constancy of an idea as act, which is indeed a constancy compared with the wide variability of an idea's contents, for absolute constancy. Ideas as acts can change, and that the change does not concern their content is shown by the fact that the object to be apprehended by the ideas remains unaffected by the change.

5. Cf. the illuminating discussions by St. Witasek in his *Grundlinien der Psychologie* (Leipzig, 1908), pp. 73 ff.

Transitions from sensations (*Empfindungen*) or perceptual ideas to imaginative ideas are the most obvious examples. I can reproduce in memory the tone C, which is now given to me by a tuning fork. The pitch will not remain absolutely exact, but this inexactitude does not represent what is characteristic in the imaginative idea. It is, so to speak, only an accident that the heard C and the reproduced C bear less similarity in pitch than the C heard at time t and the C heard at time t', which also will not be absolutely the same. In principle, the pitch, i.e., the apprehended or apprehensible object, is not affected by the fact that it is at one time perceived and at another time imagined. Here, at least in principle, the act has undergone modification, while the content has remained unchanged.

It is obvious that there are two main thoughts which play an important role in the differentiation of content and act in the idea as experience: on the one hand, we infer from a difference in the apprehended objects to a difference in the apprehending ideas. On the other hand, we infer from two sorts of variability in our ideas, one concomitant with their objects and the other independent of these, that there are two components in these experiences. Both of these points give reason to inquire more deeply into these matters, to which, on this occasion, we can only refer in passing.

What justification is there to pass from differences in objects to differences in the experiences which apprehend them? Mere experience, e.g., induction, has as little part to play in these matters as it has in the case of the axiom of parallels or the theorem of Pythagoras. Whenever apprehension becomes knowing (*Erkennen*) (i.e., when it achieves something which often has been called "adequacy" but which might be called, in a more general and characteristic manner, the relationship of apprehension), we unquestionably have an ideal relation [6] and one, therefore, which is primarily a matter of *a priori* knowledge. Is the following statement true, that, if an ideal relation R holds between A and B, it does not hold between A' and B unless the B becomes B' in order to enter into the relationship R to A'? This certainly is not true in all cases. When we deal with space-points, there is no difficulty in finding a point A' which is just as far from, and therefore stands in just the same distance-relation to, B as does A. And

6. Cf. *Über Annahmen*, pp. 265 f.

that this is also possible where we are dealing with the relation between apprehension and the apprehended object is proved by the fact that the same idea-experience is suited to apprehend completely different objects, according as to whether the experience in question is intro- or extroverted, or as to whether it involves a reference to an object's being or to its being thus-and-so. The situation is different when, instead of considering the undoubtedly complex, total fact of apprehension, we focus our attention on presentation and at the same time assume that all other circumstances that, as it were, complete the apprehension are the same, and especially that we have a case of that extroversion (*Auswärtswendung*) that represents the normal case of the intellectual processing of ideas. By virtue of the very nature of the relation of apprehension—though, at present, so little is known of it—it is immediately clear that different objects can—*ceteris paribus*—only be presented through different ideas. How else, then, than by means of the characteristics of the presenting experiences themselves could one tell that the one refers to this object as "its object," while the other refers to another?

The same reasoning by which we conclude that object-different ideas differ from each other leads us to the conclusion that ideas that have the same object are alike. The claim that perceptual and imaginative ideas of the same tone or of the same color must be similar in one respect cannot be better proved than the claim that two successively experienced perceptual ideas of the same tone must agree in being ideas of that same tone, and that two imaginative ideas of different tones must agree insofar as they are both imaginative ideas. We can, however, be satisfied with this simple assertion. We have therefore discovered two variable aspects, one of which concerns the object and one of which is in principle independent of the object. Elsewhere I have already maintained that this necessarily implies a duality of components, the phrase of course understood broadly enough.[7] One might ask in return whether there should not also be two components for red and blue, since those two objects, besides being different, are similar in that they are colors.

7. "Bemerkungen über den Farbenkörper und das Mischungsgesetz," *Zeitschr. f. Psychol. u. Physiol. der Sinnesorgane,* XXXIII (1903), 20 (*Gesammelte Abhandlungen,* I, 515).

I doubt whether this consequence is very frightful, since the whole subject matter, especially in its object-theoretic aspects, is quite obscure. For our present purpose we do not have to concern ourselves with a solution of such doubts, since that aspect of the idea as experience which varies with its objects is not only collated with a constant moment of those experiences but also with a moment which, in the transition from perceptual to imaginative ideas, remains unaffected by the change of objects but is variable in other respects. It does not help us if we draw an analogy with genus and species, unless the same species is permitted to fall under different genera.

If the claim that there are two components in ideas as experiences therefore holds its ground even before strict examination, we still may have to justify the use of the terms "act" and "content." Perhaps we need not justify the use of the term "act," since traditionally it has not been used in a fixed manner. If someone should object that "act" then means a pure *abstractum*,[8] the foregoing passages show that act is related to content, not as color is related to blue, but rather as color is related to extension or shape (*Gestalt*). But as regards the traditional use of the expression "content," I must admit, as already indicated, that I once read my own meaning into other people's language (as one so easily does) and that I claimed greater freedom of expression than I was conscious of. One might, however, expect that the situation would rather be obscured than clarified if I suddenly gave up my previous use of this well-seasoned word. In fact, this seems to be the less advisable, the less other conventions concerning these matters can be clearly and firmly stated. This becomes especially evident in attempts to arrive at a sufficiently workable differentation between "content" and "object." Usually it seems that what is called "content" is itself an object, by preference an object of apprehension, and a more immediate rather than a remoter object. However, these or other determinations have never led to any sort of precise demarcation.

Otherwise regarded, however, the metaphor involved in the word "content" deserves a certain amount of consideration. Of an "immanent object" it may well be said that it is "contained"

8. See A. Marty, *Untersuchungen zur Grundlinie der allgemeinen Grammatik und Sprachphilosophie* (Halle, 1908), I, 453, footnote.

in the idea. However, once it has become apparent that the object in question is only pseudo-existent,[9] we have absolutely no justification for still calling this object the "content" of the apprehending idea. It must be added that what I have called "content" seems to be important enough to be preserved as a concept (*Begriff*), whatever happens, though we must find a new name for it. It is regrettable that what in logic is contrasted as "content" with "extension" (*Umfang*) differs so considerably from what we mean by the word; however, my proposed terminological differentiation between "logical" and "psychological" content may well suffice to exclude misunderstandings.[10]

In the foregoing passages I have attempted to set forth the contrast between the act and content of ideas, since the facts about these are in general so familiar and accessible as not to occasion controversial conceptions. But it is easy to show that this contrast is not wholly peculiar to ideas. And there are consequently contents which are not the contents of ideas. This becomes clear when we consider that there are objects—as has been repeatedly shown above—which are characteristically and in principle different from these objects which have just been considered in connection with ideas. A color is something completely different from the existence of the color, a tone something completely different from the softness or loudness of the tone. The following objects are likewise utterly different from the objects of ideas: "That diphtheria is to be cured by a serum injection," or "That Bulgaria's declaration of independence did not have any warlike complications in its wake." Of these objects it is characteristic that they take up a position within the contrast of the positive and negative which is utterly impossible to apprehend by way of ideas. Objects of this kind I have called "objectives." And in contrast to objectives I have called objects like color and shape, etc., "objecta" (*Objekte*), whereby this latter term is with reasonable conventionality restricted in its application. As ideas apprehend objecta, so judgments or assumptions apprehend objectives; and these latter experiences allow us, without strain, to carry over the manner of treatment which led to our previous antithesis, between an idea's content and an idea as act, to our new case. Objectives

9. Cf. "Über die Erfahrungsgrundlagen unseres Wissens," § 10, and *Über Annahmen*, pp. 85 ff., footnote 3; also pp. 229 f., footnote.
10. *Über Möglichkeit und Wahrscheinlichkeit*, p. 163, footnote 3.

are not as various and manifold in kind as objecta; still, they do not lack a certain degree of variability. This is already evident in the above-mentioned contrast between positive and negative objectives and between being (*Sein*)—in the narrower sense—and being thus-and-so (*Sosein*), between existence and subsistence, and between the degrees of possibility, etc. As said before, an idea which is suited to apprehend blue must be a different experience from an idea which can apprehend green. Something similar can be said of those experiences of which the one is suited to apprehend the object "being," the other to apprehend the object "nonbeing." Here, as there, the parts of the experiences in question which are concerned with their varying objects may be called "content," which here, however, are the content of a judgment or an assumption. An act-aspect corresponds to the content-aspect of these experiences, as is vouchsafed by the fact that, as concerns the same objectives, their means of apprehension must be differentiated into judgments or assumptions. Plainly, the contrast between judgments and assumptions is itself already a contrast in act, which compares naturally with that between perceptual ideas and ideas of imagination (*Einbildungsvorstellungen*).[11] Within the domain of judgments, degrees of certainty, or rather uncertainty, in our convictions are to be recognized as differences in act, which have, in principle, nothing to do with the content of the experiences or with their apprehended objectives.

It has already been shown in our previous discussions of emotional presentation that, as in the case of ideas and judgments (or assumptions), emotional experiences also, that is, feelings and desires, can be differentiated into two components, which likewise can be called "act" and "content." Accordingly, we can summarize the matter thus: the content is that part of an experience which is so coordinated with the object to be apprehended by the experience, and immediately presented by the latter, that it varies or remains constant with, and in dependence upon, the object. The act is that part of an experience which is independently variable in respect to its object. Our previous discussions of presentation have, however, led to another result, which might make the notion of content seem somewhat questionable, to the extent that this notion presup-

11. *Über Annahmen,* pp. 344, 376 ff.

poses that there is a part of an experience which, in all its variations, is especially coordinated with the object. We know that in total presentation the whole experience stands over against the object, while, in the case of abstractly considering the act, the act alone stands over against the object. What right have we, then, to isolate a part of experiences which is, as regards presentation, the preferred correlate of the presented object, and to subsume it, and it alone, under the concept of content?

It was natural, when the notion of content was first beginning to be clarified and the fact of self-presentation had not yet been made sufficiently clear, that the content should have been regarded as the only aspect of experience capable of presentation and that the essence of the content should have been primarily seen to consist in that exclusiveness. It must now be admitted that there is no such privilege. This does not, however, prevent the part of experiences which has been incorrectly characterized by this privilege from assuming an especially favored position in matters of presentation, so that its special qualification as "content" is still justified.

That this is so can be seen from one of our previous findings, in connection with which we used the name "partial presentation." There we were able to say that partial presentation occurs whenever, out of the whole experience, only its content acts as presentative. And now we can reverse the position and say that the content is the part of an experience which is suited to be a partial presentative when conditions are favorable. It is thereby contrasted with acts to the extent that, if the latter take a greater part in the apprehension of an object, they must do so by means of and through the total experience, that is, by an abstraction from the rest of the experiences (i.e., mainly from the content). Where, however, the content alone functions as presentative, no process of abstraction takes place in order to isolate the content. To have an idea of red or blue, I need not first ignore that moment of the idea which belongs to the idea (of red or blue) as such, that is, the act, whereas the act can never be used as presentative without abstracting it from the content. Partial presentation was the first form of presentation to be made an object of theoretic reflection, long before the other kinds of presentation were considered. It is therefore important to formulate a special notion to cover the basis of such partial presentation. Partial presentation, in fact, is the proper role of ideas and is one of the main functions of thought-experiences. It is of less importance in emotional experiences, where apprehension becomes an exceptional case.

But there is a circumstance which makes it very clear why partial presentation can be used to characterize a certain part of experiences. We saw previously that the relation of the apprehending experience to the apprehended object depends partly upon the experience and partly upon the object. Considering this, it is an amazing, and still unexplained, fact that these characteristics of the objects and the experiences do not uniformly manifest exact or partial likeness, on the one hand, or diversity, on the other. Looking to the ancient tendency to regard so-called adequacy as similarity or congruence, it is worthwhile contemplating the possibility that there might be a primary relationship of dissimilarity in such a case. It is characteristic of partial presentation insofar as the presentative, as is always the case, is psychic, whereas the presented object is either physical or ideal, i.e., in the latter case neither physical nor psychic. But the fact of self-presentation shows that this is not true of all presentations, and the same is shown by such cases of other-presentation as are either direct cases of total presentation or abstracted from the same. There we are always dealing with something psychic; and the limiting case of identity in simultaneous presentation (*im Gegenwärtigkeitspunkte*) [12] shows that the greatest possible similarity or congruence (*Übereinstimmung*), is, so to speak, the ideal goal of all that sort of apprehension which is here being considered. At first it seems amazing that this goal is unattainable in other-presentation of the previously mentioned sort; it cannot, however, be denied that this is so. It cannot, however, be said that dissimilarity plays the same role in the one case that similarity plays in the other. Even if similarity is not identical with the relation of apprehension, it still is more natural to assume that an experience apprehends an object through its similarity with the latter and not through its dissimilarity. There is, however, no other way to take account of the facts than to set presentation by dissimilarity (*Unähnlichkeitspräsentation*), and presentation by similarity (*Ähnlichkeitspräsentation*) side by side. [13]

12. Cf. "Über die Erfahrungsgrundlagen unseres Wissens," p. 68.
13. Cf. *Über Möglichkeit und Wahrscheinlichkeit*, pp. 253 f.

To this we may at once add that presentation by dissimilarity always takes place where the contents of the experiences serve as presentatives. Partial presentation and presentation by dissimilarity go together. Whatever is characterized by the former has additional weight, since it will, at the same time, be characterized by the latter.

It cannot, therefore, be said that contents can only function as presentatives by dissimilarity (*Unähnlichkeitspräsentanten*), for contents also play a role in self-presentation and in the cognate case of other-presentation by similarity (*Ähnlichkeitsfremdpräsentation*). But in that case we have no proper partial presentation, only, in the first place, total presentation, and then an abstractive elaboration of such presentation as is also obtained, in similar fashion, when the act-moment is abstractively isolated from the total presentation. One can hardly go astray if one says that genuine partial presentation is always presentation by dissimilarity. That part of an experience which under favorable circumstances is coordinated with the object, and accordingly is a partial presentative and, at the same time, a presentative by dissimilarity, is the part which can appropriately be called the "content" of the respective experience—according, that is, to our present knowledge of presentation.

8 / Psychological Presuppositions and Founded Objects

TURNING AGAIN to the special facts of emotional partial presentation, we see that the objects presented in that manner deserve to be studied in much greater detail. It might be of help in our investigations not only to study those objects directly but also the character of the corresponding apprehending experiences. For if we find differences among those experiences, we may expect analogous differences among the presented objects. Such a conclusion by analogy seems justified by the situation in the field of intellectual experiences, where the difference between ideas and acts of thought corresponds to the difference between objecta and objectives. There is, in general, reason to presume that what is emotionally presented will be characteristically different from that which is intellectually presented and that, within the emotional domain, characteristically different experiences will prove to be presentatives of characteristically different objects. In this connection not only difference between feeling and desire may be of objective importance but likewise specific differences within the domain of feelings. These specific differences are, in fact, particularly favorable to object-theoretical treatment. We shall not be deviating too far from the main line of our discussion if we dedicate some of our attention to the sorts of feelings just mentioned.

For this purpose we will make use of the notion of psychological presupposition, of which we have repeatedly and advantageously made use above.[1] A renewed attempt will

1. See above, pp. 5 ff.

therefore be made to clarify this notion, especially since the advance of our research calls for a modification of its previous formulation. The need for a notion of psychological presupposition made itself evident to me when I became interested in the facts of emotional life (*Gefühlsleben*); and this notion will be especially helpful in our study of the emotions (*Gefühlstatsachen*). It might, therefore, be appropriate to pin down our concept on so-to-speak neutral territory, that is, in the field of the intellectual experiences.

We can take as our starting point the self-evident fact that judgments are always [2] dependent upon ideas but that ideas are not likewise dependent upon judgments. This dependence does not merely mean that nowhere in experience do we meet with judgments apart from ideas; it also means that we are dealing with a relation founded on the nature of the judgment, and which is most clearly to be apprehended when considered from the standpoint of objects. As it is out of the question, by the very nature of the matter, to have an idea which is not an idea of something, so it is out of the question to experience a judgment without judging something. Before notice had been taken of objectives, it was believed that judgments must have objects just as ideas do. Today we know that, with respect to judgments, that which is judged (*geurteilt*), rather than that about which the judgment is made (*beurteilt*), corresponds to that of which we have an idea.[3] Thus the parallelism is sustained, and it is as impossible for judgments not to judge something as it is for them not to pass judgment *upon* anything (*beurteilen*). One cannot be mistaken in this matter, and it is even more evident in regard to the passing of a judgment *upon* something (*Beurteilung*) than in regard to the judgment *of* something (*Urteilung*), the latter having been long enough overlooked. Though judgments need objects about which they judge, they cannot themselves provide the object to be apprehended out of their own resources. They cannot immediately apprehend such an object, but depend upon an experience which can do so. This prerequisite experience presents the object which is to be judged about. In the simplest case, it is an idea which does this, and which therefore serves best as a

2. Strictly speaking, only sometimes in a somewhat complicated manner; cf. above, pp. 10 f.
3. Cf. *Über Annahmen*, p. 44.

paradigm. This is the experience that I called a "psychological presupposition."

It has already been mentioned that for an object to be dependent upon another object generally means that the former cannot exist if the latter does not. This means that such a dependence assumes a different form according to the sort of being that it helps to constitute. One has, in particular, a dependence of existence, if an object cannot exist unless another object exists. If there is a causal principle, then in this sense all beginning is dependent upon something. There is also a dependence of subsistence, as is exemplified in the fact of the dependence of being an equiangular triangle on being an equilateral triangle.

The following is very important: there are dependences which have so little to do with existence and subsistence that one is tempted to talk of a dependence of being thus-and-so in addition to a dependence of being. Any object of higher order can be taken as an example. Difference is doubtless thus dependent, since there can be no difference without something which is different, and a something which must also be in the plural. It is immediately clear that this is not necessarily an existent something. Even a man who does not believe in the existence of secondary qualities knows that there is a difference between green and red, and he can therefore take red and green as *inferiora* for the *superius* difference. But the *inferiora* do not even have to subsist: the round square is surely different from the oval triangle, though none of the objects here functioning as *inferiora* subsists. One may therefore be inclined to surmise that being does not matter in this respect, but only being thus-and-so. This means that, if there is to be any meaningful talk about difference at all, we must presuppose beings which are thus-and-so with a "thus-and-so" such that "difference" can be applied to them. If there were nothing but the quality red—which it is strange enough, but not absurd, to suppose—then there could be no difference. Indeed, nothing more essential could be raised against these considerations than the question as to what could be meant by the "there were nothing but" in connection with these objectives of being thus-and-so or the material with which they are concerned. Naturally, neither existence nor subsistence is meant, and so again we come up against one of those peculiar cases where only an appeal to *Aussersein* can be of any help. In fact, if there could "be" no plurality of objects differing from one another in the sense in which being apprehended vouches for being given, then there could also "be" no difference, not even in the sense of *Aussersein*. For even if there "are" different objects in the sense of *Aussersein,* the difference between them will have not merely *Aussersein* but also genuine subsistence. We see, therefore, in the case of this sort of dependence, that the difference between being and being thus-and-so is not so important as the difference between being in the proper and narrow sense and *Aussersein*. In respect, therefore, both to the present and to all other objects of higher order [4] one might appropriately talk of a characteristic dependence of *Aussersein*.

It seems to be immediately evident that the relation between *inferiora* and their *superius* is not convertible, as A. Höfler pointed out long ago, or, as one says in modern but hardly clearer language, that the relation is not symmetrical.[5] This claim must not, however, be interpreted psychologically as meaning that one cannot think of a difference without thinking of what are different, e.g., green and red, while one can think of red and green without needing to include a thought of the difference. No doubt the latter is correct. But the way the former is to be judged depends upon one's theory of abstraction and also upon the feasibility of one's practice of abstraction.[6] But things are different if we presuppose the previously given objective characterization. If difference could not be or could not even have *Aussersein*, if there could be only red and nothing else, then red could still *be* and have every claim to *Aussersein*. Thus the relation of being different is dependent upon the property red, but red is not dependent upon being different. In this sense red is "logically prior," a notion which object-theory could not drop without loss, especially if it is considered from the viewpoint of implication.[7] This is clear in virtue of the fact that all implication is a matter of objectives,[8] whereas in the

4. Cf. also below, pp. 93 f.

5. A. Höfler, *Logik (philosophische Propädeutik I)* (Vienna, 1890), p. 53. [Meinong erroneously puts *"transitiv"* instead of *"symmetrisch."*]

6. Cf. B. Russell, "Meinong's Theory of Complexes and Assumptions," *Mind*, XIII (1904), 209.

7. Cf. *ibid.*, pp. 207 ff.

8. Cf. E. Mally, *Gegenstandstheoretische Grundlagen der Logik und Logistik*, pp. 4, 65 f.

case of red and difference we are dealing with objecta and not with objectives.

It would have worse consequences for the theory of objects and for epistemology if an attempt were made to eliminate or reduce the notion of necessity [9] than if the notion of the logically prior were relinquished. We must mention the notion of necessity at this point, for it does not apply to all relations between a *superius* and its *inferiora,* since besides ideal *relata* and ideal complexes [10] there are also real *relata* and real complexes. For one principal group of objects of higher order the notion of necessity is essential, and these objects I have labeled "founded objects" (*fundierte Gegenstände*). This expression, in virtue of its history up to date, leads us back to "psychological presuppositions." When I was myself still uncertain in respect to the differences between content and object, I used to talk of "founded contents" (*fundierte Inhalte*) instead of "founded objects." [11] The expression was borrowed by other authors, but the meaning that I had assigned to it was changed, and it unfortunately became ambiguous.[12] However, one aspect of the meaning, that most in need of correction,[13] curiously enough remained unchanged: I mean the combination of the expressions "foundation" (*Fundierung*) and "content." Thus, one is quite frequently confronted with a contrast expressed by the terms "substance-like" content, on the one hand, and "founded content" (*fundierter Inhalt*), or also "founded content of consciousness" (*fundierter Bewusstseinsinhalt*), on the other—the latter of these names a dependent experience in contrast to an independent experience,[14] and feelings are reckoned among

9. Cf. my discussions in *Über die Stellung der Gegenstandstheorie im System der Wissenschaften,* pp. 55 f. (also *Zeitschr. f. Philos. u. philos. Kritik,* CXXIX, 160 f.); see also *Über Möglichkeit und Wahrscheinlichkeit,* pp. 232 ff.

10. In respect to the originally proposed change of the expression, see E. Mally's contribution in *Untersuchungen zur Gegenstandstheorie und Psychologie* (edited by me) (Leipzig, 1904), p. 142, footnote 2.

11. See "Zur Theorie der Komplexionen und Relationen," *Zeitschr. f. Psychol. u. Physiol. der Sinnesorgane,* II (1891), 253 ff. (*Gesammelte Abhandlungen,* I, 288 ff., with additions on p. 302).

12. Cf. *Über Annahmen,* p. 15, footnote 2.

13. See *ibid.,* p. 15; also pp. 10 f.

14. Cf. E. Becher's recent article "Gefühlsbegriff und Lust-Unlustelemente," *Zeitschr. f. Psychol,* LXXIV (1915), 143 ff.

such "founded contents." Naturally, names are here of small importance, but it might help in clarifying matters to point out that, in the sense in which I introduced and applied the terms, the relation of an experience, e.g., a judgment, to its psychological presupposition is primarily a matter neither of content nor of the relation of a founded to a founding (*fundierend*) (object), nor even that of a superior object to its *inferiora*.

By touching on the two moments of logical priority and necessity, we have nevertheless discovered some helpful aspects by means of which the relation between experiences and their psychological presuppositions can be further described. A logical *prius* must always be acknowledged wherever there is an object, called by us a *"posterius,"* for which the *prius* is a prerequisite, whereas the reverse is not the case, the *prius* not depending on the *posterius* for its being or its *Aussersein*. This is precisely the case in regard to psychological presuppositions. Judgments cannot exist without underlying ideas, whereas there is no objection in principle to ideas being given without judgments. This is an existential priority, that is, as expressed some time ago, a priority which concerns existence, whereby the idea does not need to exist earlier in time, nor does the logical or timeless *prius* need to be a temporal *prius*. Once, in fact, I used the expression "psychological presupposition" in place of the more familiar expression "partial cause" (*Teilursache*) in order to leave open the possibility that they should be contemporaries.[15]

It is especially interesting to note how the priority of the idea is founded on a completely different sort of priority. If this priority rests, as we saw, on the fact that by their nature judgments require an object about which they judge, and that they also require an idea as the experience which presents the object to the judgment, then, so to speak, the first *prius* is that object, which, however, is not necessarily an existent object, since it may merely subsist, and which is not even necessarily a subsistent object, since it may merely have *Aussersein*. The dependence of judgments upon ideas is founded on a peculiar dependence of judgments upon the objects which are to be judged about. Let us for the time being

15. See *Psychologisch-ethische Untersuchungen zur Werttheorie*, p. 34.

designate objects with uppercase letters and the experiences which present the objects with lowercase letters, and let us reserve the first six of the lowercase letters to designate ideas, the next six to designate judgments or assumptions, the next six for feelings, and the remaining letters for desires. We can then say: g is dependent upon a, which is to be explained by the relation between A and g and not directly by the relation between a and g. This requires special consideration, because we will have to deal with the relation between A and G and also its emotional analogue. The relationship between *inferiora* and their *superius*, which we considered earlier, would on our present scheme have to be described symbolically as the relation of A and B to F. Whether we may go beyond the domain of ideas will be discussed immediately.

Concerning necessity we have already mentioned that g's demand for A, and therefore for a, is not only empirically evident but is also necessary. Conversely, that g is judged of A and not i of A may nonetheless lie in the nature of A, if, e.g., the judgment is a negation of being (*Seinsnegation*) and A a complex of incompatible determinations (qualities, *Bestimmungen*). But the situation does not have to be that way, and, even if it is, there is no necessary connection between A and g, but only between A and G, i.e., the objective presented by g. Even less does necessity hold between A and g in respect of the properties of g. Therefore it can be said that G is necessarily dependent upon A and a but it is not necessarily dependent as regards its properties or those of its objective.[16] It cannot even be said to be empirically dependent in virtue of a regular concomitance.

Our findings concerning the relationship between dependent experiences and their psychological presuppositions within the intellectual domain, or, more particularly, between judgments and ideas, can readily be carried over to the emotional domain, insofar as we can expect the situation there to be similar. Following our proposed symbolism, we have to substitute an n or a t for g, where the presupposition may contain, besides the A and some other self-presenting object, also a G in case we are dealing, not with an idea-feeling (*Vorstel-*

---

16. The terms "independent" (*selbständig*) and "dependent" (*abhängig*) are used according to St. Witasek's use in his treatise "Über ästhetische Objektivität," *Zeitschr. f. Philos. u. philos. Kritik*, CLVII (1915), 105; see also below, p. 92.

lungsgefühl), but with a judgment-feeling (*Urteilsgefühl*). If, however, we are dealing with a desire, we may have to take an N into consideration, so that the presupposition, besides A and G and a and g, may also contain an n. If, in particular, we take the feeling n into consideration, it indicates a subsistent A or an A that has *Aussersein,* and, through A, an existent a, without being, in a strict sense, "founded" on the latter. It would not accord with our analogy if we treated any feelings as sensations (*Empfindungen*) and therefore as independent experiences; as a matter of fact, I do not believe that there are any examples of feelings which are not based on psychological presuppositions.[17] On the other hand, one must not expect that the characteristics of A can be very closely tied to those of n. This is shown by the different ways in which the feelings of the same individual, and even more the feelings of different individuals, react to the same intellectual presuppositions at different times, and also the associative transference of a feeling from one presuppositional object to another, and so forth. Nevertheless, in assorting a repertoire of relevant facts, one should rather be too scrupulous than too generous. I find it especially hard to believe in "sensuous unpleasantness" (*sinnliche Unannehmlichkeit*) at the mere aspect of "worthless combinations of sounds" (*Tonverbindungen*), though none less than C. Stumpf testifies to it.[18] At any rate, though the dependence of emotions is readily accessible to *a priori* insight, their dependence upon their psychological presuppositions is often not distinct enough to be known *a priori,* so that any attempt to discover lawfulness here seems to be at first exclusively an empirical matter.

17. Cf. E. Becher, "Gefühlsbegriff und Lust-Unlustelemente," pp. 144 f.
18. "Über Gefühlsempfindungen," *Zeitschr. f. Psychol.,* XLIV (1907), 37.

9 / Additional Remarks Concerning the Notion of Psychological Presupposition and Its Formulation

THE PRECEDING DISCUSSIONS and the following paragraphs had been in print for several months when I learned (being kindly informed by the author) that Dr. Stephan Baley had critically examined the notion of "psychological presupposition" in his work *Über Urteilsgefühle*.[1] This criticism at least deserves some brief attention at a time when I am again explicitly taking up my old notion after more than twenty years. His criticism is, on the one hand, concerned with the determination of the notion in question, and, on the other, he is concerned with its use in cases which seemingly did not need to be subsumed under their own peculiar notion. The relations of psychological presuppositions to feelings receive particular consideration. The author speaks in particular of the "psychological presupposition of feeling" (*psychologische Gefühlsvoraussetzung*).

The author pays explicit attention[2] to the fact that A. Höfler defines the psychological presupposition of feelings as "those psychic phenomena (*Erscheinungen*) 'in' which and 'through' which we take pleasure or displeasure,"[3] and he also pays some attention to the fact that St. Witasek talks of a "double" function of the presupposition of feeling;[4] he therefore

1. Lemberg: Verlag der Schewtschenko-Gesellschaft der Wissenschaften, 1916.
2. *Über Urteilsgefühle*, pp. 5 ff.
3. *Psychologie*, p. 389.
4. *Grundlinien der Psychologie*, p. 322.

also asks, in reference to my discussions in *Psychologisch-ethische Untersuchungen:*

> What is the essential character of the notion of the psychological presupposition of feelings that we need to know this in order to do justice to the previously mentioned discussions by Meinong? It is neither the act-content relation as such, nor the causal relation. What is essential to the notion is the dependence of feelings upon the intellectual elements in a quite general sense, the "priority" (*Primärsein*) of the latter to the former, as becomes evident in one or the other of the named relationships. . . . If we stop at this wide version of the notion, we have to admit that it is vague, and that it does not give much positive information as to the intellectual element that is to be subsumed under it.[5]

Baley thinks that "the mutual relationship between feelings and intellectual elements in various kinds of dependence had not been at all sufficiently investigated *before* the notion of a presupposition of feeling was built upon it" and that "on the contrary this notion was first constructed and only later were the manifold interlockings (*Ineinandergreifen*) of these relationships of dependence subsumed under the ready-made notion."[6] This "had many bad consequences," and the author therefore concludes that "the manner in which the notion of a psychological presupposition of feeling is built upon the notion of content and of cause of feeling needs to be made more precise in order to be at all useful as a clear psychological notion."[7]

We have, in particular,

> two distinct problems: to enumerate the relations of feelings (*Gefühlsbeziehungen*), as they appear to the considerations of a naïvely thinking person, and to attempt a scientific explanation of them. . . . The synthetic construction of the notion (of feeling-presuppositions) is something that should follow the solution of both problems. The first problem is not easy, and the second problem, i.e., the scientific interpretation of the different kinds of feeling-relations (*Gefühlsbeziehungen*), will be difficult in more ways than one.

This is in fact true of the causal relation, and he continues:

> it is doubtful whether the "directedness" (*Gerichtetsein*) of feeling to an object, which is a well-known fact of everyday life, is

5. *Über Urteilsgefühle*, pp. 10 f.
6. *Ibid.*, pp. 12 f.
7. *Ibid.*, p. 13.

reducible to an act-content relationship. There are, after all, psychologists who refuse to admit that there is an act-content relationship between feelings and ideas.[8]

To my preference for an "a priorism" in these matters, the author opposes the view that

> the directedness of feelings . . . is not something primary, having an *a priori* connection with their essence, but . . . is interpolated between feelings and ideas (or objects) by our consciousness on account of certain special circumstances.[9]

He explains this by "the fact that emotional and intellectual changes run in parallel fashion." [10]

> As well as making use of the causal relationship, the naïve consciousness very often relates feelings to intellectual elements by way of hypostasizing feelings as qualities and, as such, attributing them to objects.[11]

> This case stands in contrast to the case where the feeling seems to be something independent. . . .[12]

In the same way, "sensations (*Empfindungen*) can be connected in different ways with objects," referred to them, very much as in the case of feelings. It often happens that we, e.g., "have the sensation of warmth but do not localize it or relate it to something outside us." [13]

> It is, therefore, natural to assume that the causes which produce this appearance of relatedness are the same in both cases, and there is no prior reason to reject such an assumption.[14]

> Thus, if a song seems to us sad, one can assume that it does so in virtue of the same psychic laws by which an oven appears warm and ice appears cold.[15]

> When feelings are combined into a group with sensations and ideas, so that they appear and disappear together, they fall under similar psychic conditions with the latter and are therefore sub-

8. *Ibid.*, p. 15.
9. *Ibid.*, pp. 16 f.
10. *Ibid.*, p. 18.
11. *Ibid.*, p. 19.
12. *Ibid.*, p. 20.
13. *Ibid.*, p. 22.
14. *Ibid.*, p. 23.
15. *Ibid.*, p. 24.

jected to the same processes. Just as with ideas and sensations, they assume the character of properties, states (*Zustände*), and activities. But they essentially require a substratum or an object to which they are attached. . . . To assume a special relationship by which the reference of feelings is explained would be superfluous as long as one is dealing with the forms of reference familiar to the naïve consciousness.[16]

"How it comes about that we relate a certain feeling to a certain object"[17] the author

does not feel obliged to decide. The theory as to the character of the reference which puts ideas (or objects) into relation can and may at least tentatively be used to explain the relations that connect feelings with ideas (or objects). We have no reason to assume that the situation is quite different as regards the reference of feelings, as long as we have not demonstrably failed in our attempt to regard it as something similar to other cases of reference.[18]

And just as it is not necessary to hold that the sensation of a tone has an *a priori*, essential "directedness" (*Gerichtetsein*) to something in order to apprehend the reference of the tone to the violin, so it is also not necessary, in order to explain the fact that we, e.g., relate our well-being to nice weather, to assume that the feeling of well-being has an *a priori* and essential directedness to something which is inseparable from its essence. It is, moreover, not necessary that, in all cases where we say and believe that we have referred a feeling to something, a complete, conscious act of reference should be present. . . . If we are well acquainted with a relation, and if the circumstances under which the terms of the relation occur are so clear that there can be no question as to the nature of the relation which is founded on those terms, then we do not explicitly perform an act of reference, for reasons of psychic economy, but we act *as if* we had performed such an act and therefore usually say later on that we *did* relate the terms of the relation to one another.[19]

In the same way, we usually say "of our feelings that we referred them to something, and we do not find it hard to name the objects to which the feelings were referred."[20]

16. *Ibid.*, pp. 24 f.
17. *Ibid.*, p. 26.
18. *Ibid.*, p. 28.
19. *Ibid.*, p. 29.
20. *Ibid.*, p. 30.

If we try to discuss the foregoing inadequately excerpted quotations, we note in particular how the manner in which consciousness "refers" (*bezieht*) feelings to intellectual elements is treated. An object *B* is referred by us to another object *A* in that *B* is apprehended in a relation *F*. If it is said, as a result of this sort of apprehension, that *B* stands to *A* in the relation *F*, this not the same as saying that one has referred *B* to *A*. I have to relate red to green in order to find them different, and the activity of the subject is more noticeable in such comparison than on many other occasions. But the difference between red and green is there, whether I relate them to each other or not. When I say, therefore, that a feeling is directed to an objectum and that the feeling presupposes the idea of this objectum, I certainly cannot do that without "referring" (*beziehen*) the feeling to the objectum or to its idea. But my main point is not to insist on this referring, which must take place anyway, but that what I assert is not this reference, which must be present whether my statement is right or wrong. In keeping with prevailing prejudices, this is often left out of consideration, and it is widely believed to be a sign of a better scientific attitude if one speaks of the apprehension of a thing rather than of the thing itself, as if the apprehension were not itself a "thing" in respect of which one must in the end be either right or wrong. In regard to a widespread psychologism of this kind, I must surely not presume to forget how uncertain I myself am whether I *did* avoid it sufficiently when I formulated the notion of "generable complexions" (*erzeugbare Komplexionen*).[21] But it is evidently too early to construct the psychology of an error on the mere suspicion of "interpolations" before the error has been established as such.

It is not right, similarly, to make the position, to which our author is opposed, a matter of the "naïve consciousness," to which he occasionally refers in order to contrast it with the higher authority of science.[22] This "naïve consciousness" is not in all cases to be held in contempt; but what I said as to the directedness of feelings and psychological presuppositions does not at all mean that the naïve consciousness will be tempted to

21. In the essay "Phantasievorstellung und Phantasie," *Zeitschr. f. Philosophie u. philos. Kritik*, XCV (1889), 174 f. (*Gesammelte Abhandlungen*, I, 207 f.; cf. appended notes, p. 275).
22. Cf., e.g., p. 18 of *Über Urteilsgefühle*.

form an opinion about them under certain circumstances. More-over, I believe myself to have stated facts which have nothing to do with what the naïve or the sophisticated person thinks about them. By no means, however, can I see justification for opposing my views, under the aegis of "scientific method" (*Wissenschaft-lichkeit*), because they are often supported by the attitudes of the naïve consciousness.

The center of the author's argumentation lies in a parallel-ism between emotional-intellectual and purely intellectual re-lationships. In respect to such a parallelism, it is remarkable that the author speaks of a hypostatization of feelings as properties of things, whereas even exponents of a radical subjectivism do not readily speak of a hypostatization of sensations in a similar sense; and it is more important that we should answer the question whether, in an exclusively intellectual domain, relation-ships show sufficient uniformity as a basis for conclusions go-ing beyond the intellectual realm. Is it in this respect really much the same whether we are dealing with a stove that is warm, or with red and green, which are different, or with Castor and Pollux, which form a pair? It is sufficient to refer to Section 11, below, where reasons are given to show why, in the two latter examples, an object of higher order is imposed on objects of lower' order. This is not the case in the first example, where the property warmth stands in no *inferius-superius* relationship to the other properties of an oven. If it is further asked whether the sadness of a melody follows the analogy of warmth or that of difference, the just-mentioned paragraph will make it clear that sadness is an object of higher order and is not, therefore, on the same functional level as warmth. If the temporal proximity of the data is important in order to find the stove warm, it is not at all relevant for the difference between red and green; and there is hardly any reason to believe that the case is different in regard to the sadness of a song.

In order to avoid the danger of a vacillating attitude, which at one time favors objects, at another time favors the ex-periences that apprehend the objects, let it be said that the sad-ness which can be taken to be a sort of property of a song is not itself a feeling and also not a "hypostatization" of a feeling. If what we said in the preceding section is right, sadness is an object apprehended by way of feeling-presentation. So that the like treatment which our author administers to sadness and warmth is itself to be taken as a sort of sign of the existence of emotional partial presentation, if the necessary reservations are made. Whatever I have said regarding the directedness of feelings and their psychological presuppositions refers to the feelings and not to this object peculiar to themselves and presented by them.

More specifically, as mentioned in the preceding section,[23] the claim that there is such a directedness requires that there is also a dependence of feeling upon an object not presented by it and, therefore, a relation which cannot be rejected as impossible because it subsists neither between warmth and a stove nor between the idea of warmth and a stove. It should rather be compared to the relation between the idea of difference and the objects which stand in the relation of difference, without which, regardless of their great variability, the difference could not be apprehended, except perhaps abstractly. There would, however, not be any directedness in such a case, whereas, in the case where a feeling is directed to its borrowed (*angeeignet*) object, we can forgo the demand that the connection be very tight; we cannot do this in the case of difference and the like, since in such cases a *superius* is not merely dependent upon its subordinates but has, as regards its character, even an *a priori* dependence upon them.[24] Often an *a priori* connection between the borrowed and proper object of feeling has its place taken by an empirical connection, so that in this respect the analogy to oven and warmth finally gets due credit. And so the point is indicated at which our author could have begun with a quite correct observation.

Nonetheless, this would not give the author the right to contrast feelings with their borrowed objects in the same way as the tone is contrasted with the violin; even moderately careful observation will show such an externalizing treatment to be illegitimate. How much insight we have into the fact of directedness will perhaps become clear if we begin by considering judgments or assumptions instead of feelings. An experience which apprehends a case of being (*ein Sein*) cannot do so, except perhaps abstractly, without apprehending something which has being (*ein Seiendes*), to which it is directed. Whatever the characteristics of this thing which has being may be can in a given case only be known empirically. But the directedness to its object does not consist in the mere simul-

23. See above, pp. 59 ff.
24. See above, pp. 64 ff.

taneity of the psychic event. The situation does not differ in the case of feelings, where an associative interpretation of directedness has already been rejected expressly and correctly,[25] and where likewise any other interpretation must be rejected which makes do with so-to-speak object-free feelings which acquire objectivity (*Gegenständlichkeit*) as a sort of irrelevant external trimming. This means, as far as I can see, that direct experience has never encountered object-free (*gegenstandsfrei*) feelings, and it is therefore needless, in our disagreement with the author, to invoke the dispositions or "attitudes" (*Verhaltungsweisen*), the latter of which he likes to mention more than is necessary.[26]

It can be gleaned from the preceding section [27] that there is only one remaining step, and that a legitimate one, from where we are to the notion of a psychological presupposition. The trouble which our author took to derive difficulties from the alternatives "act-content relation" and causal relation has been in vain; in vain also for the special reason that the notion of psychological presupposition had already been formulated with the very intent to keep it free of the causal notion.[28] It was also vain because the notions of "act" and "content" had been revised since then (the results of the revision are summarized in the preceding pages),[29] of which revision, however, the author neglected to take notice.

Even if these disquisitions regarding the "bad consequences" of premature "constructions" hardly give us a good impression of our young author, I have to admit to my critic that the manner in which I introduced the notion of a psychological presupposition, thereby satisfying provisional demands, was far less precise than might be desired. This, however, I ad-

25. See E. Husserl, *Logische Untersuchungen*, 2d ed. (1914), II, 389.

26. I am referring to the main theme of his work, the processing of judgment-feelings, to which I will recur expressly on another occasion.

27. See especially pp. 63 ff., above.

28. See above, p. 64, near footnote 15.

29. See § 7, above. That there are psychologists who do not even want "to hear of the act-content relationship between feelings and ideas" (also not of the content-object relationship and other things) is the less important counterargument the more voluntaristic it is understood to be. If I am right, those psychologists must give up the "will to ignorance."

mitted in the preceding section, before I knew of St. Baley's investigations. But I derived some benefit from his critical remarks, for I now see that the name "psychological presupposition," as standing for the notion with whose expression I have always been more or less consciously occupied, has been from the very beginning insufficient because unclear.

Of course, the idea whose object is judged about or valued (*wertgehalten*) can naturally be called the "presupposition of the judgment" or the "presupposition of the feeling." And the adjective "psychological," since it refers only to an internal event, can be criticized only inasmuch as "psychic" would have been more adequate. But, disregarding this rather incidental point, I acknowledged,[30] when I introduced the term "psychological presupposition," that there are enough experiences which are in this sense the psychological presuppositions of other experiences but which do not exhibit the particular situation in regard to which one can speak of the "directedness" of judgments or feelings to the objects of the ideas in question. If, for example, I value (*werthalten*) an O because it is the cause of a P, by which I set store (*dem ich Wert beimesse*),[31] my feeling of value is in fact directed to O but not at all to P or to the causal connection between O and P. But the judgment regarding this connection is naturally a presupposition for the feeling in question, and thus it is of course a psychological presupposition in the above sense of the word.

However, the notion of a "psychological presupposition," which is characterized by its "being directed," has shown itself to be so important, since it was first thought of, that we cannot refuse to satisfy the need for its terminological fixation. For the sake, however, of continuity, the importance of which I shall again mention in this book,[32] I want to avoid a completely new expression, since I have so often called the cases which have the particular characteristic of being directed to something (*Gerichtetsein*) "psychological presuppositions" for short. Under such circumstances a clarifying remark might help us out: in the following sections, where we deal with the fact of being directed to something (*Gerichtetsein*), we shall occasionally and experimentally use the expression "psychological object-

---

30. See *Psychologisch-ethische Untersuchungen*, pp. 34 f., 53.
31. Cf. the still quite insufficient discussion, *ibid.*, pp. 59 ff.
32. See below, pp. 134 f.

presupposition" (*psychologische Gegenstandsvoraussetzung*). We hope that thus the essential objective (*gegenständlich*) moment will become sufficiently clear. The expression must not, however, be taken to mean that the object of the judgment or feeling is the presupposition. And it is not in favor of the new term that such a restriction must be made. But we hope that the drawback is more than compensated by the previously mentioned advantage of continuity.

10 / On the Characterization of Feelings and Desires in Accordance with Their Psychological Object Presupposition

AT FIRST IT WILL REMAIN undecided whether feelings can be profitably subdivided in accordance with the classification of elementary feelings, psychological object-presuppositions not being considered as their possible basis. The special fitness of these presuppositions to be such a basis was made clear by St. Witasek's [1] convincing statement that not only the difference between ideas and judgments or assumptions but also the difference between act and content is of importance for the characterization of the feelings which depend on relevant intellectual experience for their object-presuppositions (*Gegenstandsvoraussetzung*). This is still in need of clarification. The main point seems, however, to have been sufficiently established for it to be used as the basis for the following investigations. The parallelism between sensuous feelings as idea-act-feelings and aesthetic feelings as idea-content-feelings, on the one hand, and what I long ago [2] distinguished as knowledge-feelings and value-feelings in the domain of intellectual feelings, on the other hand,[3] is quite obvious. One must therefore ask the question

1. See his *Grundzüge der Ästhetik* (Leipzig, 1904), pp. 195 ff., and especially the summary of his *Grundlinien der Psychologie*, pp. 324, 328.
2. In *Psychologisch-ethische Untersuchungen zur Werttheorie*, pp. 36 ff.
3. It is hardly too early if, more than two decades after the formulation of my notion, I express the suspicion that contemporary value-theory has neglected to consider the basic notions behind my statements, misled by the rather external circumstance that very often the word "value" was used in a broader sense, which is similar

whether the resultant four classes constitute a correct division of elementary feelings in accordance with their psychological object-presuppositions.

One must, in the first place, notice that, in the juxtaposition of "idea-act-feelings beside idea-content-feelings, and judgment-act-feelings beside judgment-content-feelings," assumptions are not being considered. If they are included in our consideration in view of their similarity to imaginative ideas, their analogy with ideas indicates that they belong to the same class as content-feelings, even if the contrast between judgments and assumptions concerns the "act." For assumptions are related to judgments as imaginative ideas are to serious ideas,[4] while idea-act-feelings are in the first place sensuous feelings, that is, serious feelings rather than imaginative feelings. Indeed, assumptions could not readily furnish the object-presuppositions of knowledge-feelings, though they doubtless play a role in value-feelings, to the extent that the magnitude of a value is determined by both counterfeelings,[5] of which one, at least, must have an assumption as presupposition.[6]

As I tried to show elsewhere,[7] it will not do to deny that assumptions can furnish the object-presuppositions of aesthetic

---

to that which will be mentioned at the end of this work (pp. 153 ff., below). To use "value" in this broader sense naturally does not prevent the characterization of an important part of the value-field by its relation to judgments. I for myself still believe that it is these matters with which the untheoretically thinking person is concerned when he speaks of "value" and when no meanings are borrowed from other fields. In the following, therefore, we shall use "value" in this narrower sense.

4. Über Annahmen, § 65.
5. On counterfeelings, see below, pp. 110 ff.
6. See Über Annahmen, pp. 332 ff.
7. Ibid., pp. 318 f. In connection with the question there touched upon as regards the meaning of the change from quoted speech in prose, I accidentally found a postscript which is extremely interesting. In Book XI of Goethe's Aus meinem Leben: Wahrheit und Dichtung there is the following passage: "I honor rhythm and rhyme, through which poetry becomes poetry; but whatever is profoundly and thoroughly effective in poetry, whatever is truly formative and beneficial, is whatever remains over after a translation into prose. Then we have the pure, perfect content, which often is not really present under the dazzling illusion of form and which often, when present, is concealed by that form" (Propyläen edition of Goethe's Sämtliche Werke, XXV, 159; Cotta's edition in 36 vols. [1867], XII, 46).

feelings. This is obvious by reason of the fact that, as proved by the so-called verbal arts (*redende Künste*), objectives also count as objects of our aesthetic attitudes, and as among the most important ones.[8] Aesthetic feelings cannot, in short, be described as idea-feelings or, more particularly, as idea-content-feelings, although there are certainly many aesthetic feelings which can be described in this manner. At any rate, such cases also suffice to prove that aesthetic feelings cannot simply be characterized as assumption-feelings; this has already been made evident by the feelings of value (*Wertgefühle*) just mentioned, for which assumptions furnished the psychological object-presuppositions.

The demand, therefore, arises for a more adequate characterization of aesthetic feelings, and it might be better fulfilled from the viewpoint of the object than from that of the content of their presuppositions, if at the same time feelings of value are also taken into consideration. In my first discussion of these matters [9] I called feelings of value simply "existence-feelings" (*Existenzgefühle*); but in doing this I went too far, since that which subsists cannot be excluded from valuational consideration. Nevertheless, in the domain of values, we must definitely accord being a precedence over being-thus-and-so. For even though a being-thus-and-so is very often valued, it is always the being-thus-and-so of something that is, without regard to the further fact that each factual (*tatsächlich*) being-thus-and-so always has factual subsistence (*Bestand*) and that this is likewise true of each *possible* being-thus-and-so. So that even the latter is a kind of quasi-value-object in an objective of

---

8. E. Landmann-Kalischer defends the "aesthetic indifference" of objectives ("Kunstschönheit als ästhetischer Elementargegenstand," in *Beiträge zur Ästhetik und Kunstgeschichte* [Berlin: W. Moser, 1910], pp. 28 f.) but acknowledges the "internal" or "logical connection of events" as possibly being a "peculiar aesthetic elementary object" (*ibid.*, p. 29). This is hardly acceptable if logical connection is, as I believe, above all a matter of objectives. Quite free from such *ad hominem* argumentation is the consideration that objectives cannot be aesthetically indifferent if determinations, which can only be treated as differentiations of objectives, are not thus indifferent. No work of the verbal arts will permit change without alteration of its aesthetic character from positive to negative, or from factual to possible, and vice versa. Changes of these kinds, however, concern objectives.

9. See *Psychologisch-ethische Untersuchungen*, p. 16.

subsistence (*Bestandobjektiv*). We can summarize the matter thus: value-feelings are essentially feelings of being (*Seinsgefühle*), even if the being which is relevant in their case is the being of something which is thus-and-so (*eines Soseienden*). To formulate matters in this way leads on to the next question, as to whether there may not be a class of feelings which are essentially feelings-of-being-thus-and-so (*Soseinsgefühle*). In aesthetic feelings we may have such a class before us.

The cases mentioned above, where aesthetic feelings have to do with objectives, confirm this immediately. There too, however, we have objectives of being (*Seinsobjektive*), as is shown by phrases such as "There was a child who never wanted to go to church," or "There was a king in Thule," etc. The role of objectives of being is even more evident in the fundamentally important case of references by way of being,[10] not to mention the obvious fact that each being-thus-and-so allows us to recur to its own being or, better, to its subsistence. But experience shows that this moment of being is never of importance for aesthetic feelings. This is evident in the fact that such feelings never depend on the actual (*tatsächlich*) being of the objects in question. Even the factuality (*Tatsächlichkeit*) of being-thus-and-so seems likewise to be eliminated, since mere assumptions suffice to apprehend an objective of being-thus-and-so. Nevertheless, how differently matters stand in regard to objectives of being-thus-and-so is made clear by the facility with which the assumptions in question pass over into judgments and in the, as it were, astonishing sovereignty of poetic or, more generally, artistic imagination over objects. So, for example, in modern drama, exact information is frequently given as to the age or other characters of the persons in the play. At first this information can only be of the order of assumptions. But, once such assumptions are made, the persons in question are indeed of the indicated age, as if the poet had the right of free disposal regarding them. He has, in fact, nothing beyond the right to make analytic judgments in Kant's sense, according to which the golden mountain is in fact (*tatsächlich*) made of gold. In respect of these rights of poets, being is at a disadvantage in relation to being-thus-and-so.[11] It can, therefore, be seen that, in

10. See *Über Annahmen*, § 45; also *Über Möglichkeit und Wahrscheinlichkeit*, § 26.

11. Cf. *Über Möglichkeit und Wahrscheinlichkeit*, pp. 278 ff.

this way too, being-thus-and-so has a prerogative over being.

However, any further attempts to attribute constitutive importance to being-thus-and-so for *all* aesthetic objects of feelings are opposed by everything that compels us to attribute aesthetic dignity to objects of sensation or to higher-order patterns founded on those objects. But even if a color, a form (*Gestalt*), or a chord is not a being-thus-and-so (*ist kein Sosein*), it is, at any rate, a thus-and-so (*ein So*). A thus-and-so is present in any case of being-thus-and-so, and whoever explicitly apprehends the thus-and-so also implicitly apprehends [12] the being-thus-and-so, so that it cannot be wrong to subsume these cases under the standpoint of being-thus-and-so.

Remembering that ideas and assumptions play a role in contemplative apprehension,[13] while judgments play a role in penetrative apprehension, and considering also what has just been said, one will not find it very hard to characterize aesthetic feelings from the standpoint of their object-presuppositions. With respect to the contemplative characteristics of the latter, feelings could be determined as feelings of contemplation (or contemplative feelings) (*Kontemplationsgefühle*). But again the previously mentioned fact comes in the way, that assumptions can even function as presuppositions for feelings of value, so that it does not seem suitable to label feelings of value "penetrative feelings" (*Penetrationsgefühle*). But whoever lets such points discourage him overlooks one important point. Assumptions can certainly function as presuppositions for value-feelings, but only, however, for imaginative, not for serious, feelings of value. The situation is not the same in regard to aesthetic feelings. Aesthetic feelings whose presuppositions are assumptions are primarily serious feelings, and it is thus shown that aesthetic feelings are really indifferent whether their object-presuppositions are serious or imaginative. The value-feelings are clearly sensitive to changes from contemplation to penetration, inasmuch as, if they have an imaginative presupposition, they themselves take on an imaginative character. Their sensitivity, moreover, consists in the fact that proper value-feelings react only to serious presuppositions (*Ernstvoraussetzungen*), whereby the word "proper"

12. Cf. *ibid.*, pp. 270 ff.
13. See *ibid.*, § 34.

must be taken in the sense that, if anyone wishes to call assumptions "imaginative judgments," he might call serious judgments "judgments proper." Imaginative feelings of value are surrogates for serious value-feelings, surrogates regarding which it is at once known how they assist in the contemplative apprehension of values. Even if they are one of the factors which help to determine the magnitude of values (*Wertgrösse*),[14] the value itself is never really felt in them and through them. This latter sort of feeling takes place only when the psychological object-presupposition is of penetrative character. In this sense, value-feelings are exclusively penetrative feelings. This second characterization could then be combined with our first characterization, if we defined aesthetic feelings as feelings presupposing the contemplation of something's being-thus-and-so, and value-feelings as feelings presupposing the penetration of something's being.

It is, accordingly, not too hard to draw a line between aesthetic and value-feelings, but the question remains open whether these two kinds of feelings suffice for an exhaustive disjunction covering the whole domain of content-feelings. In fact, side by side with contemplation of something's being-thus-and-so and penetration of its being, there are also, according to the preceding, contemplation of something's being and penetration of its being-thus-and-so. But, empirically speaking, these two kinds of attitudes are barely noticeable as presuppositions of feeling. Being, except being-thus-and-so, seems to be of no import for contemplative thought, and being-thus-and-so without reference to a case of being is of no import for penetrative thought. There is practically no danger when the difference between these two doubtless possible kinds of feelings is at first disregarded. Even if doing this involves a certain danger of imprecision, it will, comparatively speaking, be at most a superficial defect, should experiences, for which the previous description of the two kinds of content-feelings is appropriate, not be readily subsumable under the two expressions "aesthetic feelings" and "value-feelings." Since the arts are at once thought of when the expression "aesthetic" is used, one might hesitate to call feelings directed toward temperature or taste, even in cases of pure contemplation, "aesthetic." Similar hesitations [15]

---

14. Cf. *Über Annahmen*, p. 331.
15. Th. Lessing's (see below, p. 111, § 12, n. 14).

may be felt in respect to the word "value," though my personal sense of words experiences no such scruples. All this, as far as I can see, provides no reason against conventional disregard for such inconsistencies in the use of the terms in question, for the sake of simplicity in theoretico-technical usage.

It will, therefore, be intelligible when, in what follows, I treat aesthetic feelings and value-feelings as subspecies of the genus "content-feeling" and when I set them beside the two kinds of act-feelings, i.e., sensuous and logical feelings. The differentiation between idea-content-feelings and thought-content-feelings, which is in certain respects more obvious, will not thereby lose any of its importance. The new division, nevertheless, meets the demands of theory and practice much better.

It is further important to mention that, as regards penetrative experiences, the relation between content-feelings and act-feelings still needs to be clarified. It is not difficult in practice to distinguish between the basic facts which are relevant for the whole differentiation. For nobody has any doubt that, for example, a person interested in the genuineness of a document as the basis for important legal claims has a different attitude toward it from a person merely interested in its genuineness as that of an interesting historical document. It seems quite natural to speak of a value-feeling in the former case and of a knowledge-feeling in the latter case,[16] though the former expression may seem to be a little more natural than the latter. For the situation of the historian can most easily be described by saying that he does not really value the genuineness of the document but only the knowledge of its genuineness, so that, in the latter case also, we should have to do with a value-feeling and should feel qualms about using our previous expression in order to differentiate between the two cases. But it is also advisable to rename the second case, for which we could use the quite characteristic expression—invented by St. Witasek—"knowledge-value-feeling" (*Wissenswertgefühl*).[17]

There is no doubt that there are such knowledge-value-feelings, but it certainly would contradict our experiences if all knowledge-feelings were taken to be knowledge-value-feelings. Even if the experience of holding something in esteem (*positive Werthaltung*) can be described as an elementary feeling of

16. Cf. *Psychologisch-ethische Untersuchungen zur Werttheorie,* § 12.
17. See *Grundzüge der Ästhetik,* pp. 255 ff.

pleasure regarding an objective,[18] this does not apply to knowledge-feelings, even if it cannot be denied (as I once did)[19] that these feelings have their objectives. Knowledge-feelings have, indeed, objectives; but the difference between knowledge-feelings and value-feelings is not to be found in such objectives, since the moment of knowledge is not in any way a necessary part of the material of such a feeling. Thus, in our previous example of the document: not only the person who has a direct interest in it, but also the historian, usually thinks only of the genuineness of the document and not in the least about his knowledge of that genuineness. There is, however, a fundamental difference between the two cases, and our theory is therefore faced with a by no means easy task. This task is not simply performed if we point out that, in the one case, the content-aspect of the presuppositional judgment plays the predominant role, while, in the other case, the act-aspect plays the predominant role, since such a predominance cannot alter the "feel" of the experience. At this point, feeling-presentation (*Gefühls-präsentation*) renders us welcome aid: one can easily imagine that, according to the predominant role played by act or content, a different feeling-experience results whose peculiarity expresses itself, as it were, in the peculiarity of the presented object.

The fact that act-feelings and content-feelings do not differ in respect of their presuppositional object is not really amazing if one remembers the relevant reasons given for the differentiation between these classes of feelings; the reasons are not that one is, in any case, dealing with presuppositions that are acts without contents or contents without acts but that, in the case of knowledge-feelings, the contrast between the Yes and the No of the presuppositional judgments, which is so fundamental for value-feelings, has lost most of its relevance. The same is the case, strictly speaking, in regard to the contrast between factuality (*Tatsächlichkeit*) and possibility, which in its "ontic level" (*Seinshöhe*) points to the content of judgment.[20] The act-feeling does not, therefore, lack a presuppositional content, nor the content-feeling a presuppositional act; and the opposition

18. Cf. "Über Urteilsgefühle, was sie sind und was sie nicht sind," *Archiv. f. d. gesamte Psychologie*, VI (1905), § 1 (*Gesammelte Abhandlungen*, Vol. I).
19. *Ibid.*, § 3.
20. See *Über Möglichkeit und Wahrscheinlichkeit*, pp. 265 f.

between these two classes of feelings should by no means be taken to mean that in each single case it will be clear at once to which of the two classes a given experience of feeling belongs. In fact, it quite often happens that we take up the role of a theoretical, disinterested observer toward the reality around us, including the facts of value (*Werttatsachen*) which are present in this reality. As far as idea-feelings are concerned, we can find an analogous case in the way in which, in sensuous pleasantness, the quality of the objects of sensation plays a definite role, so that the characteristic attitude we have to aesthetic objects becomes manifest. We shall not here consider how matters stand as regards feeling-presentation (*Gefühlspräsentation*) in such intermediate cases. We shall, at first, investigate the facts of presentation in such clearer cases as are also easier to deal with.

In order to understand the contrast between knowledge-feelings and value-feelings correctly, it might be advisable to consider the classes of desire (*Begehrungsklassen*) correlated with these two sorts of feelings. Traditionally, only the relation between value and value-feelings, as only the relation between value and desires, has been considered. Disregarding many possible uncertainties, one can here clearly see that value and valuing (*Werthalten*) are the logically prior pair. One will think it "logical" to desire what has value and will think that it is an inversion of the natural state of things if someone declares something to be valuable because he desires it. Nonetheless, the valuation directed to an objective cannot really be taken for the psychological presupposition of the desire directed to that objective. For valuation in a strict sense, that is, serious as opposed to imaginative valuation, has as its presupposition a judgment of being and, in the special case, a judgment of existence. I cannot, however, desire anything which I believe exists. Matters are similar in respect to non-being and in the primary case, nonexistence, as will be shown in greater detail.[21] Thus it can be said, in general, quite briefly and perhaps a little imprecisely, that an objective which, if it could be judged positively or negatively, would occasion a valuation also occasions, at least in favorable circumstances, a desire, in circumstances where not a judgment, but only an assumption, can be made. The objective then is the presup-

21. See below, pp. 143 ff.

positional objective of this desire. The desire is extinguished as soon as the judgment takes the place of the assumption; this is the subjective aspect of what, at least in one of the two possible cases, is called the fulfillment of the desire. In respect to all this, one could range objectives of fulfillment (*Erfüllungs-objektive*) alongside presuppositional objectives, the two being identical in character in our case.

Now we cannot deny that knowledge-feelings are correlated with desires in much the same way as value-feelings are. If, as we say, knowledge-feelings and value-feelings have in principle the same objective, they can also have the same presuppositional judgment. And, as in the case of value-feelings, so in the case of knowledge-feelings, a desire is occasioned if only a presuppositional assumption takes the place of the presuppositional judgment. The similarity of these two kinds of desires is seen even in the fact that they share a common name, which, however, does not designate the actual experience of desire but only the disposition to desire. Even in prescientific discourse one speaks of "interest," in which everyday language then draws a distinction, albeit a rather vague one, between being interested in something and having an interest in something. In more technical language, one distinguishes between theoretical and practical interests. The dispositional turn (*Wendung ins Dispositionelle*) becomes evident in the word "knowledge," which is part of the expression "knowledge-feeling," and we are accordingly moved to range a "knowledge-desire" alongside a "knowledge-feeling." In the same way as in the case of ordinary desires, there is a state in which knowledge-desires are fulfilled and thereby, as it were, annihilated. The objective of fulfillment is in this case in no way identical with the presuppositional objective, since the contrary of the presuppositional objective, if it be a fact, also is a fulfillment of the desire. Here, apparently, what is important is not that the presuppositional objective has become a fact but that the presuppositional assumption has been replaced by a presuppositional judgment, by the fact, that is, that ignorance has become knowledge. Thus, when knowledge occurs, our desire is fulfilled, and one might try to describe it thus: that a desire directed upon knowledge is described as a knowledge-desire. If this is understood as meaning that it is knowledge which is desired and not being, as in the case of ordinary desires, then it is not quite correct, since usually the person who has the desire does not think of knowledge in the manner in which the treasure-hunter thinks of a treasure. We conclude, therefore, that, as in the case of the two kinds of feeling (i.e., knowledge-feeling and value-feeling), the two kinds of desires have the same presuppositional objects but that they differ from each other as regards their objects of fulfillment, which does not happen in the case of feelings at all. Under these circumstances, the expression "knowledge-desire" (*Wissensbegehrung*) is ambiguous, but the situation is no better in the case of the term "knowledge-feeling" (*Wissensgefühl*). Since the latter expression has already been proven useful, the former does not need to be rejected; and ordinary desires might then be called "value-desires" (*Wertbegehrungen*). It would, however, be of advantage if the examination of objects of experience were to put even clearer terms at our disposal, a matter to which I shall return later.[22]

In support of what has been said, let us briefly make two further points. First of all, that, quite beyond the region of theoretical interest, there is at least one well-known case where the desire to know has attracted prescientific notice. In such a case we do not have to do with a mere disposition but with an actual experience, for which our language has a special and clear expression; it is, namely, the fact of the "question."

Elsewhere [23] I have already pointed to W. Frankl's important observation that the person who asks a question naturally thinks of the object of his question but not readily of his state of knowing, and perhaps this consideration was one of the original factors which instigated the previous investigations.

It is clear without more ado that what has been said about knowledge-desires can be applied without reservations to questions, at least to the extent that questions demanding decisions are concerned. It is regrettable that J. Kl. Kreibig's otherwise instructive monograph [24] did not enter into these matters, which are so centrally illuminating for the essence of questions. The situation is a little different in the case of determinative ques-

22. See below, § 11.
23. *Über Annahmen*, p. 124.
24. "Beiträge zur Psychologie und Logik der Frage," *Archiv f. d. gesamte Psychologie*, XXXIII (1914).

tions (*Bestimmungsfragen*),[25] in respect to which the presuppositional objective is not apprehended through an assumption but through a judgment. For when we ask who was the real originator of the war-events of 1914, these events are not merely assumed but believed, and they are also believed to have had a cause. But the indeterminateness with which the object of the question is here apprehended is characteristically contrasted with the determinateness of this object in the objective of fulfillment. Apparently the transition from the indeterminate to the determinate here replaces the transition from the assumption to the judgment as the latter occurs in the question which demands decision. Knowledge as the explicit goal of desire seems to be dispensable in either case.

The second point which needs to be considered here is that there are other desires besides knowledge-desires which are not value-desires. A man who is hungry or thirsty desires, and so does a man who merely reads a play in a book or a tone-poem in a score or in a pianoforte selection. And when the objects of such desires have to be described, there is the same danger of a fictitious reduction to value-desires as in the case of knowledge-desires. Then it is said that it is the existence or, more subjectively, the enjoyment, of the food or the work of art that is desired. Such a way of thinking is even more obviously artificial than it is in the case where knowledge is interpolated. One must therefore also differentiate between presuppositional object and object of fulfillment in this case. Then, just as above, the presuppositional object of the desire in question is plainly the same as the object of the feeling which goes with it, but the presuppositional object is again apprehended rather imperfectly by an imaginative idea and not by a serious one. Again the fulfillment is the more perfect experience of apprehension, though it cannot be said that the person who has the desire consciously envisages the experience which annihilates his desire as his goal. Perhaps this provides a clue for a truly general description of desires. Side by side with value-desires and knowledge-desires, one can set at least two coordinate kinds of desires which may provisionally be called "sensuous desires" and "aesthetic desires," respectively. They stand beside the knowledge-feelings and value-feelings in an opposition to sensuous

25. See E. Martinak, "Das Wesen der Frage," *Atti del V. congresso internazionale di psicologia* (Rome, 1905), pp. 4 ff. of the offprint.

feelings and aesthetic feelings. This quadripartition can be preserved even if the original characterization, which is got with the
help of the oppositions "act" and "content," "idea" and "judgment," did not quite stand up to testing.

I do not wish to conclude my treatment without spending a
little time on facts that seem to be quite important, and to
which my attention was called by the question of a young
colleague,[26] namely, whether the four classes just described are
also similar to one another in that the contrast between serious
experiences and imaginative experiences holds for them all,
and not solely for value-feelings. In fact, whenever we speak of
imaginative feelings, we usually think of imaginative value-
feelings. And closer investigation confirms our suggestion that
value-feelings take precedence over other feelings in regard to
the contrast in question. This has its roots in the law that,
whenever suitable judgments occasion value-feelings, the pertinent assumptions as a rule furnish object-presuppositions
(*Gegenstandsvoraussetzungen*) for imaginative value-feelings.
These imaginative value-feelings can be evoked at will, as can
the respective assumptions. As an illustration, consider our
imaginative interest in the characters of a drama [27] and compare it with the aesthetic feelings which may, in favorable
circumstances, occur at the same time and which preserve
their serious character (*Ernstcharakter*) even when all their
psychological presuppositions are not serious, but imaginative,
experiences. It is easily understood that this lies in the nature
of these feelings as content-feelings. Since, for content-feelings, not the act-aspect of their presuppositions, but only their
content-aspect, is important, variations in the act-character of
such presuppositions will plainly not matter. One might
quite reasonably doubt whether there are aesthetic imaginative
feelings at all. And the indifference shown by aesthetic feelings
in regard to their presuppositional act (*Voraussetzungsakt*) is
paralleled in effect in the case of the logical and sensuous feelings by the fact that the act-moment of their presuppositions is
essential. It is indeed a recognizable peculiarity of sensuous
feelings [28] that they fail to be aroused when their object-pre-

---

26. Cand. jur. Ernst Seelig in Graz.
27. Cf. *Über Annahmen*, pp. 128 f.
28. Cf. St. Witasek, *Grundzüge der allgemeinen Ästhetik*, pp.
198 f.

suppositions take on an imaginative character. And, as concerns logical feelings, the epithet "logical" seems obviously inapplicable wherever we have to do with assumptions instead of judgments. We therefore suspect that in the case of logical, as in that of sensuous, feelings, imaginative experiences play no part.

At first, however, the premises which lead to such a conclusion are in need of revision. It does not violate any experiential law that logical imaginative feelings can take the place of logical serious feelings when assumptions take the place of judgments. Likewise it is not evident that, when a sensuous object is imagined, there can be no act-feeling but only a content-feeling. Content-feelings or aesthetic feelings seem to be insensitive to the transition from serious experiences to imaginative experiences in respect to their object-presuppositions. An imagined major chord arouses serious feelings, though they are often weaker than those aroused by a chord that is actually heard. But, generally speaking, this insensitivity is something quite different from an utter inability to evoke imaginative feelings; and that such a capability is present in each of the classes of feelings, despite their differences, is made clear by the fact that each of the four classes of feelings is accessible not only to perception but also to memory. If we were previously right [29] in inferring, from the fact of self-presentation in perceiving, that there is other-presentation supported by correlative imaginative experiences in memory or in merely assumptive apprehension, we have reason to believe in the certain occurrence of imaginative experiences in the domain of sensuous, aesthetic, and logical feelings, inasmuch as we can certainly remember feelings belonging to these classes or think of them without remembering them. Naturally, we must now ask the question what the cause of the arousal of such experiences may be if the imaginative presuppositions concerned do not suffice to do the job. Doubtless this question deserves full attention. The answer will, however, not be too difficult if we are willing to widen the psychological laws of reproduction (Reproduktionsgesetze) in a suitable manner.

29. See above, pp. 24 f.

11 / The Objects of Emotional Partial Presentation

THE QUADRIPARTITION, which we have just shown to be justified, would seem, to the extent that it concerns feelings, to be especially suited to effect a transition from presenting experiences to the objects presented by them. Through our division of feelings into four classes, our attention has been automatically called to the objects Pleasant, Beautiful, True, and Good, though the meaning of these expressions has not been made sufficiently clear by their mere correlation with those classes. The use of the term "true" seems especially dubious in this context, and we will return to this point later.[1] On the other hand, it is clear that expressions such as "good" and "beautiful" can be used with claims that are more or less exacting, something that still needs some additional justification.[2]

In the field of desires, obligation (ought, *Sollen*) and instrumentality (*Zweckmässigkeit*) are obviously our objects of presentation. We have already mentioned the possibility that our four forms of feeling will be correlated, under appropriate conditions, to forms of desire that are correspondingly differentiated. This differentiation may also have relevance for the objects presented by the desires in question, and we may have occasion, if pressed, to speak of value-obligations, beauty-obligations, etc. There will be no valid objections against introducing similar differentiations in respect to instrumentality (*Zweckmässigkeit*). The objects of emotional presentation,

1. See below, pp. 117 ff., 153 f.
2. See below, §§ 13 ff.

however, require the rudiments of a general description before we concern ourselves with such relatively special questions. This shall be attended to first.

The theory of objects is without doubt an *a priori* science, if not, indeed, *the a priori* science. The subsistence (*Bestand*) and *Aussersein* of objects can be known *a priori* from the nature of the objects in question. Nevertheless, this knowledge of being can be traced back to a direct apprehension of these objects, as a sort of quasi-experience by means of which the theory of objects is in a position to take an inductive path from below upwards, just as the empirical sciences do. The characterization of the objects of emotional partial presentation accordingly has the advantage that a limited group of these objects, the aesthetic objects, has already been subjected to a fairly profound study from the point of view of the theory of objects.[3] So it becomes quite natural to continue the investigations.

There is a profound parallelism between objects and the experiences which apprehend them,[4] a parallelism which has understandably favored a subjectivistic interpretation of facts concerning objects (*gegenständliche Tatsachen*). In our field this parallelism makes itself most obvious in the fact that, just as our presenting experiences have other psychological object-presuppositions which are primarily intellectual experiences, so the objects which are presented by these experiences and which are, in our special case, aesthetic depend for their being and their being thus-and-so upon that which is apprehended by the presuppositional experiences.[5] The property "beautiful," like the property "red," not only requires something of which it is a property, but it requires another property or complex of properties as its basis, which is as much a necessary condition for its occurrence as a red thing is for the property red. The property beautiful depends upon the characteristics of its basis, as, for example, this form (*Gestalt*) is beautiful, that one ugly, this more beautiful than another, that one less. This has an obvious analogy to the relationship of *relata* and complexes to their *inferiora*. There would be no similarity without similar objects. Whether two objects are similar at all, or to

3. By St. Witasek in the above-mentioned treatise "Über äs-thetische Objektivität" [see above, § 8, footnote 16].

4. Cf. *ibid.*, pp. 188 ff.

5. *Ibid.*, pp. 105 f., 108 ff.

what extent they are similar, depends throughout on their characteristics.

Still, there are reasons which exclude a simple subsumption of aesthetic objects under the notion of objects of higher order.[6] *Relatum* and complex stand, so to speak, between their *inferiora* and connect them. Beauty, on the other hand, does not connect the tones of a beautiful melody, but the already unified object melody is its basis. And such a basis does not necessarily consist in a plurality of objects, as seems necessary in the case of *inferiora* of relations (except in limiting cases, as, for example, that of identity). Beauty is grasped by a perceiving-like intuition (*wahrnehmungsartige Anschaulichkeit*) and not by a productive process, such as the one by which similarity is apprehended. And while the knowledge of similarity has the characteristic necessity of *a priori* knowledge, judgments as to the beauty of an object are always of an empirical cast. Of these four characteristics, the latter two are of less crucial interest, since they are more connected with the theory of apprehension than with the theory of objects. This will be evident [7] in respect to the fourth characteristic, which is the absence of the *a priori*. Regarding the third characteristic, i.e., the general lack of productive activity, we must observe that this activity, which arises in apprehending accredited objects of higher order, is obvious in very different degrees. It cannot, for example, be overlooked in the comparative apprehension of a difference, but it is often not noticeable with certainty in the apprehension of a melody. The first two characteristics, on the other hand, which can be taken together under the notion of the "oneness" (*"Einsheit"*) (in contrast to the plurality) of the object which is the basis, are doubtless a matter of fact and peculiar importance. Still, the subsumption under the notion of objects of higher order can be maintained if this notion is somewhat modified in a manner that has been rendered necessary by the progress made in our knowledge of the theory of objects.

The notion of objects of higher order was initially formulated in connection with *relata* and complexes. It was not known at the time, at least not in a strict theoretical sense, that objectives were to be counted as objects as well as objecta. Only

6. See *ibid.*, pp. 180 ff.
7. See below, pp. 95, 118 ff.

objecta, therefore, were counted as objects of higher order. When objectives had also gained consideration in the theory of objects, it became apparent that there were different levels among them. In comparison with the objective "*A* is *B*," the objectives "It is a fact that *A* is *B*" or "It is true that *A* is *B*" must without doubt be considered as objectives of higher order; and this is in general true for each objective that itself includes an objective in its "material." We can also express this as follows: Each objective is an objective of higher order with respect to another objective if the latter occupies the place of an objectum in the former.

It is thereby already presupposed that objectives take the position of objects of higher order with respect to the objecta of their material. Thus, in general, we can say that all objectives as such are objects of higher order.

It is now quite easy to find reasons for what has just been said in the nature of objectives themselves and also in the general nature of objects of higher order. Our picture of the various levels of order is only an indication of the fact that objects of higher order are based or built upon objects of lower order and that the former could not be there if the latter were not there first. The "being there" is to be understood, as we have already seen,[8] not only in the sense of existence or subsistence but also in the sense of *Aussersein;* and the "at first" is meant in the peculiar, timeless sense of the logically prior. All this applies, without the slightest difficulty, to objectives.

Of course, it may at first glance look strange that we can speak of the being (or even *Aussersein*) of a being (*eines Seins*). On a closer look we see that it is equally unavoidable and no worse than when the theory of knowledge becomes a knowledge of knowledge, which leads to a peculiar but not untenable situation.[9]

It would clearly be senseless to talk of a being which was not the being of something and, therefore, to talk of an objective which had no basic material. The objective's material may, in its turn, contain other objectives (of lower order) but only such objectives which are at least based on objecta. Thus it is shown that all objectives are essentially objects of higher

8. See above, pp. 18, 61, 64 f.
9. Cf. *Über Möglichkeit und Wahrscheinlichkeit*, § 54.

order and that no objective can assume the position of an *infimum*.

If this is true, then it is not right to attribute to all objects of higher order what is common to *relata* and complexes, that is, to objecta of higher order. The foregoing holds especially of most *inferiora*. Disregarding possible limiting cases, relations must have at least two members, complexes (*Komplexionen*) at least two components. The same holds for objectives of (an object's) being thus-and-so, whose material must be bipartite. Contrariwise, the objectives of (an object's) being, existence, and subsistence—and no less the objectives of (an object's) *Aussersein*—are by nature monadic, and it does not make any difference whether they have a simple or complex material of objecta. It can, by the way, also be seen that the characteristic dependence of the *superius* upon its *inferiora* is by no means always an *a priori* or necessary dependence. This can readily be seen in connection with real *relata* (*Realrelate*) and real complexes (*Realkomplexe*), which were counted by me from the very beginning among objects of higher order. The same holds of objectives and is substantiated by the very simple fact that there is other knowledge besides *a priori* knowledge and that the lack of necessity in the former is not to be explained by our insufficient intelligence. There is no object whose existence follows *a priori* from its nature. Existence is, nonetheless, as much an object of higher order as subsistence.

We can readily apply these results to aesthetic objects. Their lack of self-sufficiency and their dependence on the substrates presented by the psychological object-presuppositions of aesthetic feelings have already been recognized by St. Witasek as a sign of the status of aesthetic objects as *superiora*. The main reason against appraising them as objects of higher order was the oneness, the monadic character, of the substrates. Now, having regard to objectives, we may say that this is a no more valid reason than is the fact that the connection between substrate and aesthetic object is not necessary. Thus aesthetic objects are indeed subsumable under the notion of objects of higher order.

Likewise, it can easily be seen that all which has been shown to hold for aesthetic objects can be generalized in regard to the other objects of emotional presentation. The objects "pleasant," "true," and "good" also lack self-sufficiency and depend upon the presuppositional objects of the feelings which present them. They likewise do not require a plurality of substrates. The same can be said of the exclusive objects of desire, that is, oughtness and end (*Sollen* and *Zweck*). This affords a modest beginning to the characterization of the objects of emotional presentation, but it is, nonetheless, a genuine first step when we say: The objects of emotional partial presentation are objects of higher order.

We should be taking a second step in the same direction if we could gain clarity as to those consequences of our results previously arrived at which are relevant for the basic classes of objects and for the most characteristic properties of those objects. The classification of objects is undoubtedly influenced by what has just been said. This becomes clear when we consider that, even if objects of feeling and objects of desire are objects of higher order, and objectives also are so, we cannot forthwith hold that the objects of feeling and desire are objectives, and they are also not to be reckoned as objecta. We understand this when we remember the reasons against considering objectives merely as a special class of objecta.

That they are not to be considered as special objecta is already made clear if we merely regard their external aspects. Objecta, in contrast to objectives, occur in a great multitude; there is nonetheless greater similarity between the most different of those objecta than between the objecta and the being or being-thus-and-so of these objecta. Further, the outstanding peculiarity of objectives is the dominating contrast between the positive and the negative. Objecta also show contrasts, as for example the physical contrast between warm and cold or the psychic contrast between affirmation and negation; but none of these dominates the whole manifold of objecta, since there are psychical objecta which are neither warm nor cold and physical objecta which are neither affirmative nor negative. More characteristic, perhaps, is the fact that the contrast between positive and negative not only dominates the objectives but also, by way of them, so to speak, the objecta, by the formation, that is, of the so-called negative notions.[10] If it thus becomes clear to us that objectives form a basic class of objects on their own, separate from objecta, then it does not seem to be unreasonable to draw an analogous consequence

10. Cf. also *Über Annahmen*, § 2.

in the case of the objects of feeling and desire. Here, also, we see a complete difference in external aspect, as well as the complete domination by a contrast which is sufficiently similar to the contrast between positive and negative that it can often even be called that of "positive" and "negative" without danger of distortion. This contrast is occasionally attributed to objecta and objectives when, for example, a certain objectum is given as pleasant or unpleasant, beautiful or ugly, good or evil. Neither objects of feeling nor objects of desire are therefore to be regarded as objecta.

The just-mentioned similarity in respect to the contrast of positive and negative [11] (between objects of feeling and desire and objectives) might lead us to ask whether the objects of feeling and desire may not also be objectives. But we shall find that they present a very different aspect from objectives, even if, as will be mentioned below, we cannot deny a certain affinity between objectives and the objects of desire. The heterogeneity is especially evident in that property which I have just described as the possibility of applying the contrast of positive and negative to objecta. While, in the case of objectives, the contradictory contrast in a way develops from the contrast of contraries, in respect to the objects of feeling and desire the same contrast does not lead to such fundamental developments.[12] The contrast seems even to depend upon objectives of (an object's) being thus-and-so as the means by which it is applied. This must not, however, be taken to mean that negative value (*Unwert*) is the proper negation, that is, negation by way of an objective (*Objektivnegation*) of value, or that "ought-not" (*Nichtsollen*) is the negation by way of an objective (*Objektivnegation*) of ought (*Sollen*).

Elsewhere I have pointed out [13] that evidence is lacking that the disjunction "objecta or objectives" is exhaustive, and we shall see that the expectation that there may be yet other objects is much less "academic" than I could ever have guessed at the time.

The objects of feeling and desire are indeed objects of

11. No doubt, it is the noteworthy main motive of the Windelband-Rickert discussions.

12. Cf. the discussions (divergent, however) by F. Rickert in *Der Gegenstand der Erkenntnis*, 3d ed. (Tübingen, 1915), pp. 264 ff., which unfortunately we cannot further consider here.

13. *Über Annahmen*, p. 61.

higher order, but plainly they are neither objecta nor objectives; and we shall now have to find out whether we can add something in positive description to our negative determination.

The first question is: Have we then found, in addition to the known classes of objects, i.e., the objecta and objectives, one or more classes of objects of a different kind? Remembering that the duality of the classes "objectum" and "objective" corresponds to the duality of the classes of apprehending experiences, i.e., ideas and judgments (or assumptions), we tend to have a prejudice in favor of a duality of additional classes of objects; for here, too, we have to do with two kinds of apprehending experiences, and so can speak of the objects of feelings and desires. Such a prejudice has, as a natural development, that we often feel a certain similarity between passive experiences, such as ideas and feelings, on the one hand, and active experiences, such as thought and desire, on the other. And following that prejudice we may provisionally accept it as a heuristic principle that the objects of feeling, without regard to their peculiarities, will have a certain likeness to objecta and that the objects of desire will have a certain likeness to objectives. If one thinks, as is traditionally done, of "categorical judgments" whenever one thinks of "judgment," or if one thinks of bipartite objectives whenever one thinks of objectives, then the monadic object "ought" seems to preclude our seeing any analogy to the character of objectives. But there are, as is seen in all cases of being, in a not too wide sense of the word, monadic objectives as well, though the bipartition peculiar to objectives of being-thus-and-so never occurs in objecta. There seems, however, to be a precise counterpart to this bipartition among the objects of desire. We have already indicated above that an end (*Zweck*) is an object of desire. It is not to be too sharply differentiated from what ought to be, as long as it is not treated as an opposing correlate to its means. The means are something which ought to be for something else's sake, which then can be, but does not have to be, the end. This "ought (*Sollen*) for or because of something" we can call, more briefly, "for-sake-being" (*Fürsollen*). It is related to the simple ought in much the same manner as being-thus-and-so is related to being. If the objects of desire really fall into two such classes, it can clearly be shown that they are more closely related to objectives than to objecta.

The general aspect of things seems to confirm our view, and

this not only in the case of objects of desire but also in the case of objects of feeling, which appear, by our recent discussion, to have been put into a certain analogy with objecta. This is to some extent substantiated by the fact that objects of feeling are natural *priora* to objects of desire, just as objecta are *priora* to objectives. We have said above how naturally it comes to us to desire something because it has value, in the case, that is, that one values it. This does not, however, mean that the object of the feeling in question therefore at once becomes the borrowed object of desire, as the objectum becomes the borrowed object of thought.

There will, however, in the long run, be felt to be what is at least a superficial lack of coherence if, of the four main resulting classes, the first two are named according to a principle which is completely different from that applied to the last two. The expressions "object of feeling" and "object of desire" were derived from our apprehending experiences or, to be more exact, from our presenting experiences. On the other hand, the name "objectum" originated from a relation of something to apprehension. But to free the meaning of this word, and the meaning of the word "object," from such a relation [14] is of vital interest for the theory of objects, and the term "objective" will automatically be affected by such a separation. It is therefore recommended that we should find new expressions for our two new classes of objects, expressions that do not refer to apprehension or to anything characterized with reference to apprehension.

In respect to objects of feeling, the following fact might aid our purpose: that there we are not always dealing with values in the proper sense, but nonetheless with something sufficiently value-like for the term "value" to be intelligently applied to it.[15] If I for my part do not want to speak in favor of a more general use of the word "value," [16] yet the step from "value," "worth," to "worthiness" (*Würdigkeit*) is not too great, and it is a step which has altogether the character of a generalization and perhaps suggests less subjectivity than may be desirable in the intentions of a term which should beg as few questions as possible. Nothing would be gained if "worthiness"

14. *Ibid.*
15. Cf. "Für die Psychologie und gegen den Psychologismus . . . ," *Logos*, III (1912), 13.
16. Cf. below, § 15.

(*Würdigkeit*) were replaced by "dignity" (*Dignität*); but the still-unused expression "dignitative" (*Dignitativ*) is less pretentious than "dignity." I therefore propose to use the expression "dignitatives" for objects of feeling, which will be correlated with "desideratives," standing for objects of desire. The ending of the words "dignitative" and "desiderative" to some extent mitigates their relationship to presenting experiences, though this still remains prominent. So, for the time being, the following quadripartition for all objects suggests itself: objecta, objectives, dignitatives, and desideratives; and the addition of "for the time being" will emphasize once more that we are not in a position to tell whether this classification is complete or not.

The new classes of objects must obviously set the same tasks to object-theoretic investigation as objecta and objectives have already done. Our first task is to describe the objects of the new classes [17] qualitatively and quantitatively, the latter because they can be directly pronounced to vary in intensity. The fact that this moment of intensity is a matter of the emotional objects themselves also deserves special attention in connection with the presenting experiences, since the long-observed capacity of the presenting experiences for graded increase must thus be a matter of their content.

There has always been talk of differences in the strength of feelings, or of differences in the strength of desires; and to the question whether those differences depended upon the act or content of the experiences in question, universal consent would favor the act. The reason for this was primarily that by the "content" of a feeling or of a desire men in some manner understood its intellectual object-presuppositions. But even one who has learned to be exact in these matters will think of a strength of acts in the case of the more-or-less of pleasure or displeasure; and he will see in it an analogue to the more-or-less of certainty in judgments. But in fact the more-or-less in beauty or value is proportionate to our stronger or weaker feelings; and if these feelings have the function of presenting those objects, then the relevant gradation in feeling must be a matter of content. This raises the question whether acts of feeling are at all capable of gradation.

It is possible that there should be such a gradation and that it should be directly proportionate to that of contents. We should not be amazed by our great uncertainty in these matters, since the situation is not very different in the case of ideas, which, as we saw, are in many ways analogous to feelings. When we ask how quality and intensity are, so to speak, distributed in our ideas, the answer no doubt is that, in the case of strong or weak noises, it is not our hearing that is strong or weak but, in the first place, only the objects of sensation and then, perhaps secondarily, our experiences, to the extent that these present those objects, that is, to the extent that their content is concerned, and not their act. It is easily seen that any attempt to show differences of degree (*Stärkeverschiedenheiten*) in ideas as acts is not readily successful. The contrast between seriously having an idea and having an idea imaginatively is qualitative—it is always qualitative where we have to do with serious and imaginative experiences.[18] I have sometimes suspected that the changes in ideas as experiences which are effected by attention are quantitative changes in ideas as acts, but this is only a very uncertain presumption.

Without doubt, the situation is better in the case of our thought-experiences, where the variability of thought-content corresponds to the variability in the level of being (*Seinshöhe*);[19] and degrees of certainty also have a clearly quantitative aspect, particularly as regards the certainty of judgments. It further accords with the already mentioned analogy which holds between experiences of thought and experiences of desire (or between their objects), that in desire there are clear differentiations in the strength of acts which cannot well coincide with the strength of the contents correlated with the presented strengths of the objects, since these show themselves in differences in the strengths of the "oughts."

At first one may be inclined to deny that the more-or-less in an ought has anything at all to do with strength of oughtness. The ambitious person's desire that his actions should be publicly acknowledged is often more lively than his concern that his actions accord with his duties. And yet his duty goes with a clear ought of obligation, whereas there may be no such ought in connection with his recognition. Still, in this incongruity between strength of desire and the ought of obligation,

18. Cf. *Über Annahmen,* p. 344.
19. *Über Möglichkeit und Wahrscheinlichkeit,* pp. 265 f.

it becomes apparent that whoever attributes obligation to duty, and possibly denies it to recognition, is considering the special ethical ought of obligation, and therefore a perhaps especially objective or impersonal ought; [20] but for the time being we are dealing with the ought presented by a certain desire, however subjective a matter this ought may be. If this is accepted, then it is also understood that a strong ought will be correlated with a strong desire as its possible presentative, and only the following question remains open: whether, that is, the strength of the desires concerned is to be taken as a matter of act or of content, and whether there is in desire yet another kind of variability in strength.

The first part of the question will be answered if we remember that whatever varies with the presented object will usually be the content. We easily see, however, that it is not plausible to believe that every change in strength of desire affects the content of desire, but there are also reasons which substantiate this view. Will (*Wollen*) and wish (*Wünschen*) seem to be the emotional counterparts to certainty and conjecture, respectively. [21] This is shown by the fact that willing as much represents the maximal limit of wishing as certainty represents the maximum of degrees of conjecture. But it is also shown by the fact that some difficulties remain unsolved by this description. Degrees of desire and oughtness cannot be held to be directly proportional, as may be added in verification of the above, above all not in the sense that higher degrees of oughtness correspond to being willed, and lower degrees of oughtness correspond only to being wished. When something is willed, when something is at most wished, depends upon quite other moments than the degree of oughtness. Laws of connection between degrees of oughtness and desire can, however, as little be excluded as we can exclude laws connecting possibilities and degrees of conjecture, laws such as we have in probability, [22] even though possibilities do not always go hand in hand with corresponding degrees of conjecture, as if presented by the latter.

In respect to the quality of dignitatives and desideratives, we have already pointed out that they exhibit a contrast in

20. Cf. below, § 14.
21. Cf. below, pp. 144 f.
22. Cf. *Über Möglichkeit und Wahrscheinlichkeit*, especially Part II.

which they correspond without exception either to positive or to negative objectives. This correspondence, however, will not allow them, as mentioned before, to be reduced to corresponding kinds of objectives: "unpleasant" is not to be interpreted as "not pleasant," and one must waive such an interpretation even in cases where our linguistic expressions at hand are imperfect enough to suggest it. This seems to be obvious in respect to the contrary (*Gegenteil*) of an ought (*Sollen*). One has to use the expression "ought not," which as little means the "contradictory opposite" of "ought," as "not wanting" means the "contradictory opposite" of "wanting"—only that for "not wanting" there are positive substitutes, such as "resisting," whereas there are none for "ought not."

Differences of species are of course matters of the quality (of dignitatives and desideratives) which has already been indicated in connection with the psychological object-presuppositions of the presentatives involved. If in this sense the dignitatives are divisible into the four classes of the pleasant, the beautiful, the true, and the good, there can be no doubt that the obvious qualitative differences among these classes must correspond to qualitative differences among the presenting contents. So it is made clear that, in the case of elementary feelings, there are, besides the differences between pleasure and displeasure, other qualitative differences which are not reducible to differences in psychological presuppositions. The division of desideratives into oughts and instrumentalities (*Zweckmässigkeiten*) can be seen to rest on the fact that their presuppositional objects have either one or two members. But the difference is, as we saw,[23] directly evident, just as is the difference between objectives of being and objectives of being-thus-and-so. In precise analogy to being, there is, besides an ought in the narrower sense, an ought in a wider sense. For instrumentality (*Zweckmässigkeit*) can be said to be an ought in the same way as (an object's) being-thus-and-so can be said to be a kind of being taken in a broader sense. There is no such obvious correspondence, in the case of dignitatives, to objectives of being and objectives of being-thus-and-so. Thus the valuing of an objectum for another object's sake is often not taken to be a genuine valuation, and this gives us reason to suspect that, since in fact there are cases of such valuation

23. See above, p. 98.

or there are such values, that which is known as mediation or valuation (*Werthaltungsvermittlung*) or transmission of valuation (*Werthaltungsübertragung*) might really be derived from desires or oughts. If, *cum grano salis*, something ought to be if it has value, so, conversely, something will have value if it ought to be. And what ought to be for something else's sake can be called "valuable" (*wertvoll*) for the sake of that something. But this quite offhand statement will have to be reconsidered. Nevertheless, the relationship between desideratives and dignitatives has always been thought to be an obviously close one. This is the reason why, as we saw on the preceding pages, a quadripartition of the desideratives corresponds to our four classes of dignitatives.

12 / On Knowledge (*Erkennen*) by Means of Emotional Partial Presentation. Justified Emotions

EVERYTHING WHICH IS PRESENTED is as such apprehended, if the word "apprehend" is understood in a broad enough sense, so that it also includes that "incomplete apprehension" (*unfertiges Erfassen*) which is present in the form of ideas which occur without thoughts.[1] Assumptions and judgments apprehend what is presented by their content; and, as we mentioned at the beginning of this book, they do not apprehend "authentically" (*eigentlich*) but "completely." [2] Which of these intellectual paradigm cases does emotional presentation follow? We have already had occasion to point out that feelings often behave like ideas and that desires behave like thoughts. This analogy would entail that feeling-presentation would be incomplete apprehension, and presentation by desires would be complete apprehension. But in this respect the likeness breaks down. Presentation by desires as such does not effect more than incomplete apprehension, and one might even ask whether the presenting emotional experience, considered in itself, apprehends things at all, even if only incompletely. This brings out the very characteristic fact that, for intellectual experiences, apprehension is to that extent their natural destiny, so that, even in cases where, strictly speaking, apprehension is not yet accomplished, i.e., in respect to ideas, it is quite natural to speak of at least incomplete apprehension. This is not the case in regard to feelings and desires, since

1. See *Über Möglichkeit und Wahrscheinlichkeit*, p. 248.
2. Cf. *ibid.*, p. 249.

they can and indeed do occur without functioning in any way as a means of apprehension. Still, it would be somewhat arbitrary to deny that emotional presentatives are in some sense a case of "incomplete apprehension." Nevertheless, it is important to note that the presentatives in the domain of desires are likewise incapable of complete apprehension and that they depend in this respect, as do also feelings, upon superadded thought-experiences. Presentatives of feelings and desires function under favorable conditions, in the very same way as ideas. That is, they require to be supplemented by assumptions and judgments whenever that which is presented by them is to be apprehended actually and "completely." For apprehension is ultimately always an intellectual operation, of which emotional experiences by themselves are not fully capable.

Whatever holds of apprehension naturally also holds of knowledge and cognate experiences. Knowledge is the penetrative apprehension of something factual or possible, wherein this apprehension has that moment of internal legitimacy which is known as evidence.[3] There seems to be nothing that would prevent knowledge from taking possession of everything with which it is presented. It is not, therefore, amazing if our knowledge, or possibly at least our wholly sincere striving for knowledge, turns, among other things, to the pleasant, the beautiful, the good, and the instrumental. On the other hand, an emotional experience, despite its capacity to function as presentative, can as little know as it can apprehend completely. This is also especially true of desires, whose similarity to judgments obviously again breaks down at this point.

There are reasons for lingering a while over this practically self-evident state of affairs. The just-given characterization of knowing can also be formulated in this way: Knowledge is internally justified judging [4] (as opposed to merely externally justified judging) that satisfies the demands of truth or probability.[5] Being justified is therefore a property of certain judgments. It is both striking and worth considering that being right or not being right, or, in short, having a certain justification or lacking one, is also noticeable in emotional experiences. We talk of good and bad taste in art, of a sensitive and in-

3. Cf. *ibid.*, p. 414.
4. *Ibid.*, p. 416.
5. *Ibid.*, pp. 416, 472 f.

sensitive conscience in ethical matters, and usually defer to a sensitive conscience without denying that such a conscience might possibly be too sensitive. In this way we would think someone wrong who, in a conflict of choice between personal comfort and great cultural treasures, such as the honor of the threatened fatherland, would decide for the former. In respect to this and to other instances, to which we shall recur later, it might be suspected that we have nothing beyond a seeming justification. However, its seeming presence is a fact; and before it is taken to be delusive, one should attempt to compare this seeming justification with a case which is not merely seeming, where the moment of justification is generally acknowledged to be of the highest significance. The easiest way to proceed would be to treat emotional experiences as we treated judgments and to make room for the possibility that under favorable conditions they may have an external, and then perhaps also an internal, justification. This doubtless is what is meant by Brentano's reference to a "right (*richtig*) love" and a "right preference," [6] but it is not sufficiently worked out theoretically [7] to permit me a definite judgment as to the extent to which the following discussions relate to it. Without initiating a direct controversy, I will simply ask whether an appeal to evidence or to an evidence-analogue can explain the moment of justification in emotional experiences.

Evidence owes its significance in the justification of an experience of knowledge not merely to the fact that it is itself a peculiar moment in such an experience but to the relation of this peculiarity to truth, that is, in the end, to the factuality of the objective apprehended by the experience.[8] (Let us for simplicity's sake consider only the evidence which justifies certainty.) In the same way, we cannot get closer to the justification of emotions by pointing to some qualitative peculiarities of these experiences. It is rather necessary that this property should be related to the carrying-out of an apprehension (*Erfassungsleistung*), for which purpose that which is apprehended must be factual. Emotional presentation complies

6. Brentano, *Vom Ursprung sittlicher Erkenntnis* (Leipzig, 1889), pp. 20 ff.

7. For interpretation see O. Kraus, "Die Grundlagen der Werttheorie," *Jahrbücher der Philosophie*, II, 13 ff., 19 f. For a critique see Chr. v. Ehrenfels, *System der Werttheorie*, I, 43 ff.; II, 217 ff.

8. Cf. *Über Möglichkeit und Wahrscheinlichkeit*, pp. 414 ff.

with such a demand to the extent that presentation is a kind of apprehension, as we have already seen. But, in order to be factual, the presented object must, as far as we know, be an objective. The proper objects of feeling are incapable of being objectives, as has already been shown; and even if the proper objects of desire could be called "objective-like," it is not any easier to determine their factuality, or their levels of possibility below their factuality, than it is in the case of objecta. We must be clear on this point and must realize that oughtness or instrumentality do not simply lack factuality in each and every sense or that they are not simply indeterminable in this respect. In a very inexact manner, factuality is even attributed to many objecta.[9] This does not mean that objecta themselves admit of modal determination but merely that they stand in some objective which is factual in contrast with many nonfactual objectives with other material. The same may hold for oughtness, though it may be no more modally determinable than objecta. This would, however, have to be the case if the manner of apprehension pertaining to desideratives were to be accessible to evidence or the like.

As just remarked, dignitatives and desideratives cannot be completely apprehended by their presentatives but require a supplementation by assumptions or judgments. So it is natural to suppose that a possible part of the evidence of emotional justification does not lie in our emotional experiences themselves but in additional judgments. It is now, however, easy to decide how far these viewpoints would retain their validity if, instead of evidence proper, an evidence-analogue were taken in the determination of the experiences in question. But the fainter the similarity is, the less will it do justice to the affinity which seems to subsist between emotional and intellectual justification, and which it was the special task of the theory to render more intelligible.

Having thus far failed, do we have to say that there can be no antithesis of the justified and the unjustified in the emotional domain, inasmuch as this contrast, like that of true and false, belongs exclusively to the domain of judgments and their objects? Once I took up such a position [10] and tried to explain the fact that we talk so readily of value-errors (*Wertirrtümer*)

9. Cf. *Über Annahmen*, p. 69.

10. *Psychologisch-ethische Untersuchungen zur Werttheorie*, § 26.

by calling attention to the role which error plays in regard to the ever present intellectual presuppositions of valuations (*Werthaltungen*). The question with which we are at present concerned does not exclusively refer to values. It may, however, be useful to proceed in our answer from the domain of values, since it is a relatively well-known region, and to state that, as far as I can see at the moment, value-errors are not explained by a mere appeal to their intellectual aspect. Certainly anybody is also simply intellectually wrong who values a sugar pill for its healing power. By this we do not deny, but, on the contrary, rather imply, that there is something in the emotional aspect of the experience of valuation which cannot indeed be called error in the ordinary sense of the word but must be called "error" in an extraordinary sense of the word. In this extraordinary sense, the valuation itself, and not only its presupposition, can be significantly said to lose its justification, and that on account of something in the valuation itself which depends precisely on its false presupposition. This seems to be similar to "right" conclusions drawn from false premises. Primarily the premises are false, and the conclusion validly follows from them; but, nevertheless, it is false too.

We have just given an example which was analogous to falsehood. In other cases of values there is an analogy to truth, which is no less clear than the cases where we have an analogy to falsehood; it is even clearer than the latter, since its justification cannot be pushed across to the intellectual part of the experience. The similarity to intellectual experiences holds to the extent that we can see a definite correspondence to cases of immediate evidence, on the one hand, and mediate evidence, or mediation of evidence, on the other. There are, above all, valuations which somehow seem to justify themselves, and there is no need to have recourse to external data. A few examples have already been given at random,[11] to which others can be added. For anyone who considers the facts, and is not merely making deductions from ready-made theories, cannot well deny that justice, gratitude, and benevolence carry the guarantee of their worth in themselves in a way in which their opposites not only lack such a guarantee but also carry a guarantee to the contrary. We have often enough had occasion to find out, during recent years, how our valuation declares itself in favor

11. See above, pp. 106 f.

of those who continue fighting and dying on a sinking ship, instead of surrendering themselves.

Just as the legitimacy of judgments is more generally acknowledged where it rests on proof, i.e., where their evidence is mediated, so also in mediated valuations the moment of justification is more apparent than it is in the case of immediate evaluations. The evidence of the Principle of Deduction (*Schlussgesetz*) is correlated with a law of mediation of value which often makes us aware of its *a priori* character. So it seems to be evident that anybody is right who values the cause when he values the effect, or who really values things which he believes to have value. It is also evident that anybody is palpably wrong who behaves in the opposite manner.

A well-known procedure of syllogistic logic (*Schlusslehre*) now leads us to see a counterpart to what I have called an "implicit quasi-premise"[12] regarding the mediation of evidence, which can easily be formulated hypothetically thus: "If B is rightly valued and A is its presupposition, then A also is rightly valued." At first sight this is just a judgment like any other judgment. But what it is about is important for us. If the moment of justification is left out of the valuations which are here judged, what we have is as meaningless as a rule of inference in respect to judgments whose justifications are completely left out of consideration. As a rule, of course, in respect to the rules of inference, one is concerned with objectives, and has a choice among several equivalents. But one may also occasionally consider judgments, though one is not then allowed to say: "If I judge that A is B and that B is C, then I also judge that A is C." For it may happen that I judge the premises but not the conclusion, or even add another seeming conclusion. I must rather say: "If I am justified in believing that A is B and that B is C, then I am also justified in believing that A is C." That the situation is similar in the case of valuations is obvious. We certainly ought not to say that if I believe that A is the precondition for B and B is valuable to me, then I must unfailingly experience a valuation of A: this valuation may not occur for a variety of reasons. But we may say that if things are as they are said to be and I am justified in valuing B, then a valuation of A would not lack justification, while indifference to A, or even negative valuation of A, would be

12. See *Über Möglichkeit und Wahrscheinlichkeit*, pp. 672 f.

unjustified. Taking the rules of syllogistic inference which apply to objectives, one can easily find a counterpart which applies to valuations. One must, however, be able to take account of the factuality of the values in question (and not only of the valuations), just as one takes account of the factuality of the objectives in question in the former case, if one is to say: "If *A* is the precondition of *B* and *B* has (factual) value, then *A* also will have (factual) value."

Certain relationships which appear in the case of counter-feelings are very instructive,[13] though they are not affected by the complications with which the mediation of valuation is afflicted. They are especially instructive since relations for which a justification of the feelings in question is essential stand side by side with others for which this is not the case, or, at least, not to the same extent. Relations of the second kind already become evident when counterfeelings are taken from the binary combinations which result automatically out of joy over the existence,[14] and sorrow over the existence (*Daseinsfreude, Daseinsleid*), and out of joy over the nonexistence and sorrow over the nonexistence, of one and the same objectum. It surely has *a priori* evidence that, if I rejoice over the existence or nonexistence of a thing, I cannot feel sorrow about it at the same time in the same respect. Similarly, if the existence of something pleases or grieves me, the nonexistence of the same thing cannot please or grieve me in the same respect. The question is not whether the joy is justified or unjustified. Thus, considering all the resulting sorts of incompatibilities, we find ourselves left with only two cases of counterfeelings, joy in existence and sorrow over nonexistence, and joy in non-

13. Cf. "Für die Psychologie und gegen den Psychologismus," p. 5.

14. Why Th. Lessing (*Studien zur Wertaxiomatik*, 2d ed. [Leipzig, 1914], p. XVIII) denies that joy in existence is subsumable under value-feelings has not been made clearer to me by his peculiar example of the cancer of the wealthy aunt (*Erbtante*). For the unsympathetic legacy-hunter the cancer certainly has value in the most natural sense of the word (though not of course, an "impersonal" value; cf. below, p. 136). The additional sentence is clearer: "Every living thing feels joy in regard to its own existence. Does this mean that it respects the object of its joy?" Indeed, every feeling of respect is a value-feeling, but not every feeling of value is a feeling of respect. So there is no reason against subsuming existence-joy under value-feelings in the indicated manner.

existence and sorrow over existence, whose members are mutually compatible. Now it is easily seen that in a certain sense it is not sufficient that counterfeelings are capable of combination. It seems natural that, whenever the existence of something pleases me, its nonexistence will grieve me, and matters are similar as regards the other three cases. How is this obvious fact to be understood? Does it mean that a joy in existence cannot occur without a sorrow in nonexistence? Apparently not, for experience convinces us of the contrary. It may please me to receive a present whose nonpossession, to which I was used, did not make me feel deprived in any way. More often sorrow at nonexistence arises with the loss of something regarding whose existence no joy was felt, as a result of long familiarity. Still, there is good reason to appeal to the mutual belongingness of the counterfeelings, and this becomes clear when the moment of justification applying to those feelings is introduced. Whoever feels joy over the existence of something will "rationally," one might say, feel sorry regarding its nonexistence. Relative to the presupposed joy, he is justified, and he is unjustified if he is indifferent to its nonexistence. And if he was justified (period) in his joy in existence, then he will be justified in his sorrow over nonexistence, and unjustified (period) in the lack of it. We are here dealing with a certain consistency among valuations that is taken to be similar to consistency in judgments and that definitely requires the addition of justification for its conception. Besides, consistency in valuations is not only evident in the case of counterfeelings. Consistency also works relevantly toward guaranteeing our adherence to a certain valuation and against capricious changes in valuations.[15]

That we at times almost have *a priori* evidences [16] for such

15. Whereby the difficulty which was considered in *Psychologisch-ethische Untersuchungen,* p. 80, can be disregarded.
16. Th. Lessing, in his *Studien zur Wertaxiomatik* (see esp. pp. 25 ff.), has successfully worked this out; in connection with our present inquiries, we must acknowledge this especially. It does not diminish his merits if, as far as I can see, the author's distinction between *"reine Wertlehre"* or *"Wertarithmetik,"* on the one hand, and *"Wertphänomenologie,"* on the other (which latter ought, however, to "coincide to a great extent" with the former [*ibid.,* p. 7]), preserves in the notoriously ambiguous word *"Phänomenologie"* the major part of those theoretical defects which my conception of a theory of objects tried to eliminate.

lawfulness (*Gesetzmässigkeit*) makes it reasonable to deny at this point the misunderstanding which regards this evidence as itself providing the justification which we attribute to the value-feelings in question. Evidence is not legitimacy (*Rechtmässigkeit*), but it is concerned with, or, to be more exact, evident judgments are concerned with, legitimacy. And "in the same sense . . . as *a priori* forms of logic can be called rules of correct thinking, so the *a priori* value-propositions can be understood as categorial determinations of correct valuation."[17] If it is clear that whenever I feel joy over the existence of something I also rightly feel sorrow over its nonexistence, then the legitimacy of the nonexistence-sorrow in question is understood. The legitimacy of the feeling is, however, no more constituted thereby than the sum of the angles in a triangle is constituted by the insight that it amounts to two right angles.

All that has here been said about feelings has counterparts and supplements in the domain of those desires which are concerned with values. To desire what has value and because it has value, to desire more strongly what is more valuable rather than what is less valuable, to give preference to the more valuable over the less valuable in cases of conflict,[18] to want the means because one wants the goal, and so on, are all obvious to us in the sense of seeming "rational." It is not the case that, under given circumstances, such desires must necessarily occur. They need do so as little as it is inevitable to judge the conclusion of an argument when the premises are given. And all that is so clear and so multiform in the case of values and value-desires will not be wholly lacking in the case of the other dignitatives and the desires which are based on them. And in fact not even a theoretically open-minded person will go so far in his tolerance as to allow it to be a matter of taste whether truth as such is respected by someone, and whether or not he stands up against error or falsity without regard to possible practical disadvantages. And even in the aesthetic realm we should not be so restrained, by the caution which the history of art has taught us, as not to prefer Beethoven's *Fifth Symphony* to a street song, or Goethe's *Faust* to a modern horror movie.

17. Th. Lessing, *Studien der Wertaxiomatik*, p. 26; see also pp. 35 ff.

18. In reference to the very characteristic analogue to this provided by the conflicts of surmises in the intellectual domain cf. *Über Möglichkeit und Wahrscheinlichkeit*, p. 547.

Considering all the confirmations for our theories streaming in from different sides, it simply cannot be denied that there actually is a moment of justification in the field of emotions. But our theory is therefore set before the task of describing these states of affairs in a way which cannot simply be achieved by a quite useless transfer of the notion of evidence from the intellectual to the emotional, but which must employ quite a different mode of treatment. A hint as to how to begin is given when we consider that emotions, on account of their presenting function, have a place in knowledge, and have thereby also a possible justification as knowledge, whereby the expression "justification" can, in a transferred sense, but without loss of clarity, be applied to the presenting emotions themselves.

How this is to be understood may become clear when we think of the analogy of ideas. For a long time, and quite correctly, it has been denied that truth and falsehood are a matter of ideas. But it is nonetheless often said that someone has a right or a false idea of something, and what is meant by this is simply that by means of the ideas in question one may make a true judgment or a false one. If in fact, under certain conditions, a feeling or desire is substituted for an idea as the means of presentation, one must not be amazed to find that, when the judgments made are justified or the reverse, the justification is also attributed to the emotions. If no objections can be raised against someone who says it is correct to have an idea of aluminum as light and not correct to think of a telephone as a kind of speaking tube, then no objections can be raised against one who says that a man is right who refuses to cling to life at any price, and not right if he values truth only as a means to practical results—if, that is, life or truth presents to our feelings or desires such characteristics as preclude (or call for) such an attitude. These two examples, however, are rather too complex, since in their case we not only have to do with the causing or preventing of something, but rather with a justified preference for or a turning-down of such. But it will not be too hard to avoid such a mistake if we go back to simpler situations.

On a closer look, it is easily seen that a feeling or desire is never said to be justified or unjustified per se, but always relative to an object to which the emotion in question is directed, and which is its presuppositional object. If we have a feeling, for example one of pleasure, no one will say that it is justified or unjustified to feel such a pleasure, but one may well be justified in being pleased with A and unjustified in being pleased with B. This runs parallel to the fact that no one will think it correct or incorrect to have an idea of the object "light" per se, but that he will think it correct to have an idea of aluminum as "light" and incorrect to have an idea of lead as "light." If such an idea is said to be correct since the judgment whose predicate is apprehended by the idea is true, it is quite appropriate to call a feeling justified if it presents an object whose designation is the predicate of a true judgment and whose presuppositional object's name is the subject. I am justified (right, *im Rechte*) in being pleased by the successes of the allied Central Powers during the present war to the extent that such a feeling of pleasure presents an object that can rightly be attributed to the successes in question (*zugeurteilt werden*), since it in fact applies to them. It can therefore be said in general: If P is an object presented by an emotion *p*, then it is justifiable to attach the emotion *p* to an object A if P in fact applies to A (*dem A zukommt*), and the judgment "A is P" is therefore correct. "Correct" and "incorrect," when they are in this sense attributed to emotions, doubtless do not mean the same as "correct" and "incorrect" when used in connection with judgments, yet the new use of the expressions derives from their use in connection with judgments. An evidence-analogue for feelings and desires is therefore not required.

One thing, however, must be presupposed and carefully considered. That which is presented to us by our emotions must be fit to be used under favorable conditions as a basis for truths and adequate probabilities, that is, for a knowledge through whose evidence the justification of the emotions in question can be legitimized. Can we rely on whatever is emotionally presented to furnish us with such a basis? For the present inquiry we can again make use of the fact that much thought-provoking consideration has in recent years been devoted to this question, especially in regard to certain aspects that it covers. By these aspects I mean those of aesthetics: E. Landmann-Kalischer has thoroughly and intelligently drawn a parallel between aesthetic judgments and judgments of sensation (*Sinnesurteile*) and has argued for the "knowledge-value of aesthetic judgments."[19] St. Witasek, however, in his frequently quoted last publication,[20] denies that that which is presented by aesthetic feelings[21] is of use for knowledge and, to that extent, has decided against the "objectivity" of aesthetic objects. He came to this conclusion after he had especially examined, in his diligent and thorough manner, the object-theoretic facts. I myself owe to his paper "Über den Erkenntniswert ästhetischer Urteile" the essential stimulations for my own conceptions, despite initial doubts of principle[22]—which are more fully developed in the present book—so that it is obvious that Witasek's objections apply to my conceptions. Indeed, it is possible that what holds for aesthetic feelings cannot simply be generalized to apply to all feelings and all desires. But in matters that have to do with presentation, a prejudice in favor of general homogeneity has been sufficiently confirmed so as to furnish a warranty that Witasek's counterarguments have an importance beyond aesthetics.

E. Landmann-Kalischer's paper primarily intends to shed light upon the similarity between aesthetic judgments and judgments of sense. Without doubt, such important similarities will be found in great number even when the "agreement (Übereinstimmung) with other judgments" does not seem to suffice as the single "great criterion" for the truth of a judgment.[23] But one must in this respect agree with Witasek that the very character of dignitatives and desideratives is such that it is not of much help to use sense-judgments as a standard of comparison. For even if the term "sense-judgment" is understood broadly enough, anything that falls under it gets its characteristics from perception in the proper sense of the word: the demands which an object must fulfill in order to be a perceptual object[24] are not, however, fulfilled by emotional objects. The clearly empirical character of most aesthetic judgments seems, however, to point to judgments of sense. But

19. "Über den Erkenntniswert ästhetischer Urteile," *Archiv für die gesamte Psychologie*, V (1905), 263 ff.

20. "Über ästhetische Objektivität," *Zeitschr. f. d. Philos. u. philos. Kritik,* CLVII (1915), pp. 102 ff., 190 ff.

21. *Ibid.,* pp. 193 ff.

22. See "Über die Erfahrungsgrundlagen unseres Wissens," p. 74.

23. "Über den Erkenntniswert ästhetischer Urteile," p. 305.

24. Cf. "Über die Erfahrungsgrundlagen unseres Wissens," §§ 4 f.

the judgments of internal experience are also, after all, empirical, and Witasek in fact refers to them, since to him a road through sense-experience and one through *a priori* knowledge seem alike to be rendered impossible by the very character of aesthetic objects.

If, on the other hand, we have not found [25] that this feature stops us from subsuming aesthetic objects under a sufficiently widened notion of objects of higher order, we are also entitled to ask whether we can be right in denying them the ideality [26] by which those objects of higher order are characterized which form the most appropriate terrain for *a priori* knowledge. In fact, considering the total aspect of things, there is little doubt that "beautiful" has more essential affinity with "similar" than with "blue." But if we keep in mind perceptibility [27] or capability of existence [28] as the mark of contrast between "reality" and "ideality," then we are dealing directly with the characteristic by which sense-judgments differ from aesthetic judgments. Like similarity, it seems that beauty can neither exist nor be perceived: it belongs therefore to the field of *a priori* knowledge. Nevertheless, there is a clear discrepancy between this conclusion and our lack of *a priori* knowledge in aesthetic matters, for which only experience, so it seems, provides a substitute. Perhaps we can eliminate this lingering want of clarity if we also turn for counsel to the other classes of emotional objects, instead of dwelling on aesthetic objects alone.

Let us begin with one group of feelings or desires which has been neglected in our present inquiries, with those desires, namely, which are connected with truth. A certain diligence was necessary in our considerations in order not to confuse the judgment-act-feelings in question with a special kind of value-feelings, i.e., truth-value-feelings. No care can alter the fact that the matters (*Tatbestände*) to which these feelings attach are true objectives or judgments; we may disregard the fact that truth, here as elsewhere,[29] is the limit of probability and that probability also attracts similar feelings. Feelings of this kind may very well be called "truth-feelings," whereby proba-

25. See above, pp. 93 ff.
26. Cf. St. Witasek, "Über ästhetische Objektivität," pp. 181 f.
27. Cf. "Über die Erfahrungsgrundlagen unseres Wissens," p. 25.
28. Cf. *Über Möglichkeit und Wahrscheinlichkeit*, pp. 61 f.
29. See *ibid.*, pp. 472 ff.

bility is so to speak included *a potiori* among the objects to which those feelings refer. It then apparently becomes merely a matter of analytic judgment that truth is their presuppositional object. Leaving aside all question of definitions, it may be asked how we know that these feelings, which, as we saw, can be clearly enough characterized without referring to their presuppositional object, will have truth as their presuppositional object and not, for instance, falsehood. Can we believe that falsehood, too, could take on the role of the presuppositional object, and that we have to learn from experience that it cannot take on that role? No truly unprejudiced person would want to answer "Yes." It clearly lies in the nature of the feeling and of its presuppositional objects that truth claims the positive dignity and falsehood the negative dignity. We do not have to rely on mere experience. The connection between feeling and presuppositional object is a necessary one and is known *a priori*.

This may have influenced the manner in which issues regarding truth have been treated in the theory of knowledge and in other disciplines. Nothing is more common than the popular way of speaking, according to which truth is "felt." The modern theory of knowledge, as is well known, shows quite emphatic, intelligently grounded tendencies to consider truth as a value, where "value" plainly does not have its usual meaning, and also does not have the narrow meaning given it in this book when we contrasted knowledge-feelings with "value-feelings," but is used in a broader sense, for which the word "dignity" (*Dignität*) seemed most appropriate. "Dignity" means something closely enough related to truth for it to be successfully used in the description of truth's essence. In a different context [30] I talked of a notion of truth as pertaining to objectives and a notion of truth as pertaining to experiences, and I still think that these notions are very close to the meaning ordinarily attached to the word "truth." But at present it seems as unobjectionable as it is important to characterize truth from the point of view of dignity. The connection of this dignity-notion, or (in a broader use of the word) this value-notion of truth, with the objective-notion or the experience-notion seems to be a paradigm case of the *a priori* relationship between a proper

30. *Ibid.*, pp. 414 f.

object (*Eigengegenstand*) and a presuppositional object of feelings.

When the multiplicity of our value-feelings (the word "value" understood in our special narrow sense) is contrasted with the relative uniformity of the objective side of truth-feelings, there is, in the former case, a great lack of the clarity met within the latter. Still, there is not a complete lack of *a priori* insight, as is shown by the laws of the mediation of value and desire, provided these laws are not, as previously indicated, taken to be mere laws governing factual value-attitudes or desire-attitudes (*Verhalten*). That whoever values a goal will usually also value its means is as much an empirically attested truth as that whoever believes in a ground normally does not doubt its consequence. But just as the argument-principle of the *modus Barbara* does not concern the occurrence or nonoccurrence of judgment-experiences, so the law of end and means does not concern the occurrence or nonoccurrence of valuations or desires. It concerns the natural mutual belongingness of values, regardless as to anybody's attitude toward them. Here, as there, it is clear that the approach is *a priori*. But what is the sense of all that has been learned? I can find only one natural interpretation. According to this, we can say that, to the extent that the object which is our end (*Zweck*) in fact has the property presented by the value-feeling or value-desire, the object that is our means will also have that property. Of course, the rules of inference are formally valid even in the case of suspended or false premises and conclusions. But they only bind these together if the premises are true. And if there were to be no true premises nor conclusions, the rules of inference would be without meaning. Matters are similar in respect to the value-laws mentioned above and their like. There we have *a priori* insights which presuppose true judgments having emotionally presented objects in their material.

We have to presuppose this expressly, since any attempt to find inherently legitimate, that is, evident, judgments whose predicates designate the peculiar objects of emotions (*emotionale Eigengegenstände*) leads to much better results in the domain of the truth-feelings than in that of the value-feelings. At present no object can be named to which a value-dignitative can be attributed with the same *a priori* evidence as a truth-dignitative can be attributed to a factual objective of apprehension (*Erfassungsobjektiv*). Still, in the case of high ethical goods, our experience of their goodness (*Gutcharakter*), and of their relationship with one another, are at times so obvious that it is hard to believe that our knowledge of such goodness lacks all *a priori* insight. We may therefore hope that clearer insight into the character of these goods will one day render it possible for us to have a clear *a priori* apprehension of the interconnections among such goods. Even at present we have made some progress in respect to a few ideals. Love, justice, truthfulness, e.g., stand only a little behind what we met with in the realm of truth-feelings. I should not unreservedly dare to stake a claim for *a priority* in this field, but reserve the right to conjecture that there is such an *a priority* to be found, much as one may likewise conjecture that the laws of mechanics have more of the *a priori* in them than our mathematics and dynamics can vouch for.

Continuing our comparison with mechanics, we may pass to the further question as to what stock of definite knowledge we can build up or strive for in the domain of values, besides building up mere conjectures and hopes. In mechanics, experience begins where the *a priori* ends, and this is so because mechanics, as a part of physics, deals in the end with reality, that is, with existing things. In contrast to this, dignitatives have been recognized to be ideal objects of higher order. How could experience have access to these?

We find ourselves, in fact, in a special knowledge-situation whose peculiarity is not greatly lessened by its similarity to a situation in the intellectual domain. Whoever believes something also believes that he is right in his belief. It seems hardly more than the obvious consequence of his belief. It is much less evident that someone who is not the judging subject also in consequence becomes inclined to hold the same belief, at least to the extent that for him the fact of that belief yields either a strong or weak presumption in favor of the truth of what is believed. This does not only hold in the case of authorities. The fact that any X believes this or that clearly impresses any Y in the sense of giving him a tendency to believe the same thing unless especially paralyzing circumstances cloud the issue. Is this tendency to be explained by some induction according to which people are more often right than wrong in their opinions? The similarity is faint, but we are certainly reminded of this when we notice that whoever attaches a feeling, that is, primarily a value-feeling, to a certain presuppositional object also believes himself to have quite a right feeling and is ready without further consideration to criticize any divergent attitude. It is no easier to tolerate those who value differently than those who think differently, though there are occasions enough to practice ourselves in that art. And when somebody learns this art, and occasionally learns it all too well, life has corrected an instinctive exaggeration which plainly had an initial legitimacy. Its point of departure can best be thus formulated: If *A* is the presuppositional object of a value-feeling *p* which presents the proper object *P* (*Eigengegenstand*), then the simultaneous givenness (*Zusammengegebensein*) of the objects *A* and *P* gives reason to presume that *A* has *P*. It must not be overlooked that this is not a case of evidence-for-certainty but a case of evidence-for-surmise, which up till now has not been introduced. Matters are quite similar to what they are in the case of judgments of external perception.[31] Like these, our present presumptions also require a verification, and possible lack of verification hurts the legitimacy of these presumptions as little as it does in the other case.[32] At one point we at least see a characteristic difference from perceptions, provided we are right in holding that all dignitatives, even those of the value-domain, are ideal objects. For in their case the presumptions in question are not concerned with existence, as perceptions are, but with subsistence. All the facts that we are here dealing with are facts based in the objects concerned and are therefore matters of *a priori* knowledge. We come to such knowledge by taking a very peculiar roundabout course through experience, since our capacities are so imperfect.

Summarizing, we can say that we have some access to the knowledge as to whether a given object has a value-dignitative or not. Nevertheless, besides some so-to-speak divinatory approaches, we practically have no such *a priori* insights as the matter on hand by its very nature should afford. On the other hand, we can make legitimate surmises, even if they are very weak. But they make it possible for us to go on from our actual valuations and experiences, which confirmed these surmises, to increasingly stronger surmises concerning value-dignitatives, and we can do this through our increasing dependence on the experi-

31. Cf. "Über die Erfahrungsgrundlagen unseres Wissens," § 18.
32. See *Über Möglichkeit und Wahrscheinlichkeit*, pp. 436 f.

ences in question and through other indirect moments used for our purposes of knowledge in the same manner as we use the aspects of perception. Nonetheless, the use of experience for this purpose involves considerably more difficulties than does the processing of perceptions.

It is not difficult to transfer what was said about the realm of values into statements about aesthetic feelings and the relevant desires. We are hardly likely to obtain any insights into *a priori* valid laws of mediation, but by means of intuition we apprehend the eternally beautiful in things great and small. It is much easier to assume that for this sort of intuition especially gifted talents are required, much more so than for the apprehension of values. History knows only of a few ethical geniuses in comparison with the relatively large number of great names in art. We have in addition the rich material of facts included in our attitude to aesthetic objects, and each single case of a feeling based on an objective (*gegenständlich*) presupposition involves presumptive evidence for the judgment that the proper object of the feeling is indeed a property of the presuppositional object. And again it is, as a matter of course, important whether and where the reliability of this presumption can be significantly increased by any method of processing it. That the empirical route has a tendency toward *a priori* goals is more evident here than it is in the case of values. For value-feelings are in the main existence-feelings, while aesthetic feelings are in principle feelings toward an object's being thus-and-so, quite regardless as to its existence (*daseinsfreie Soseinsgefühle*). They attach themselves to their objects without regard to those objects' existence or nonexistence. Thus induction proper is rendered impossible, even if we leave the character of the objects of aesthetic feelings out of consideration.

Matters are even worse in the case of sensuous (*sinnlich*) feelings. There seem to be no internally evident cases of lawfulness, and as far as the relationship of the different feelings to their presuppositional objects is concerned, our experience of great individual divergences has pushed the natural consciousness of legitimacy right into the background. Still, instinctive intolerance cannot always be silenced, and once in a while, even in respect to these lower pleasures, it looks as if a real understanding and justification stood opposed to our lack of knowledge and even capacity. Such a lack may often be ethically more desirable in view of the circumstances and conditions on which an opposing knowledge would have to rest. On the whole it cannot be denied that the feelings and desires of this group give us reason for surmises (*Vermutungen*). These surmises are similar to those pertaining to objects of value and aesthetic objects, though we do not in any way feel as strong an impulse to go on from these to laws which will be more or less acceptable and certain.

We therefore arrive at the result that a knowledge in which the proper object of an emotion is the predicate, and the presuppositional object of the emotion is the subject, achieves factuality or at least possibility in some cases. We have therefore laid the ground for a differentiation between justified and unjustified emotions. Emotions are justified if the judgments which attribute their object to their presuppositional objects are justified. We do not, however, have to add that the justification of such judgments does not conversely imply the justification of the presenting emotions, since the judgments can be negative and can point to the illegitimacy (*Unrechtmässigkeit*) of the emotions in question.

13 / Personal Value and Impersonal Value

WHAT HAS BEEN SAID regarding the extent to which emotional presentation bears on knowledge has, it seems to me, its most important application and verification in the suggestion that it may open up the way to the solution of a very old, apparently insoluble problem. This apparent insolubility has given rise, as in similar cases, to the tendency to label the whole problem a "pseudo-problem" and to push it aside. Here we have a situation with which, on a closer look, the whole domain of emotional presentation is concerned, but which is particularly acute in the case of one relatively special domain, and which for this very reason may perhaps prove all the more amenable to theoretical consideration. I am thinking of the domain of values, with which we shall concern ourselves in what follows. We shall then see whether any of our results can possibly be used in the other domains of emotional presentation.

We shall be dealing with what counts as a most indubitable basic axiom in almost all modern value-theory, and which goes under the label of the relativity of all values. This indubitability has not always been obvious to the naïvely thinking person. This is made clear by the fact that popular belief so eagerly ascribes marvelous properties to gold or precious stones. There are especially three factors responsible for the fact that men have more and more ceased to believe in value as an intrinsic property of a valuable thing. First, the value of a thing very often depends on the value of another thing of which the former is a part, cause, condition, or the like. When we consider the great number of such possible complications, there is perhaps no objectum (*Objekt*) that, in differing circumstances, could not at one time be an objectum of value, at another time an objectum of disvalue (*Unwertobjekt*), so that the property of an objectum of being valuable or disvaluable (*unwertvoll*) does not depend on its definite characters. It may become especially clear in how external a manner value attaches to the nature of an objectum when we consider that, in certain conditions, an objectum can preserve its position as an objectum of value even when the basis for this position, the relation of the objectum to some intrinsic value (*Eigenwert*) or even the intrinsic value itself, has long ago perished.[1] The second factor is of importance when the magnitude of the value depends on the stock of (material) goods. This dependence is called in modern political economy the law of "marginal utility" (*Grenznutzen*),[2] in virtue of which the same objectum, e.g., a certain quantum of water, may, in special circumstances, be either very valuable or completely worthless. A third factor is evident in the fact that, all else remaining equal, the character of the subject most concerned will decide the value, as, when, e.g., the same food has value for the hungry but not for the sated. These and other experiences have directed theoretical attention away from the nature of the value-objectum to the existence (*Vorhandensein*) and nature of the value-subject, and especially to certain characteristic experiences, to the "value-experiences," of the subject.[3] Value-feelings primarily, and secondarily the desires coordinated with these, have been recognized as value-experiences. Value could, in consequence, be defined as the capacity of an object to attract interest upon itself as a value-objectum.

I have no desire to minimize the importance of the results that I myself helped to confirm. However, with all due respect for their importance, it is advisable to keep in mind that by no means all the tasks which have been set to value-theory by the facts have thereby been solved. This will be shown in the following section by adducing certain very striking circumstances.

Nothing is in general more natural than to deny that an

1. Cf. Chr. v. Ehrenfels, *System der Werttheorie*, Vol. I, §§ 46 f.
2. See *ibid.*, § 25.
3. Cf. "Für die Psychologie und gegen den Psychologismus in der allgemeinen Werttheorie," *Logos*, III (1912), 3 ff.

objectum has value for a subject if he feels no interest in that objectum. But, from this point of view, reading and writing are valueless for all but a very few school-children, and this difficulty is not diminished if we point out that what the children learn in school will be of value for them later on, since our difficulty consists in the fact that the disinterested person already sees value for the child in what the child is now learning. The difficulty grows in the case of value-subjects for whom there can be no appeal to a possible future. This applies to hopeless mental defectives, who are not expected to value food, clothing, housing, etc., but for whom these and other things are nonetheless thought to have value. The thought of value here seems to indicate something not taken care of by referring to the interest of the subject in question—unless by "interest" we already mean "value."

The facts which were called value-errors in preceding sections point in the same direction. The fitness of an objectum to attract interest does not depend upon the truth or falsity of the judgments which are its psychological presuppositions. Thus the divining rod seems to have no less a claim to the name of "value" than a medicinal plant. I once tried to take account of this difference by proposing that one should in the latter case talk of "objective" value, and in the former case only of "subjective" value. But then "subjective" value is also accepted as value, whereas no ordinary judge would like to admit that the divining rod has the property of being valuable.[4]

Another relevant point of view is what I have elsewhere [5] briefly called "potentialization." [6] If value is treated as a fact

4. If value is to be defined in such a way that reference to the subject becomes obligatory, it is not enough to say "The value of O lies in the fact that an S is interested in O." I thought that one's meaning should be completed by adding "could be interested or ought in right reason to be interested" ("Für die Psychologie und gegen den Psychologismus," p. 9). However, when I went on to say, "but in this last remark the exclusively psychological treatment of value has been transgressed," I deserved Th. Lessing's reproach: "In this definition the normative notion of value and the psychic fact of value are confused" (*Studien zur Wertaxiomatik*, pp. XVIII ff.).

5. "Für die Psychologie und gegen den Psychologismus," pp. 6 ff.

6. It has been objected to this notion that in it a "logical operation with notions (*logische Begriffsoperation*), the develop-

relative to the subject and his surroundings, then it becomes natural to include the subject and his surroundings explicitly in this fact of value, so that the value will, for one thing, arise and perish with its subject. Considered in this light, potentialization has doubtless a tendency to make values independent of all such presuppositions. At first, of course, the subject and his surroundings still seem to be brought in, and the categorical judgment merely replaced by a hypothetical judgment. But the matter does not usually end with the objective apprehended by the hypothetical judgment, as is noticeable in the case of all thought regarding dispositions. When someone is said to be a good shot, it means that he hits well when he shoots. But nobody will predicate an "if-then" relationship, or something similar, to him as a property but will rather seek in this round-about way to characterize a property which is itself in most cases essentially unknown but which is nonetheless the heart of the matter—i.e., precisely what I have called "the basis of a disposition" (*Dispositionsgrundlage*). This basis can often only be relatively characterized, but this does not make it a relative matter itself. The case of potentialization in respect to values is doubtless similar. We may therefore surmise that whatever strives for recognition in potentialization is not merely a relative determination of value.

In somewhat less theoretical form, but more effectively, our point can be expressed thus: If the essence of values is constituted mainly by the attitude of the subject, then the value will in consequence arise and perish with this subject, and the subject, being the last condition of all values, will, so to speak, embrace value in himself. But then the existence of the subject, being the basis of all value, will be superior to every particular value. Life will be the greatest good. Occasionally such a conclusion has been drawn; but no time has drawn such a conclusion practically and *ad absurdum,* or has exposed its inherent frivolity more plainly, than our own.

---

ment of a thought out of a thought, is confused with an empirical change in a real fact" (Th. Lessing, *Studien zur Wertaxiomatik,* p. XVIII). If a "real fact" means that which actually happens in our apprehension, I must summarily reply to such a summary critique that "the development of a thought out of a thought" or "an operation with notions" always happens in a thinking subject, and that, at the same time, abstraction and determination, despite their psychic character, preserve their logical meaning.

We have therefore automatically entered the special domain of ethical values, from which we shall gain, as I believe, the most decisive standpoints from which to view our problem. No unbiased observer will have any illusions as to the fact that there is hardly a domain of human judgment where assurance in conviction so much contrasts with the actual extent of our knowledge as in ethics. Nevertheless, any person fit to be taken seriously has at least some fundamental ethical beliefs in terms of which he measures the value of his own and other people's actions, and in relation to which he can attain clarity as to the sense of the concept of value, even in the event that some of his fundamental opinions should fail to stand up to his own future criticism and to the further progress of theory. But there are some things in relation to which one never really becomes uncertain, despite all readiness to be taught differently. Whoever has given the best of his life's strength, as so many have done, to the fight against untruthfulness and injustice, or against faithlessness and unkindness, may well ask, hoping for some theoretical answer, whether there is a sufficient basis for the ideals for which he has striven and according to which he has lived. There must, he would argue, be some reason why there are people who, on account of their special character, react to such matters with experiences of satisfaction and approval, and who do not react similarly to their opposites, even if, strictly speaking, nothing prevents right from being turned into wrong, and good into bad, for people with different characters.

Such objections against the relativity doctrine can be met by pointing out that, in the case of ethical values, we are often, strictly speaking, not dealing with values proper but with functional or rather effect-values (*Wirkungswerte*). But the relations that connect these latter with values proper are completely objective, and they are, therefore, in particular, independent of the subjects of the values and of their tendencies. I myself once looked for such relations in the special case of dispositions toward altruism, not, however, in the belief that altruism can exclusively be regarded from the standpoint of effect-values.[7] Since then the meaning of such attempts has become even more questionable to me. But even if one could succeed in showing fundamental ethical values to be function-

7. See *Psychologisch-ethische Untersuchungen*, § § 56 ff.

values, nothing would be gained for the relativity view in the just-mentioned respects. For function-values lead back unavoidably to values proper, in regard to which an appeal to the subject, whose nature is always external to the objecta in question, would, as before, be quite unsatisfactory. The connecting relations in their objectivity may quite well be independent of the subject's nature; but that, from such connections, new facts of value can result, i.e., those very function-values, can only be explained in the sense of the relativity view by supposing that there are subjects whose nature leads them to transfer their valuations or desires from one object to another according to a strict law, provided that these objects stand to one another in a certain relationship. In such a case, things could also be different for subjects of another character, and possibly a basis for completely different values or disvalues may here be given.

In the face of such difficulties, one might ask the simple question whether it is in all circumstances as essential and as obligatory to include the value-subject in the notion of value as contemporary value-theory thinks that it is. In that case, it is hard to rid oneself of the suspicion that relativity to a subject is no more helpful in this case than it is when subjective experiences and relations to such are made constitutive of truth and even of factuality. In fact, the statement "The truth is what is believed by a subject" does not seem to be very different from the statement "Something is valuable if it evokes an experience of positive valuation or desire in a subject." And if there is indeed a false psychologism in the theory of knowledge, then we may well ask how one can have a right to feel free from the danger of an equally false psychologism in value-theory.

The doubts expressed on the preceding pages can be silenced by pointing to associations, developments, etc., and by "psychologically" explaining their origins and so getting rid of them. The history of philosophy has shown this to be possible in so many previous cases, whether for good or for bad causes. And merely because such procedures can be applied, one can hardly escape the duty to take a deeper look at the facts. Emotional presentation and the knowledge based upon it promise us help in such attempts.

It was clearly inevitable, when the dates of origin of the relevant conceptions are considered, that the doctrine of the relativity of values should not have taken account of the possibility of emotional presentation. The predicate "valuable" was not taken to differ characteristically from the predicate "beautiful." The latter was taken to mean the capacity of an object to attract aesthetic feelings to itself, and in the former a value-feeling merely took the place of an aesthetic feeling. But it is also clear that, quite regardless as to what the character of the value-feeling and the pertaining desire may be, this character of the presentative need not be evident in the presented object. If value is the object presented by the value-feeling, just as beauty is the object presented by the feeling of beauty (*Schönheitsgefühl*), then in neither of these objects must a relation to the apprehending subject necessarily be included. Likewise we have in ideas a presenting experience, but in objects like color and sound there is no bringing-to-light of an apprehending experience or of its subject. Naturally there is no reason why, for special purposes, values should not be indirectly characterized through apprehending experiences, as colors and sounds can, by a different detour, be described by way of frequencies. But, this being admitted, these moments (of apprehension) are as little constitutive in the one case as in the other, and there is no reason why values should more readily be regarded as relative than colors. Value, then, does not primarily consist in the capacity to attract value-experiences to itself but consists simply in what is presented by value-experiences. Here, as in the case of all fundamental facts (*Fundamentaltatsachen*), we must forgo a proper definition in favor of direct experience.

If in fact we succeed, as I think we have succeeded, in obtaining from the presentational achievement of emotional experience a notion of value which is free from relativity, we have not yet completely eliminated subjectivity from this notion. This is seen from the parallel case of the secondary, and also of the primary, qualities, whose phenomenal character does not imply relativity. But these very qualities show that, even if we acknowledge such a phenomenal status, we by no means wish to ignore their importance for knowledge. In both cases it is important to realize in what sense and to what extent the phenomena in question can be a basis for knowledge. In the preceding paragraph we reached the result that something emotionally presented is quite capable of providing such a basis. The notion of values based on emotional presentation is quite capable in favorable conditions of fulfilling the demands made on it of unconditional objectivity, to which our attitude to ethical issues bears witness. To what extent conditions are really favorable to such a fulfillment is a different question, which cannot be answered in the state of our present ethical practice, let alone in the state of our present ethical theory. But we have gained not a little ground if the preceding discussions have succeeded in removing difficulties which made it appear as if the profound demands in question were incongruous with the nature of all value and must therefore once and for all be held to be illusory.

If such convictions as mine are represented among our contemporaries,[8] so-called public opinion is nonetheless sufficiently against me. This opposition suffices to make one ask whether anyone who accepts my convictions does not thereby put himself into conflict with almost all exponents of modern value-theory, demanding of them nothing less than that they should retrace the path of development taken so naturally by value-theory over several hundred years. Science occasionally has had to do just that. But, statements which do not give rise to such rigorous demands for readjustment rightly inspire more trust. The theory presented here may be in this more favorable position. It does not, strictly speaking, oppose the traditions of the accepted value-theory but merely attempts to expose what is in a certain sense a new, or rather a somewhat neglected, aspect of the facts. At first sight, the opposite may seem to be the case, since my previous discussions have also been concerned with a notion of value in which, in contrast to the general opinion, an attempt was made to dig down to a relation-free moment. But this undoubtedly actual disagreement becomes less acute once one realizes that the above statements do not claim to expose *the* notion of value but only *one* notion of values (*Wertgedanke*), since there is, as far as I can see, not just one such notion but at least two, of which neither can be

8. Cf. my brief remarks in "Für die Psychologie und gegen den Psychologismus," pp. 9 f. O. Kraus's paper, "Die Grundlagen der Werttheorie," offers more details (*Jahrbücher der Philosophie*, II [1914], 12 ff.). There the following is also said about me: "In 1911 Meinong gave up his persistent denial (*sic!*) of absolute objective values" (p. 20). Since the adjoining note leaves no doubt that a *laudabiliter se subjecit* is attributed to me (of course without the *laudabilitas*), it may here be stated (for which otherwise there would have been no occasion) that F. Brentano, whose ethical writings I already knew in 1894, had no part in turning me toward nonpsychological notions in the field of value-theory.

given theoretical preference without a resultant one-sidedness. The following seems to me the posture of things.

Any other-presenting experience presents the knowing subject with, so to say, two objects. On the one hand, there is the object, *sit venia verbo,* which it other-presents. And, on the other hand, there is itself. The difference involved in this situation is frequently experienced. If two perceptual statements of the following kind are made: (*a*) that a fruit is ripe, and (*b*) that a fruit looks ripe, the perceptual idea in question is in the one case other-presentative and in the other case self-presentative. In the second case, however, a relation is also needed so as to use the experience itself to characterize the thing in the relevant way. Presenting emotions surely behave in the same way, except, of course, as has already frequently been mentioned, that they normally do not function other-presentatively, as do experiences in the intellectual realm. Self-presentation may accordingly have a certain preponderance, together with a relativistic mode of treatment. Value-experiences can, in particular, be utilized as the means of knowing the objects to which they attach. They are a means of knowing (*Erkenntnismittel*) in a double sense. First, in the sense that what is presented by the value-experience is to be attributed to the objects as their property, and secondly in the sense that the objects have the property of provoking the experience which corresponds to this object of presentation (e.g., the value). It is clear that the second interpretation remains valid even when the first does not, and even when the first cannot with right be attempted at all. Thus the second interpretation can claim to be free from presuppositions and to be of universal applicability. This appeals to our theorizing activity, especially since a nonrelativistic approach has so often broken down under the influence of extraordinarily variable external conditions. In the preceding discussions we have attempted to deny that this takes care of everything in the pretheoretical notion of value that is worthy of preservation and further development, and we have also attempted to hark back to that aspect that we have just called the "first interpretation." It is in no way denied that the second interpretation provides the basis for a fundamental notion which is both clear and broadly applicable, but it must at the same time be emphasized that there is another notion, fundamental for value-theory, based on the first interpretation above, which is both justified and indispensable.

Which of the two resulting notions can claim to be *the* primary notion of value? At this point disagreement can plainly not be avoided; for I cannot deny that to me relation-free value, which has so far been theoretically neglected, seems to deserve our preference. Values, as given to theory, if I understand the matter rightly, contain no relation whatever: this is first suggested to thought by frequent breakdowns in the notion of relation-free values, and is then impressed upon thought in the most emphatic manner. But the deepest and most burning problems of the theory and practice of values turn around relation-free values, and these problems are blurred and weakened if we make it obligatory to introduce relativity.

But anyone inclined to give primacy to the notion of relation-free value must not overlook the fact that relative value is also a fact of the greatest importance for the understanding of matters for which the notion of relation-free value may be of no help at all. That is especially clear in cases where relative value has the same significance and justification as relation-free value, or in cases where relative value does not lose its significance though relation-free value is completely absent. It is a common experience that different people take different degrees of interest in the same fact and yet that no one can thereby be known to be wrong. A patient is concerned with his own illness or wounds in quite a different manner from even the most sympathetic person in his immediate or remoter surroundings. Among the many things we live with, quite a few are rendered less valuable or even totally worthless by the death of a person connected with them. We can, of course, not always deny that the existence of a subject was one of the conditions under which such a thing had a relation-free value. As a rule, however, and under such conditions, the value is understood to be relative to a certain individual, to be a value for this individual. One would be neglecting theoretically and practically important facts if one exclusively considered relation-free values and passed over such matters.

It must be added that we are here dealing with facts which, if there is no objection to this course, can most readily be established empirically. Relative value is always there wherever a value-experience occurs or could occur quite regardless, perhaps, of its justification. But relation-free value is not always there where it is presented or could be presented. It is only there where, so to speak, something which is correct (*etwas Richtiges*) is the object of presentation. It is no easier to decide on such correctness, but in general much harder, than in the analogous case of external perception.

Relative value therefore remains the really graspable value which is, in the best sense, positive. The whole science of value should take its first steps from this point and should remain always in the closest touch with it if it wants to deserve the status of a science of fact in the narrower sense of the word, i.e., something more than a mere theory of objects. The notion of such relative value would not lose its significance if it should prove to be a mere creation of theorizing thought, more removed from our naïve ways of thinking of values than even the notion of relation-free value. If, moreover, an agreement cannot be at once reached on this matter, it is not too great a disadvantage, as long as the natural duality of the value-notions and their respective characteristics have at least been made clear. In order to fix our results terminologically, it seems most appropriate to speak of "value" in both cases, but over and above this to make provisions for an appropriate determination of the differences to be established by distinguishing adjectives. To this end, the words "objective" and "subjective" are automatically at hand, so that the relation-free value can be called "objective," and the relative value "subjective."

For myself, however, it is especially hard to use these terms in the indicated manner, since, at a time when I had not thought at all of relation-free values, I had decided to use these words in a different way within the domain of relative values. In this domain we also have to deal with things that were above [9] briefly mentioned in connection with value-errors. Anyone who believes in the divining rod or the so-called sugar pill values the thing in question, even though for a false reason. The thing in question is in any event included in the subject's sphere of interest, so that it cannot be denied relative value in every sense. But if this value is compared with the value which frontiers have for a state which they protect from neighbors who have been proved unreliable, it is clear, if we consider the divergent outcome of false and correct presuppositions, that in

9. Pp. 108 f., 127.

the first case there is a subjectivity missing in the second case. In the latter case we may then even speak of objectivity. It was in this sense that I proposed to use the terms "subjective" and "objective" as applying to relative values.[10] And I of course did not consider any possibility that relation-free values might one day also come to be theoretically acknowledged. Since theory has changed, a change also in terminology might most appropriately take account of it, and it might indeed be considered whether a terminological change would not in fact be the most radical and best thing to effect. But I am afraid of the misunderstandings which might readily result from altering the meanings (*Bedeutungen*) of words once introduced by definition. Therefore, perhaps I had better try, for my very own working purposes, to leave the words "objective" and "subjective" unchanged in their old meaning as referring to relative values. I shall then try to find other characteristic names for the two main value-classes.

The two names "relative value" and "relation-free value," which have repeatedly been used on preceding pages, may not be quite appropriate. Instead of "relation-free," "absolute" can be used. In regard to the word "absolute," I have no doubt that anything can rightly be called "absolute" which is not relative. I shall, therefore, not hesitate to talk of "absolute value," in the sense of relation-free value, when the occasion requires me to do so. Nevertheless, the word "absolute," though harmless enough in its natural meaning, when taken, e.g., to refer to a color seen or a tone heard, has acquired in the history of its use the property of stirring up the as yet unconquered *horror metaphysicus* considerably, and not always rightly. One would therefore hardly be doing well if one introduced a principal class of value, whose recognition has not as yet been achieved, by means of a technical designation that would probably make such a recognition very difficult. It must further be said—and that also holds for the expressions "relative" and "relation-free" —that to pick out properties by names that derive from some previous and different determination of an object's nature can create the impression that one has only to do with analytic judgments, whereas one in fact has insights of a completely different and more significant kind. So I searched for other

10. See *Psychologisch-ethische Untersuchungen zur Werttheorie*, § 23.

names and believed, following F. v. Wieser's usage, that I had found something quite appropriate in the expressions "impersonal" and "personal." [11] The disapproval which I reaped, especially from a quarter [12] from which I had expected the most positive understanding—despite the disagreement mentioned above,[13] which was more of a terminological than an objective character—cannot incite me to work out new changes just on account of such terminological difficulties. Things can be better done without that, since in the last resort names have no importance for me, but only things themselves, and since a final straightening of terminology is not thereby prevented.

Presupposing all this, we can formulate the main results of our preceding inquiries concerning values thus: Values can be spoken of in two very different senses, which we differentiate by use of the terms "impersonal value" and "personal value," whereby we think not of "personality" but of the "person" in the sense of the apprehending, experiencing subject, as a correlate which is absent in the one case, and whose presence is necessary in the other. In a similar way, impersonal value is that which is immediately other-presented by a value-experience, while personal value, on the other hand, is the capacity to attract a value-experience to itself. This, then, naturally is the value *for* somebody, *for* a value-subject, which is no more required in the former case than in the case of any object which, if it *is* an object of apprehension, always needs a subject while, on the contrary, essentially not needing to be an object of apprehension at all. Therefore, personal value is always relative, impersonal value always free of relativity, so that it can also be characterized as absolute value. On account of its relativity, personal value is always subjective and impersonal value objective. But within the subjectivity of personal value the contrast of objective–subjective again has importance, since, in the intellectual presuppositions of the value-experience in question, the objective facts are only sometimes decisive, and subjective opinions only loosely corresponding to facts very readily take over.

We have to return at this place to the notion of the just-mentioned object of apprehension in order to consider the

11. "Für die Psychologie und gegen den Psychologismus," pp. 2, 12.
12. See Th. Lessing, *Studien zur Wertaxiomatik*, p. XVII.
13. See above, p. 22; p. 126, footnotes 4 and 6.

possibility of reserving for impersonal value some sort of relativity to the subject. My attention was called to this problem by Th. Lessing. He remarks that the statement that "There would be no laws of value (*Wertgesetze*) if there were no preferential or rejecting interest" is "without doubt correct." [14] It is as correct as the statement that "There would be no truth or error without reason, that is, without minds (*Geister*) who judge." Here the use of "truth" is important if I am right in seeing the main difference between truth and factuality (*Tatsächlichkeit*) in the fact that truth, in contrast to factuality, is an object of apprehension. If a factual objective is called true when it is considered as the objective of an apprehending experience,[15] then truth is put into a necessary relationship to an apprehending subject even though it is not held to be dependent upon the existence or character of this or that person. In spite of this independence, truth under these conditions exhibits a relative moment of which factuality is still free. It may now indeed be asked whether the notion of value has more analogy with the notion of factuality or the notion of truth. In the preceding passages we automatically drifted to the first alternative. The just-quoted remark by Th. Lessing indicates the second. And, although it seems to me to involve a needless complication, I cannot at this point bring in anything by which such a complication could be excluded. Nevertheless, if for the remainder of the present discussion I adhere to the notion of an "apprehension-free" (*erfassungsfrei*) value, I shall hardly be committing a great mistake in the main outlines of my characterization; for, even if the notion of an apprehended value should deserve to be given preference, the moment of apprehension can quite easily be added on to my characterization, even though extrinsically.

If I was right in previously saying that impersonal value is really the notion which pretheoretical thinking hands over to the theory of values for theoretic processing, it may seem as if the modern theory of values went wrong in its processing of personal value and that it needed to correct its course. But to say this would be as wrong as to conclude, from the fact that physics or any other natural science has to deal with reality, that it does not therefore have to concern itself with ap-

---

14. *Studien zur Wertaxiomatik*, p. 104.
15. Cf. *Über Möglichkeit und Wahrscheinlichkeit*, pp. 39 f.

pearances. It seems to me clear that physics is something other than the theory of physical "phenomena." [16] But there is no telling where it could begin or could acquire its empirical legitimation if it could only make its beginning where it was undoubtedly concerned with "things in themselves." Even if we accept such a parallel for a moment, the justified demands of the theory of values would not thereby be fulfilled. For, whereas the physical phenomenon as such, the object of apprehension, is, strictly speaking, only of interest to psychology and of course also to the theory of objects, the givenness of what might be called the value-phenomenon, the inclusion, that is, of an object in our sphere of interests, is not only of psychological, but also eminently of practical, importance. It comes, therefore, even theoretically considered, under a new point of view. So we obtain as our result that the hitherto prevailing theory of values neglected to work out an important theme in over-looking impersonal value but that it did valuable and necessary work in its inquiries into personal value. Without this work the problems of impersonal value could not have been approached at all. But only the future will decide to what extent these problems can find a satisfactory theoretical solution in which what has been, or will be, found out about personal values will be utilized. To me it seems evident that any really scientific future ethical theory depends upon this.

One should not, in general, be deceived as to the difficulties which any future inquiry into impersonal values may attempt to combat. For a first appraisal, we may again most suitably make use of the above-mentioned parallelism between this and our relationship to the external world (*äussere Wirklichkeit*). Under favorable conditions there is very good evidence that there is such a world, but very bad evidence as to what its character may be.[17] In a somewhat similar manner the unprejudiced person believes most firmly in ethical values and in their impersonality (*Unpersönlichkeit*). But, confronted with this or that more or less concrete object, and asking whether it is to be placed among these values and, if so, where, we find ourselves involved in amazing uncertainties, to which not only present ethical theory but also the practical

16. Cf. "Über die Erfahrungsgrundlagen unseres Wissens," p. 106.

17. *Ibid.*, §§ 18 ff.

ethics seized upon by our "smart" literati bears eloquent witness. As is well known, the attempt has quite often been made to acquire or to preserve science's glory of strict exactitude by demanding that one should never leave the ground of what is "given." Without dwelling on the naïveté or ignorance which lies at the base of such demands, one can see how much easier it is to make out clearly what is well illuminated. Still, the question as to whether one should turn to things that are dark or dim is to be answered in accordance with their importance. For this reason people will never cease to do metaphysics as well as it can be done, and in the same way the theory of impersonal values will always press to be worked over anew. We may, however, hope that some progress will have been made now that some obstacles concerning impersonal values have been removed, obstacles which our theory itself put in its own way.

14 / Value and Existence.
Impersonal Oughtness (*Sollen*)
and Impersonal Instrumentality
(*Zweckmässigkeit*)

UP TO NOW OUR INQUIRY has exclusively been concerned with the dignitatives of the value-domain. It is natural to raise the question of relativity or of freedom from relativity (*Relationsfreiheit*), that is, the question as to the personal or impersonal character of the desideratives of the value-domain. Let us initiate this inquiry by first attempting to gain clarity regarding an intrinsically most important matter which seems exclusively to concern dignitatives. Right from the beginning, when I first tried to describe value-experiences,[1] I pointed to the essential role which in this connection is played by judgments, especially by judgments of being, and even more by judgments of existence, a role which can be described thus: value-feelings are being-feelings and, more especially, existence-feelings. In saying this, it was also suggested that we assign to being, and primarily to existence, a dominant position in the notion of value, which would then only be more or less weakened (*abschwächen*) by potentialization.[2] Evident as this always seems to me to be, the dominating position of being and existence nevertheless becomes dubious. I do not know whether these doubts have been expressed publicly, but I myself have been told of them *privatim* by very trustworthy sources. Since such doubts, once expressed, even when in principle they can be dispelled, very often uncover some actual theoretical defi-

1. In *Psychologisch-ethische Untersuchungen zur Werttheorie,* § 5.
2. See "Für die Psychologie und gegen den Psychologismus," p. 6.

ciencies, it can be taken as a sign in favor of the principal thoughts of a theory if it is capable of development in a direction where such doubts become relatively justified but are, at the same time, eliminable. In this sense it is to be counted as an unexpected but desirable result of our theses regarding impersonal values that an agreement can, on their basis, be reached regarding the position of being in relation to value.

It is immediately clear that whatever has just been said regarding the dominant position of being is true primarily of the value-experience and so, accordingly, of personal value. The question then arises whether the same statement can be made regarding impersonal values. If, under favorable conditions, impersonal value is presented by value-feelings, it is at once clear that being, or rather existence, is not a determination of the property thus apprehended. For the dignitative which is presented by the value-feeling has, as we saw, rather the character of an objectum than of an objective. If this is the case, the import of being (by which, of course, factual [*tatsächlich*] being is always meant) [3] for impersonal value does not consist in its being a constitutive part of an experience but in its being the presupposition for a justified occurrence of this experience, which can apprehend value in the sense of being presentative of it. The impersonal value is not then attached to the being of the objectum but to the being-thus-and-so of the objectum in question. I believe therefore that, as regards impersonal value, i.e., the so-called true notion of value, one is justified in denying that the being of its object is relevant.

The situation could be different in this respect as regards desideratives, and this is indicated by the fact that desideratives, as has been shown, are not objectum-like, like dignitatives, but rather objective-like. But, first of all, we must answer the question whether a transition can or must be made from personal to impersonal in the case of desideratives as it must be in the case of dignitatives. If we primarily keep in mind the case of oughtness (*Sollen*), we know that this oughtness always concerns an objective whereby each oughtness is an oughtness-to-be (*Seinsollen*), just as the "must" and the "can" are a "must be" and a "can be." [4] This corresponds to the nature

3. Cf. *Über Möglichkeit und Wahrscheinlichkeit*, pp. 108 f., 133 f.
4. See *ibid.*, pp. 233 and 87 ff.

of desires as far as they always concern an objective. Naturally, desire goes together with personal value, but adds to this a further personal moment, since desire, even where there is occasion for it, is not in each subject proportionate to the value-feeling,[5] and an ought cannot have relevance to the point of view of a subject who does not desire. On the other hand, it is also clear that justification has the same bearing on oughtness as on value and that oughtness is therefore to be liberated from the necessary relativity to a subject in the same way as value, which does not mean that the difference between oughtness and value must thereby be obliterated. Therefore it may be said that there is an impersonal, relation-free, and so absolute oughtness, just as there is an impersonal value. This is in accord with pretheoretical thinking, especially on ethical matters, since a "you ought" is never stated relatively to a certain subject. A metaphysically based ethics can sometimes veil but can hardly eliminate these facts.

The just-mentioned difference between oughtness and value still demands our special attention. We can say that all oughtness is an oughtness-to-be. This cannot be changed by the transition from the personal to the impersonal. Whereas in this transition values shed their relationship to being, such a relationship remains intact for oughtness, even in its impersonal sense. Any attempt to make clear the relationship between oughtness and its pertinent being is helped by the fact that, as we saw, the emotionally presented object is the *superius* in relation to the objects presented by the psychological object-presupposition of the emotion, i.e., the object proper is the *superius* in relation to the borrowed object of the presenting emotions. This seems to become evident in the linguistic expression "It ought to be." But such locutions as "It can be" and "It must be" are formed analogously, whereas it remains doubtful, by reason of what has been said regarding the nature of possibility and necessity, whether an analogous interpretation will do in their case.

Regardless as to whether oughtness is taken as personal or impersonal, it in itself indicates the limits within which it naturally applies. It cannot be said: "No person and no civilized state ought to identify itself with the assassination of royalty in 1914." We cannot say this, since it is well known that such

5. Cf. *Über Annahmen*, pp. 327 f.

identifications have been made by individuals and by whole states and nations. But it also could not be said even if such an identification had never occurred. An ought has no application to what is past. Only the subjunctive form, "It (should have) ought to have been" (*Es hätte sein sollen*) or, in the case of our example, "It (should have) ought not to have been," can be used in reference to the past. But similar limitations must also be imposed on the present and future. On a bright day one cannot say: "The weather ought to be fine today." This can also not be said when it is a hopelessly rainy day, and this is no more striking. For the same reasons, it cannot be said in August: "It ought to be winter in five months," and also not "It ought to be summer in five months." The first cannot be said because it will happen anyway; the second cannot be said because it certainly will not happen. The past, together with the present, can be regarded from the same standpoint, since it plainly has no advantage over present and future beyond the fact that it constitutes an especially closed domain of those facts, that "infecta fieri non possunt." Now the general question arises: Where does oughtness have its place if it applies to neither the factual nor the unfactual? The question might threaten to prove difficult to answer theoretically were it not so familiar in the theory of possibility. Possibility also applies to neither the factual nor the completely unfactual (*Untatsachen*),[6] but it applies to incomplete objects.[7] It may therefore be advisable to look for oughtness among incomplete objects. That something ought to be or ought not to be is said only of what is possible. It is to be expected that oughtness can be connected with the domain of what is factual or unfactual with the aid of implexive being,[8] as was done in the case of possibility.

In the attempt to understand the limitations which apply to the validity of oughts we are reminded of the peculiar limitations of desire which were previously mentioned.[9] In matters of desirability, also, the future seems to take precedence over the past. But in fact it means that nothing can be desired which already is the case, regardless as to whether this "being the case" (*das Sein*) concerns the past, the present, or the future. It is only true that, in the case of the past, facts are

6. Cf. *Über Möglichkeit und Wahrscheinlichkeit*, pp. 165 f.
7. Cf. *ibid.*, pp. 218 f.
8. Cf. *ibid.*, pp. 211 ff.
9. See above, p. 85.

demarcated in such a clearly knowable way. It is clear that nothing can be desired which *is* the case. It is not so clear, by contrast, that nothing can be desired which is *not* the case. At first glance one might in fact be inclined to believe that it is characteristic of all desire to be directed to what is not the case. The poor man desires riches. The unloved longs for sympathy, friendship, and love. These matters need to be considered somewhat more closely.

Can it be said of an internee or a prisoner that he desires to be free right now? If this "now" is taken to refer strictly to the present, it must be said that he cannot desire to be free now, just as he also cannot desire to have been free a quarter of an hour ago when in fact he was not free. What he desires and only can desire is to be free as soon as possible, perhaps in the next minute, at least at a time at which it is not certain whether he will be free or not, as it is certain in the case of the present and the past. One must not be mistaken about this. The present situation need not be irrelevant for the realization of a desire which normally is directed toward the future. Anyone who does not know the pains of imprisonment, or is not directly acquainted with them as is the one who is experiencing them, need not at all feel the desire to be free in the near or remote future, or need only feel it faintly. This desire, strictly speaking, is never directed to the present, to the extent that this can be determinately known. And it is no different in respect to the future. The above example about summer or winter beginning in five months' time can easily be translated into the desire of a subject in the month of August.

At this point we become aware of some points of uncertainty. Can I not wish in the summer that half a year later the days will be light and long, the flowers will be blooming, etc? Or why should it not be possible to wish that the great war of the last few years had never started, or were already finished, that it had brought less misery upon people, that the newspapers had lied less, or had promoted less hate among the nations, and many other such things? Without doubt, wishing is a case of desiring. It may, as has already been mentioned,[10] be related to willing as a surmise is related to a judgment made with certainty.[11] But can I, while the war is lasting, really wish that it

10. See above, p. 102.
11. The occurrence of other differentiating moments is not, of

never had started, as I really can wish that it may bring victory to those whom I must consider to be the representatives of justice and culture? If in both cases one tries to wish seriously and strongly, it seems clear that only in one case, in respect to the outcome of the war, does the wishing really succeed,[12] whereas in the other case only something wishlike results, which, strictly speaking, is not wishing at all. If I am right, the latter is not a serious but an imaginative desire,[13] which view is confirmed by its linguistic expression, since no one will say "I wish there had been no war" but only "I could have wished that there had been no war." The subjunctive perhaps is most naturally to be interpreted as an "I would wish if I were able to wish; but, as things are, I cannot wish." If this is the case, desires fall under the same rules as oughts. Desires have no point of application to the factual or the unfactual. They are restricted to the possible, which means that they are primarily linked to incomplete objects.

Considering the relationship which we found to hold between desires and oughts, we are not amazed at such a similarity. A further step may be accomplished by tracing this similarity back to the presentational work of the desire (*Präsentationsleistung*). Since I can desire neither what is factual nor what is unfactual, I may therefore think that, in the apprehension of the factual or unfactual, no oughts can be presented and hence that we are unable to place an ought anywhere but in the possible. Thus oughtness would become a matter of our psychic attitude, which understandably can set no further standard, since it is limited to what is purely personal. But we have already found out that the limitations of the ought, with which we are here concerned, hold as much for the impersonal as for the personal ought. Considering this, we must repudiate the attempted explanation as being psychologistic in the defective sense. Things may have to be understood reversely. If an object is to become the borrowed object of an emotion, in our case, that is, of a desire, it can plausibly be supposed that the object must be such that the characteristic presented by the emotion can belong to it as its property. Conse-

---

course, thereby excluded. Cf. H. Maier, *Psychologie des emotionalen Denkens* (Tübingen, 1908), pp. 616 ff.

12. Maier judges differently, *ibid.*, p. 618.

13. Cf. *Über Annahmen*, pp. 314 f., 379.

quently, anything which is the case, or is definitely not the case, cannot really be desired, since there is no oughtness in respect to such objects.

Of course, it is highly desirable that we should learn more about the essential characteristics of the connection which subsists between oughtness and possibility: better insight into this matter might modify our previous characterization both of oughtness and of possibility. We can now already see how the classical "Thou canst since thou shalt" can be defended, if the "Thou canst" is understood in the sense of possibility, and not in the more exacting sense of disposition.[14]

The second desiderative beside oughtness is instrumentality (*Zweckmässigkeit*). Now it is immediately clear that here, too, the transition from the personal to the impersonal can be carried out without difficulty. The relation between end and means is in itself so objective (*etwas an sich so Objektives*) that there has always been a danger of identifying it with a causal or a conditional relation. But when we consider the facts of emotional presentation, we know why the stock objection against all teleological thinking is a case of faulty psychologism. The objection is that all teleological thinking presupposes a subject for its end—that, in other words, all purpose must be personal. A subject is required for the apprehension of purpose, as a subject is required for all sorts of apprehension. In the apprehension of purpose the subject's emotions take care of the necessary presentation. Purpose or instrumentality is itself, under favorable circumstances, independent of all apprehension and is therefore quite independent of an apprehending subject.

14. Cf. *Über Möglichkeit und Wahrscheinlichkeit*, p. 55.

15 / Dignity (*Dignität*) and Desideratum. Value in an Extended Sense of the Word

In order to see the main consequences which follow from what has been said about emotional presentation, we have limited our consideration to the realm of values, which is only one of the four classes of dignitatives and their respective desideratives. In concluding our present discussions, we shall briefly consider to what extent the other three classes enable us to set up principles analogous to those established in the realm of values.

There are very definite indications that we may expect analogous results in the domain of aesthetic feelings. If, as we saw, the naïvely thinking person does not understand how values can be relative to a subject, he has even less understanding how this can be true of the beautiful. He thinks anything beautiful simply is beautiful, and that whoever thinks otherwise about it simply is wrong. To recognize that something may be beautiful to one person and indifferent or even ugly to another is to exercise a tolerance which one has acquired only after many experiences, and mostly experiences of futile controversy. Still, despite plentiful material drawn from art history, such relativistic consequences have, even today, not been drawn to the same extent as in the case of values. The statement "A is valuable" (*wert*) is felt to be linguistically incomplete, that is to say, it demands grammatical completion by a subject, e.g., "A is valuable to me." But a construction like "A is beautiful to me" or "A has beauty for me" is still completely unusual, so that any relativistic treatment has to make use of the phrase "A pleases me." This, however, was reason enough to adopt the relativistic point of view quite generally, at least in theory. In this connection it is not important whether we are concerned with the relativity of values to a single subject or to greater or smaller collectives of subjects. Thus there seems unquestionably a right to formulate a notion of "personal beauty," regardless as to whether the name itself is thought to be appropriate or not. But again the question arises whether we have any reason to contrast the personal with the impersonal in this case, the latter being relation-free.

The question has been answered in the negative on the ground that aesthetic objects have neither the existence of perceptual objects nor the subsistence of ideal objects of higher order. Accordingly aesthetic objects are to be dealt with merely as objects of apprehension, i.e., relative to a subject, and aesthetic norms are to be merely laws governing psychic attitudes.[1] The arguments against the existence of aesthetic objects can be supported by pointing out that, while beauty can doubtless adhere to the real, that is, to nature, beauty is not characteristically bound to reality, as is proved by the existence of art. Since, therefore, aesthetic properties pertain no more to the existent than to the nonexistent, it seems to be out of the question that the aesthetic character of an object can be a matter of empirical knowledge. One would therefore be confined to *a priori* knowledge, to which, however, aesthetic objects are not accessible, since they are not ideal objects of higher order. We have found, however, that these are not real difficulties. Aesthetic objects are objects of higher order, and they are also ideal objects,[2] so that the appropriate way of knowing can only be *a priori*. But there is an obstacle in the way of such knowledge. This is the *necessity* of everything known *a priori*,[3] which cannot readily be reconciled with the great variability of our attitudes toward aesthetic objects. If it can happen that the same melody is found beautiful by one person, indifferent by another, and ugly by a third, or that the same subject can feel the object of his pleasure become first indifferent and then repulsive, it seems out of the question to believe in a connection known *a priori*, and therefore necessary, between the melody

1. Cf. St. Witasek's "Über ästhetische Objektivität," pp. 198 f.
2. Cf. above, pp. 92 ff.
3. Cf. *Über die Stellung der Gegenstandstheorie im System der Wissenschaften* (Leipzig, 1907), pp. 51 ff. (also *Zeitschr. f. Philos. u. philos. Kritik*, CXXIX, 156 ff.).

and the aesthetic property attaching to it. All aesthetic matters, therefore, if they are considered to be relation-free, are accessible neither to empirical nor to *a priori* knowledge. They must therefore be put in the domain of experience, and so fall under a relativistic point of view.

It may perhaps help to clarify matters if we retrospectively apply our present epistemological considerations to the domain of values studied in the preceding chapter. They likewise, we saw, are ideal objects of higher order. However, in their case, empirical knowledge does not seem to be as utterly impossible as it is in the case of aesthetic objects. For, as we know, the value-experience or, in the first instance, the value-feeling, unfolds fully in confrontation with the existing value-object. The question, however, is still open as to how experience can deal with ideal, that is, nonexistent, merely subsistent objects. And we must keep in mind that anything which is known *a priori* is necessary. Thus we arrive at the same impasse as we did in connection with aesthetic objects, in the face of the uncertain variability of our attitudes in matters of value. In general, therefore, the situation does not seem to be too different in the aesthetic domain and the domain of value. So it may be suspected that, as regards the contrast between the personal and the impersonal, with which we now are concerned, we shall reach similar results in the case of aesthetic objects. This holds especially since the notion of impersonal, i.e., relation-free beauty, is supported by more than naïve, prescientific thinking. It is difficult to believe in "absolute relativity" if we consider certain examples of Greek sculpture and German poetry or music, despite all the persuasive teachings of the history of art.

In fact, it can easily be seen that it is no consequence of the ideality of an object that it should be inaccessible to empirical knowledge. I shall hardly be suspected of overestimating the importance of "enumerative and metric experiences" for mathematics; [4] the history of the theory of numbers nonetheless clearly shows that such experiences lead to good results as long as *a priori* inquiry is as yet inadequate.[5] The question is: how

4. Cf. "Über die Erfahrungsgrundlagen unseres Wissens," pp. 5 ff.; *Über die Stellung der Gegenstandstheorie im System der Wissenschaften*, sec. IV.
5. Cf. *Über Möglichkeit und Wahrscheinlichkeit*, p. 680.

does empiricism go about getting a hold on the *a priori*? Apparently the difficulty consists in the problem as to what perception (or remembrance) and induction are supposed to do with objects which by their very ideality are incapable of existence. In the first place there is induction from *a priori*, i.e., from not existent but subsistent, instances.[6] And then, as is especially important in the present context, it can happen that a state of affairs knowable *a priori*, that is, a necessary state of affairs (*Sachverhalt*), is connected with real (*reale*) concomitant states of affairs, in which latter a natural lawfulness may make its appearance, that can be established empirically, or rather, inductively. That in an isosceles triangle the angles at the base are equal is an *a priori* matter of fact concerning ideal objects. Still, one could try to show this equiangularity in a number of triangles by measurement and could establish empirically the coincidence of equiangular and isosceles triangles. This can be explained in the following way. The ideal equality makes real (*reale*) demands on the real bases between which it subsists, and the fulfillment of those demands can be a matter of inductive verification. Still, matters are sufficiently *a priori* here, since in our example we are dealing with comparisons or rather measurements, regarding which induction only makes plain that the equality of the legs of the triangle always offers an opportunity to execute them.

In principle, therefore, there is no more reason why we should not empirically reach relation-free results in respect to the beautiful than in respect to value. There is only one remaining question: What sort of empirical data could be used for such an end? Here again the analogy of value tenders good service. No one doubts, in the first place, that it is only by way of personal values that one can (if at all) reach impersonal values. The following may be said in an attempt to make what has here been said clearer: that an objectum *A* has the impersonal value *N* can be concluded under favorable circumstances from the fact that in *A* the personal value *N* occurs, i.e., that the idea of *A* under favorable circumstances arouses an emotion, or at first a feeling, which presents the object *N*. By reason of this presentation, it is presumed that the object *A* serves as foundation for the object *N*. The presentation here is the concomitant fact through which the induction gets hold of the *a priori* fact of the foundation of the value in the object

6. See *ibid.*, pp. 679 ff.

(*Fundierung*). We still may ask what the presentation really has to do with this foundation. But it is quickly noticed that such a connection is not only observed in the case of emotional presentation. Comparison may serve as a paradigm which never leaves the ground level of intellectual presentation. Red and green together provide the foundation (*fundieren*) for the object Difference; comparison, however, gives rise to the production of that idea which presents the object Difference (this time intellectually), and by this presentation we apprehend the fact of the foundation of one object on others (*Fundierungstatbestand*). Here, too, foundation and presentation are completely different things. They are, however, naturally, even if amazingly, connected by the fact that the knowledge-experience, rendered possible by the presentation, apprehends with evidence the subsistent relation of foundation. This leads us to ask whether, in the case of emotional presentation, the connection could not also be made by similar means. The situation is not in all respects similar. If emotional presentation carried in itself evidence for such foundation, each value-experience would reveal an impersonal value exactly as each set of comparisons, made under sufficiently favorable circumstances, yields a completely impersonal similarity or difference. But we have already noted that there is a possibility of justified surmises.[7] In the light of such surmises, it is no longer puzzling that, out of sufficiently congruous presentations, a knowledge of such foundations, or of such impersonal values, can be attained. This knowledge will count as certainty before the forum of epistemic practice (*Erkenntnispraxis*), just as do many other sufficiently high-level surmises.

That we can, *per analogiam*, make use of our results concerning value in the case of beauty need not be set forth. Only one point needs clarification, and this holds for value and for beauty alike: it is the objection urged against the possibility that aesthetic lawfulness (*Gesetzmässigkeiten*) can be *a priori* by the fact that actual, contrary (*gegensätzlich*) attitudes on the same matters make it impossible that either of them can be necessarily valid. Value is automatically included in these considerations, since experience shows that even values claimed to be impersonal can under certain conditions be unrepresented, especially in the case of subjects with a poor natural endowment.

7. See above, p. 121.

But even here we can go back from emotional to intellectual presentation and once more make use of the paradigm of judgments of comparison (*Vergleichungsurteile*). It is known that there is a domain, the region of the threshold, within which something actually different appears equal. Anything falling within or outside of this region does not have to be the same at different times, either for the same or for different subjects. Elsewhere likewise, in respect to objects of higher order, the possibility of an inadequacy of ideas has been pointed out.[8] Nobody minds this fact, and this is quite right. For if the objects A and B serve as foundation for the object C, it is not, strictly speaking, predetermined whether the experiences a and b, by means of which the subject reacts to the givenness of the objects in question, will be fit to produce an experience c that will stand to the object C in an appropriate relationship of adequacy. That this relationship so often obtains involves no more teleology than is present in so many other facts of organic and especially psychic life. That, under some circumstances, it does not obtain is no reason to deny the necessary relationship of A and B to C, but it is of course an impediment to recognizing these relationships, an impediment which nevertheless can be overcome with the aid of appropriate evidences.

Whatever can be said in this respect regarding intellectual presentation cannot in principle differ from what can be said regarding emotional presentation. However, the repeatedly mentioned general disadvantage in which knowledge here finds itself is seen in the fact that the certain evidence (*Gewissheitsevidenz*) which not infrequently accompanies intellectual presentations seems to go missing in the case of an (emotionally presented) foundation-relation (*Fundierungsrelation*). Not to find a major third beautiful, and not to find parallel fifths ugly (*Quintenparallelen*), readily seems to conflict with the nature of these objects. One cannot, however, assume the same attitude to someone who either has become, or who always was, insensitive to such matters as one does to a color-blind person, who takes red and green to be the same color. This points to the character of the evidences in our two cases, which, in the case of the third or the fifths, is much clearer than in many other aesthetic judgments and likewise judgments of value. Here we are of course not dealing with evidences for certain

8. See V. Benussi's contribution to *Untersuchungen der Gegenstandstheorie und Psychologie,* edited by me, pp. 383 ff. and *passim.*

knowledge but with evidences for surmises. Considering these, it is quite understandable that, while evident statements regarding the same objects may be incompatible with one another, the surmises in question can lead, in favorable circumstances, to considerable degrees of certainty. The consensus of the subjects is not the least of these favorable circumstances, so that we here see the possibility of inductive procedures which in no way diminish the *a priori* character of the facts thus to be established by induction.

In summary, the following can be stated: There are in reality no epistemological difficulties in connection with aesthetic objects which prohibit our going beyond what is relative to an apprehending subject. We have not thereby shown that there is a relation-free and, in this sense, impersonal beauty, but the way has been cleared to give reasons for such. What we have are, at any rate, objects of higher order, and any lawfulness holding among them is doubtless of *a priori* nature. In the unfavorable epistemological conditions which apparently prevail in connection with emotional presentation, it is not at all amazing that the *a priori* should only be accessible to us through a detour by way of experience or that impersonal value and beauty should only become accessible to us through a detour by way of personal value and beauty.

Of the four main classes of dignitatives which we previously distinguished,[9] only two remain to be examined, to see whether the contrast of relative and relation-free can be applied in their case. Of these, the dignitatives connected with the knowledge-feelings are much the more important. The theoretical situation in respect to these is especially difficult, for, as we have seen, there is a danger of confounding knowledge-feelings with knowledge-value-feelings, and the pertinent presented objects will also be affected by this mistake. If there is hope that the mistakes resulting from such confounding are to be avoided, a contrast to the previously considered classes becomes evident in the fact that here freedom from relativity and an impersonal character (*Unpersönlichkeit*) impress us more strongly than their opposites, and that this is also much more widely acknowledged. It is quite striking that while the intellectually apprehended base of the impersonal dignitative here in question automatically declares itself, the most con-

9. See above, p. 103.

vinced adherent of the impersonally valuable or beautiful hesitates to name intellectually presented objects to which these properties can be confidently attributed. The base-object here in question is truth, on whose account knowledge-feelings are quite often called "truth-feelings," and truth itself taken to be a matter of feeling. It seems to me that such an interpretation is unneeded, since in the factuality of an objective of apprehension we have a quite sufficient characterization of truth. The relationship to feeling provides a desirable justification for the traditional coordination of the three notions of the Good, the Beautiful, and the True. No unprejudiced person would now dare to think of truth as relative or subjective. The relativistic attitude has, nonetheless, never completely disappeared since the days of Protagoras. By viewing truth by analogy with the personal moment in value and beauty, this attitude is given a sort of justification. But it is hardly necessary to bother ourselves again over such an old issue.

It will at present remain undecided to what extent truth gives us reason to make a transition from the personal to the impersonal in the case of the dignitatives of aesthetics or the value-domain. The more we find it reasonable to ascribe impersonal value, in our exact sense, to truth, the more we feel ourselves caught in a terminological dilemma, since there is no expression at all for the dignitative presented by the knowledge-feelings which could function as do "value" or "beauty." I shall try to overcome the shortcoming by introducing a term in connection with which the term "dignitative" was proposed above [10] and which has also occasionally been used in the present essay.[11] It seems natural to say of an object which has value or beauty (or their contraries), in an impersonally objective sense, that it has a certain dignity (*Dignität*). In this sense dignity is to be taken generally to mean an impersonal dignitative. Truth will then also have a dignity which will be closely related to value-dignity and to aesthetic dignity, but will also be essentially different from them, and which will appropriately be called "logical dignity." Prescientific language, and often scientific language also,[12] takes account of the affinity of these dignities by using the word "value," not only in the

10. Pp. 99 f.
11. See above, pp. 117 f.
12. See above, pp. 77 f., footnote 3.

field of the value-feelings, but also in that of the aesthetic and the logical feelings. This is plainly a wider sense against which there can of course be no real objection,[13] except that the apprehension of the peculiar characteristics of what we have called "value" is thereby rendered somewhat difficult, as well as the differentiation of logical dignity from value-dignity proper. In this wider sense, such value would naturally at the same time be impersonal value, if it is to be what we mean by dignity; and it would likewise, in a wider sense, be correlated in principle with personal value.

This, however, does not answer the question whether there are such personal values, or, better, whether there are dignitatives in the logical domain which are not dignities. There is hardly doubt left on this point once it is seen that we do not only react with knowledge-feelings to true statements. Whatever may be presented by feelings which belong to false judgments cannot be dignities; they are relative to a subject; they are, that is, personal logical dignitatives.

Turning to the dignities of the logical domain, a question arises whether they must all be the same since there only is a single sort of truth. Indeed, there probably is very great uniformity among them. Some variability is, however, provided for, since it is plain that not only the true, but also the probable, has logical dignity, of course of less strength, and that in this respect also truth shows itself to be a limiting case of probability.[14] It seems very dubious, however, whether self-evidence should be accorded the privileged logical dignity that one readily tends to ascribe to it. Without doubt, the evident judgment has a great advantage over the judgment without evidence, but this advantage pertains to the experience, as evidence itself also does, whereas logical dignity pertains to the objective, if I am indeed right in making the "objective"-conception of truth more basic than the "experience"-conception.[15] The evident judgment certainly has a special dignity, but it is not a logical but a value-dignity, one belonging to the domain of knowledge-value-feelings.

Our whole concern in the last paragraph can be summa-

13. Cf. "Für die Psychologie und gegen den Psychologismus," p. 13.
14. Cf. *Über Möglichkeit und Wahrscheinlichkeit*, pp. 473 f.
15. *Ibid.*, pp. 38 ff., 414 ff.

rized in a question, which we may formulate by making use of the expressions on which we have just agreed: To what extent do dignities correspond to the dignitatives of our different domains? We have investigated the domains of the value-dignitative and the aesthetic and the logical dignitatives. In order to have a more fitting adjective, we can speak of "timological dignitatives" instead of "value-dignitatives." [16] The fourth and last domain could perhaps be called the domain of the hedonic dignitatives, and we can now raise similar questions regarding it. Comparing it with the case of logical dignitatives, we see that the situation here is precisely reversed. In the case of the latter, objective, i.e., relation-free, states of affairs stand in the foreground, but, in the case of the hedonic dignitatives, relative or subjective states of affairs do so. It is quite doubtful whether any impersonal states are to be expected. I am only influenced by indirect considerations when I hold that there probably are hedonic dignities. Quite generally one can count on a certain analogy among the different classes of dignitatives. Whatever holds of all the other classes can hardly be completely lacking in the case of the hedonic dignitatives. What has previously been said [17] regarding the contrast of the correct and incorrect must also be taken into account in the hedonic domain. Wherever this contrast is present, we must expect that there will be a going-beyond the subjectivity of the apprehending subject. And, finally, what the hedonic feelings present is not anything relative to a subject, and is, to that extent absolute and impersonal. However, it cannot now be decided whether these points suffice to establish any conclusion. If there are hedonic dignities, they certainly lack the assistance from the ethical or aesthetic quarter which was so useful in setting up the logical dignities.

The extension of the value-notion to the notion of dignity can be taken as suggesting an analogous procedure in the case

16. I followed J. Kl. Kreibig's manner of expression (*Psychologische Grundlagen eines Systems der Werttheorie* [Vienna, 1902], especially pp. 3, 194); there is only this difference, that Kreibig seems to refer to the wider sense of the word "value" mentioned above, p. 154. In my paper "Für die Psychologie und gegen den Psychologismus," p. 13, I said "axiological." In actual use the term has been either misunderstood or not understood, so that I must now try to replace it by another, more suitable one.

17. See pp. 122 f., above.

of the relevant desideratives. It is clear that, besides value-desideratives, in the narrow sense, or besides timological desideratives, there are aesthetic, logical, and hedonic desideratives. Correspondingly, besides value-oughts or timological oughts, there are aesthetic, logical, or hedonic oughts, as long, that is, as the ought in queston is taken to be personal. But if to the personal dignitative an impersonal dignity is correlated, there would be no objections to a corresponding impersonal desiderative, which might then be called a "desideratum." If we grant these presuppositions, then there doubtless are aesthetic and logical desiderata. The decision concerning the hedonic desiderata depends upon the answer to the question of hedonic dignitatives.

Whatever may be the case regarding this and many other detailed matters, it is clear that emotional presentation reveals its importance in the most varied fields of mental life and in the most varied domains of objects. Further work on such presentation promises much-desired answers to important questions, not only in value-theory but also in the theory of beauty and even that of truth.

Appendix

Additional Notes Concerning the Treatise
On Emotional Presentation

[The original of these extremely condensed and sometimes cryptic notes to *On Emotional Presentation* was found in Meinong's *Nachlass* and was added by Dr. Rudolf Kindinger as an Appendix to the posthumously published *Gesamtausgabe*. Some of the Notes throw valuable light on Meinong's intentions, even if others raise questions. They have therefore been translated and published with the present translation of the text.]

ON THE CONCEPT AND TERM "EMOTIONAL PRESENTATION"

The first question concerning the legitimacy of the expression is: Where is the verb "to present" [*präsentieren*] actually used? Consider the following locutions: "The building presents itself very favorably from this position"; "Mr. X in this place presents himself in a very favorable light"; "A faculty presents one of its members for election to the rectorship of the university"; "An official file has a presentation number."

"To present," "to offer," and "to put at someone's disposal" are similarly used. In addition to these there is [in German] an etymological relation to *Vergegenwärtigen*, "representation," in which "presentness" is implied, though there also is presentation without such presentness.

In presentations of this kind various factors can be distinguished: the presentative who presents and the recipient to whom something is presented, though it remains questionable if there is a recipient in every case of presentation. At least the recipient would not seem to have to accept the pres-

[159]

entation in every case. There is in addition some result aimed at, for the sake of which an object, which may be called the *presentatum* [*Präsentat*], is presented.

This mode of treatment has its primary, most natural application to ideas as presentatives in contrast with thoughts (judgments and assumptions) as recipients. The object is the *presentatum*, the apprehension is the result aimed at. In this situation presentation reveals itself in three ways: (1) the presentative usually comes first in time; (2) the presentative conditions the direction of thought to the object in question; (3) the presentative is by its nature so closely related to the object to be apprehended that the object, the *presentatum*, will change whenever the presentative changes.

An analogous situation occurs in the case of thinking itself. Thinking apprehends an object which is its own. But this is conditioned by a variable component in the thought itself: the *content* which we contrast with the act of thought in virtue of its correlation with the object. Here there is a difference between the presenting function of thoughts and the having of ideas [*Vorstellen*]: the presentative does not precede the resultant presentation—the apprehension—in time. But we can broaden the notion of presentation by overlooking the time-aspect and by keeping merely to the thought of a condition and a correlation. We can then speak of the presenting function of contents even in the case of thoughts. There will, however, be a difference between this case and the having of ideas. In the latter case the presentative is external to the recipient, whereas, in thinking, we may expect it to have a more internal character, whether or not the whole thought-experience or merely the act-aspect is treated as recipient. These two cases of presentation, i.e., the having of an idea and thinking (where the thought-content is the presentative) may be called "external" and "internal" presentation [*äussere* and *innere Präsentation*], respectively.

It certainly is possible to speak of internal presentation in the case of ideas. Here, the content functions as presentative, and the act of having an idea functions as recipient.

In order to avoid any misunderstanding of the term "presentation" it should be explicitly stated that the activity of the presentative, which is part of the meaning of the term in its general common use—the soldier presents his rifle to his superior, the junior official presents his work to the senior official

—is not part of the meaning of the term as *we* use it. According to *our* usage, we are never in any want of something which does the presenting. In external presentation this is an idea or other experience; in internal presentation it is a content. In the same way, the recipient, or, rather, the percipient, is given as soon as something is apprehended. But activity does not characterize the presentative as such.

NOTES TO PAGE 3

Adopting a genetic point of view, H. Spencer differentiates his "feelings" into presentative, presentative-representative, and re-representative feelings. Cf. Groethuysen, "Das Mitgefühl," *Zeitschrift für Psychologie*, XXXIV (1904), 166. — Spencer's intentions are certainly different and involve no reference to an object.

The first time the term "presentation" was used as a technical term was in *Über Annahmen*, 2d ed., p. 28, I believe.

The term "presentation" had already been used in passing in *Erfahrungsgrundlagen*, p. 62, just before the beginning of the new paragraph.

NOTE TO PAGES 17 f.

The "defective object" to which we refer at this place is the object "experience without an object, or an experience with a peculiarly incomplete object." It might impede proper understanding to use the term "object" in this twofold context, and the term should be changed if the matter ever comes to be reformulated.

NOTES TO PAGE 23

Wherever act or content is as such and by itself apprehended, we must—in accordance with the present exposition—speak of a total and not of a partial presentation, since a total presentation is only *abstractively* processed—as pointed out in

Über Möglichkeit und Wahrscheinlichkeit, pp. 252 f. Still, one may feel moved to speak of partial presentation even in this case. This kind of partial presentation might perhaps be called "improper" as opposed to "proper" partial presentation. Or should some other term be invented?

For relevant remarks see page 39, below. The term "proper" is already used there, so cannot be utilized here.

In *Über Erfahrungsgrundlagen,* pp. 61 f., the question was already raised as to whether contents require some special abstraction in order to function as normal presentatives.

Since judgments, feelings, and desires tend to be imitated, we can argue that there is emotional presentation just as there is judgmental presentation. Cf. Lipps, *Die ethische Grundfragen,* p. 23. It is of course easier to proceed from an imaginary experience to similar actual experience than it is to proceed from an idea to the object that the idea is of.

NOTES TO PAGES 25 ff.

The foregoing discussions, by showing feelings and desires to be on a level with intellectual experiences in respect of the modes of presentation *other* than partial presentation, now lead us to assert the existence of partial presentation in their case also. It really is our basic task to show that there are, in fact, partial presentations in the case of the emotions. But that it is not always easy to do so is shown, for example, in psychology, by the fact of gustatory smelling, which common belief mistakes for tasting. Some smells are likewise called "pungent," though in their case, real smelling is not meant but rather real organic sensations of pain in the nose.

If we use linguistic expressions to prove the existence of emotional partial presentation, we must note that, in the case of primarily expressed experiences, language seems to be clearer concerning the objects of those experiences than in the case of secondarily expressed experiences. Emotional experiences are usually only secondarily expressed. The reason why primary expressions are clearer concerning their objects is as follows: When I assert "A is B" in the sense of judging it, the meaning of the word or statement immediately gives us the apprehended object. This is still so in the case of some secondary expressions, such as "I judge that *A* is *B*"; but it is not the case when I say "I am making a judgment regarding *A* and *B*" where the objective is not considered. The situation comes out even more strongly in the emotional domain. The sentence "I feel pain" does not say anything about the object; and in "The child desires the apple" the objectum is named but not the objective, not to speak of any desiderative.

In these circumstances it should not surprise us that linguistic expressions of feelings and desires, if they are secondary expressions—which they usually are—do not reveal partial presentation. It is easy for opponents of partial presentation to point out that such expressions merely reveal objects of intellectual presentation. The situation is different where, as happens occasionally, emotions are primarily expressed in the predicate of a sentence rather than in the subject. The predicate in "The flower is red" is analogous to the predicate in "The flower is pretty" and exhibits an object that can only be presented by a feeling. The following sentence functions similarly: "This or that should be the case." It seems as if being is put under an obligation, for whose presentation, however, only a desire can serve as presentative (if reference to experiences and inclusion of causal or conditioning relations have to be disallowed). The situation is similar in the case of the following locution: "In order for *A* to be, *B* should or must be"— or even "In order for *A* to be, *B* is." In that connection the purpose seems to have far more analogy to being-with than to being-thus-and-so, contrary to the statements made in a later paragraph. Should there be, among desideratives, a third analogy, i.e., one to being-thus-and-so?

NOTES TO PAGE 27

The discussion at this point takes care of A. Boltunow's criticisms of W. Liel, which are partly due to misunderstandings (*Über den Strukturzusammenhang zwischen den ästhetischen Wertgefühlen und seinen intellektuellen Voraussetzungen*, Berlin diss. [1909], p. 28).

That there is a very close connection between feelings and borrowed objects comes out in the fact that we could otherwise not decide to which of two simultaneously present objects a feeling relates. W. Strich mentions it in passing in *Das Wertproblem in der Philosophie der Gegenwart* (Leipzig diss. [1909], pp. 18 f.).

NOTE TO PAGE 28

The possibility of partial presentations in feelings was first considered in *Annahmen*, 2d ed., p. 29, footnote 2.

NOTES TO PAGES 29 f.

Erfahrungsgrundlagen, p. 31, brings out that the concept of causality is insufficient for, and inapplicable to, perception. This should also be compared with the discussion of the insufficiency of the causal concept toward the end of our treatise (pp. 95 f.).

As to the analogy between "green" and "beautiful" in matters of the so-called *Objektivation*, cf. R. Müller-Freienfels, "Neue Wertlehre," *Annalen der Philosophie*, I, 350 f. His interpretation of course favors subjectivity and relativity.

NOTES TO PAGE 36

According to Rehmke, even Heyde insists that there is a double subject in obligation (*Grundlegung der Wertlehre*, p. 67).

"I ought" is related to "It ought to be" as "I can" is related to "It can be." Cf. "Allegemeines zur Lehre von den Dispositionen," *Martinak-Festschrift*. Similarities become especially apparent in the case of dispositions insofar as capabilities [*Können*] are "capabilities for a purpose" ["*Zweckkönnen*"].

On purpose, see R. N. Cossmann, *Elemente der empirischen Teleologie* (Stuttgart, 1899) referred to by Höfler, *Studien* (*Akademieschrift*), I, paragraph 19.

NOTE TO PAGES 37 f.

On "ought" as a categorical demand of facts, see Lipps, *Ethische Grundfragen,* 2d ed., pp. 140 ff.

NOTE TO PAGES 42 f.

Lipps, too, uses the image of "shadowiness" in the case of nonperceptual apprehension, which is, at any rate, a special case. See *Ethische Grundfragen,* 2d ed., p. 33.

NOTE TO PAGES 46 f.

If the proper objects of ideation are, at the same time, the borrowed objects of judgments, feelings, and desires, then it is quite clear that the object of an idea is differently related to the different basic classes [of experience]. This is what is right in Brentano's view regarding the differences among intentional relations. The present discussion is essentially different, in that we claim that every class of experiences has its peculiar object in addition to its borrowed object; this is especially apparent when we consider the objective of a judgment.

NOTES TO PAGE 46

Proper objects and borrowed objects. In face of this contrast, we should not overlook the fact that it need not mean the same thing in the case of different experience-classes. Furthermore,

1. The contrast does not hold of one particular class in whose case there are only proper objects, i.e., ideas. Borrowed objects have their origin in psychological object-presupposition. They occur only in the case of dependent experiences,

whereas ideas are independent. — To the extent that there are dependent ideas we cannot exclude the possibility that there should be analogous borrowed objects. This is the case in regard to ideas of objects of higher order. It is not meaningless, in the case of "the difference between red and green," to speak of "red" as a borrowed object of the idea "difference." That is nonetheless very different from the case where the objectum "different" as a borrowed object is given to the judgment and assumption and where "the fact of difference" as an "objective" becomes a proper object of apprehension.

2. It is a most important fact that experiences belonging to different classes behave differently toward their proper objects (Meister,[1] June 18, 1919). Thinking, i.e., judging takes a central position insofar as through it the proper object is actually [fertig] apprehended, whereas it is not actually apprehended through ideas. Still, the having of an idea is already "directed" to the proper object, and one can at times doubt whether judgments are really more directed to their proper objects than to their borrowed objects. Certainly neither feelings nor desires are directed toward their proper objects but are directed either toward the objects of ideas or their substitutes, or to objectives, or to both. The proper object remains—so to speak—in the dark and can only be brought forth in exceptional circumstances to be apprehended. By their very nature feelings and desires are not instruments of apprehension. But this is what intellectual experiences precisely are, and this seems to be their real privilege or their characteristic achievement and might perhaps be used in their definition.

Cf. also below, p. 98; concerning desires, pp. 105 f.

NOTE TO PAGE 49

Concerning the possibility that content and object should be identical:

The following may be said: If blue is not itself a content, then experience tells me nothing about contents, and I can make no statement about such things. The answer is: I can make a negative statement in saying that I know a blue-content

1. Student of Meinong, later Professor of Pedagogy at Vienna.

is not itself blue. It must, however, be admitted that we have
no great choice of positive attributes in the case of the having
of ideas. Thinking fares better, since affirmation and negation
can be directly differentiated. In analogous fashion this can
be done in the case of feelings and desires. Cannot anything
positive be found in the case of ideas? See p. 39, above.

We can plainly show in the following way that the content
and object of ideas are not identical. I can have an idea of
something that does not exist and even cannot exist. But whatever it is through which I have such an idea, and which presents a perhaps impossible object, must at any rate exist and
cannot thus coincide with an object incapable of existence.

The relationship between content and object can be
loosened by considering the degree of exactness in apprehension; cf. "Über Abstrahieren und Vergleichen," *Gesammelte
Abhandlungen,* pp. 484 ff. This thought is applied epistemologically to "semiperception" in *Erfahrungsgrundlagen,* p. 96.

NOTE TO PAGES 49 f.

If contents are here called the variable ingredients of ideas
to which acts are opposed as their constant ingredients, we
have to ask: How should we deal with that which is constant
in the apprehension of objects? Take, for example, the moment
which is necessary for the apprehension of the object-status
itself.

The answer can be given with the help of a less difficult
example. On one occasion I think of a red ball, on another of a
blue ball; on one occasion of a white horse, on another of snow.
Will what is common to our means of apprehension be counted
as part of the act? Certainly not. For I can compare the red
ball with a red cube, and now the previously constant shape
becomes the variable. The same holds for white in the
second example. Generally we may say: Whatever varies with
the object belongs to the content. The constant part as such
does not forthwith belong to the act. In the same way, not
everything variable is by itself part of the content, since even
the act is variable. Rather, everything which remains constant with constant object belongs to the content, though even
there constancy is only a symptom, not the essence of the
content. In fine, only one characteristic is important for a con-

tent, i.e., being a partial presentative. All ideas, finally, have this in common, that they are ideas of objects. And so the part of ideas which ultimately apprehends the objective nature of objects is the content alone, not the act, despite all community and invariability.

NOTE TO PAGES 51 f.

The analogy in the relation between a and b, and a' and b, must, in the sense of what is here said, be further determined as follows: b can be related to a and a' in the same way only insofar as the relation is taken, not in its totality, but merely in respect of a certain abstractive part. The distance from a to b can be the same as the distance from a' to b. But the total spatial relation between a and b, and a' and b, cannot be the same, since relative position must be considered as well as distance.

NOTES TO PAGES 52 f.

The supplementary note above (note to pp. 49 f.) touches on the fact that a possible common component of red and blue need not point to the act.

In regard to common components see (despite an otherwise very different meaning-context) Zilsel, *Anwendungsproblem,* especially his theorem of "Transmitted Reduction of Content" [*durchgreifende Inhaltsabnahme*].

NOTE TO PAGES 60 f.

On the point of view here advanced, the effect is not only dependent upon the cause, but the cause is also dependent upon the effect. Is a moment of priority not therefore also involved in independence [*Selbständigkeit*]?

NOTE TO PAGE 64 AND LATER PAGES

There are psychological presuppositions which are not object-presuppositions. Thus in the case of desires there are assumption-feelings [*Annahmegefühle*] in which the value of what is desired becomes manifest. Such pleasures should never be considered the proper objects of the desire. See also Lipps, *Ethische Grundfragen*, 2d ed., pp. 6 f.

NOTE TO PAGES 83 f.

At the end of the first paragraph the claim is made that feelings are qualitatively different. The claim is verified by the fact that there seem to be characteristically quantitative differences in feelings. In general, value-feelings are less intense than sensual and aesthetic feelings. Knowledge-feelings seem to be closer to value-feelings in this respect. Is it possible that judgment-feelings have properties in common, as idea-feelings also have?

NOTE TO PAGE 90

It seems that "true" cannot naturally be coordinated with "beautiful" and "good" (see also pp. 103, 153). It is said, indeed, that a flower is beautiful, that an action is good, that a judgment is true. But the flower is beautiful because it is blue and has such and such a shape. The action is good because another person's interest is put before one's own. But in that case "true" seems to be a parallel case to "blue" or "altruistic." It does not designate the proper object presented by the knowledge-feeling but at most the object borrowed by this feeling. In reality we are here only dealing with matters of expression. "True" has, in the first place, an intellectual meaning to which corresponds the concept of an objective and the concept of an experience. But, in addition to this intellectual meaning, there is an emotional meaning of "truth" in virtue of which something is called "true" if it attracts a justified knowledge-feeling. In this sense we can speak of truth-feelings which can genuinely be coordinated with feelings of beauty and with (so to speak) goodness-feelings.

NOTE TO PAGES 94 f.

The following is a proof that objectives are objects of higher order. The law of ordered series established for complexes and *relata* holds for them also. According to this law, an ordered series is open in the upward and closed in the downward direction.

NOTE TO PAGES 95 f.

For greater detail about the contrast of positive and negative in the case of objectives see my fourth lecture on the theory of knowledge [Carton III, Sheet 10, of Meinong's literary remains], additional notes to page 1.

NOTE TO PAGE 98

The "ought-to-be-for-the-sake-of" [*"Fürsollen"*] seems to be analogous to being-with rather than being-thus-and-so. Is their perhaps a case of desire which can be coordinated with being-thus-and-so? Cf. above, p. 103.

NOTE TO PAGE 102

A position in respect of the contrast between ideal and real may belong to the quality of dignitatives and desideratives. When we were considering justification and pertinent knowledge (p. 104), we merely pointed to the ideal character of dignitatives and desideratives. We should, however, have dealt with it more fully here. Witasek has already said that beauty is ideal (*Ästhetik*, pp. 14 f.). Cf. Witasek, p. 27.

NOTE TO PAGE 103

Qualitative objectivity in the case of an end: teleological, nonteleological, dysteleological.

NOTE TO PAGES 127 f.

The *Martinak-Festschrift*, section 2, now deals with dispositions.

NOTE TO PAGE 132

Perhaps a third kind of other-presented object will join the two classes of other-presented objects here mentioned if a noumenal object is set beside the phenomenal object. Cf. *Erfahrungsgrundlagen,* p. 98, first paragraph.

NOTES TO PAGES 144 f.

Lipps has already dealt with the subjunctive form "I should wish" (*Ethische Grundfragen,* 2d ed., p. 74).

For relevant, sometimes right and sometimes wrong statements, cf. Walter Strich, *Das Wertproblem in der Philosophie der Gegenwart* (Leipzig diss., 1909), pp. 36 f.

NOTE TO PAGE 145

Now turn to the *Martinak-Festschrift,* on pages 39 ff., or perhaps before this page, for further detail about "can" [ability, *"Können"*] in the dispositional sense of the word.

NOTE TO PAGE 146

Witasek speaks of the relativity of aesthetic determinations, which he in principle accepts, as *"Aussergegenständlichkeit"* ["externality to the object"]; see *Ästhetik,* pp. 18 and 27.

Selected Bibliography

ALL WORKS OF ALEXIUS MEINONG cited in the footnotes of *On Emotional Presentation* will be found in the seven-volume *Gesamtausgabe,* edited by Rudolf Haller and Rudolf Kindinger, in course of publication since 1968 by the Akademische Druck- und Verlagsanstalt of Graz, Austria. The reader will experience no difficulty in using cross-references since the *Gesamtausgabe* reproduces the pagination of the journals or books in which Meinong's work originally appeared. References in the footnotes and bibliography to the *Gesammelte Abhandlungen* are to the two-volume work published in Leipzig in 1912; i.e., they do not refer to the first three volumes of the *Gesamtausgabe.*

Titles of the volumes in the *Gesamtausgabe* are to be as follows:

I.   Abhandlungen zur Psychologie
II. Abhandlungen zur Erkenntnistheorie und Gegenstandstheorie
III. Abhandlungen zur Werttheorie
IV. Über Annahmen
V.   Über philosophische Wissenschaft und ihre Propädeutik
     Über die Stellung der Gegenstandstheorie im System der Wissenschaften
     Über dis Erfahrungsgrundlagen unseres Wissens
     Zum Erweise des allgemeinen Kausalgesetzes
VI. Über Möglichkeit und Wahrscheinlichkeit

VII. Selbstdarstellung, vermischte Schriften
Index

MEINONG

[Items are listed in chronological order.]

"Phantasievorstellung und Phantasie." *Zeitschr. f. Philosophie u. philos. Kritik*, XCV (1889), 174 ff. *Gesammelte Abhandlungen*, Vol. I.

"Zur Theorie der Komplexionen und Relationen." *Zeitschr. f. Psychol. u. Phys. d. Sinnesorgane*, II (1891), 245–65. *Gesammelte Abhandlungen*, Vol. I.

"Über die Bedeutung des Weberschen Gesetzes." *Zeitschr. f. Psychol. u. Phys. d. Sinnesorgane*, XI (1896). *Gesammelte Abhandlungen*, Vol. II.

Psychologisch-ethische Untersuchungen zur Werttheorie. Graz, 1894.

"Über Gegenstände höherer Ordnung und deren Verhältnis zur inneren Wahrnehmung." *Zeitschr. f. Psychol. u. Phys. d. Sinnesorgane*, XXI (1899), 189 ff.

Über Annahmen. 1st ed., 1902. 2d ed., Leipzig, 1910.

"Bemerkungen über den Farbenkörper und das Mischungsgesetz." *Zeitschr. f. Psych. u. Phys. d. Sinnesorgane*, XXXIII (1903), 20 ff. *Gesammelte Abhandlungen*, Vol. I.

Untersuchungen zur Gegenstandstheorie und Psychologie. Leipzig, 1904. *Gesammelte Abhandlungen*, Vol. II.

"Über Urteilswertgefühle, was sie sind und was sie nicht sind." *Archiv für die gesamte Philosophie*, VI (1905), 21–58. *Gesammelte Abhandlungen*, Vol I.

Über die Erfahrungsgrundlagen unseres Wissens. Berlin, 1906.

"Über die Stellung der Gegenstandstheorie im System der Wissenschaften." *Zeitschr. f. Philos. u. philos. Kritik*, CXXIX (1906), 60 ff. Separately published as book, Leipzig: Voigtländer, 1907.

"Für die Psychologie und gegen den Psychologismus in der allgemeinen Werttheorie." *Logos*, III (1912), 13 ff.

Gesammelte Abhandlungen. 2 vols. Leipzig, 1912.

Über Möglichkeit und Wahrscheinlichkeit. Leipzig, 1915.

Grundlegung zur allgemeinen Werttheorie. Graz, 1923.

OTHER AUTHORS

Chisholm, Roderick F. *Realism and the Background of Phenomenology.* 2d ed. New York, 1967.
Dawes, Hicks G. "The Philosophical Researches of Meinong." *Mind,* XXXI (1922).
Eaton, H. O. *Austrian Philosophy of Values.* Norman, Okla., 1930.
Findlay, J. N. *Meinong's Theory of Objects and Values.* 2d ed. Oxford, 1963.
Kindinger, Rudolf. *Philosophenbriefe, aus der wissenschaftlichen Korrespondenz von Alexius Meinong.* Graz, 1965.
Russell, Bertrand. "Meinong's Theory of Complexes and Assumptions." *Mind,* VIII (1904).

Index

Perceptual idea, 55
Personal value, xxv, lvi, 124, 136, 138, 141, 150
Phantasievorstellung, 24
Phenomenal object, 171
Pietà, lxi
Pleasant, liv, 32, 91, 95
Possibility, 143, 146
Potentialization, 127
Presentation, xxix, xxxiv, xli, xlv–vii, lxii, 3, 4, 5, 6, 7, 30, 38, 151, 159, 160; by dissimilarity, 57; internal, 160, 161; proper (*eigentlich*), 39; by similarity, 57
Presentative, lix, 5, 160, 163; by dissimilarity, 58
Presentatum, 160
Presenting: emotion, 132; experience, xlviii
"Presumptive" evidence, lxv
Presupposition, 27; of feeling, 68
Presuppositional: content, lxi, 27, 84; experience, 92; judgment, 86; object, xxxvii, lvi, lxii, lxv, lxvi, 9, 27, 47, 88, 118, 119, 121, 122; objective, 85, 86; relationship, 27
Primary expression, 162
Proper: content, 28; object, lxvi, 73, 118, 119, 121, 165, 166, 169
Property, moral and aesthetic, liii
Pseudo-existent, 54; object, xli
Psychic experience, 9
Psychological: object-presupposition, 75, 77, 78, 92, 142; presupposition, lxi, 6, 27, 46, 59, 61, 64, 65, 66, 67, 68, 71, 73, 75, 85, 126, 168
Purpose, 34, 67, 146
Purposiveness, 35, 38

Qualitative objectivity, 170
Quasi-intellectual, 31
Quasi-serious experience, 45

Real, 170
Realism, Chisholm's and Meinong's conception of, xxix
Reference: to an object's being, 17, 52; to an object's being thus-and-so, 17, 52

Referring, 71
Relata, 92, 93, 95
Relation, lv
Relation-free value, 133, 134, 135
Relative value, 133, 135
Relativity doctrine, 128
Representation, 159
Round square, xxxvi, 20
Russell, Bertrand, xxx, 10
Russellian paradox, 11

Secondary expression, 163
Seinsmeinen, xxxii
Self: observation, 8; presentation, xviii, xix, xlviii–li, lix, 6, 7, 8, 10, 22, 25, 39, 46, 56, 57, 90; presentative, 132
Semiperception, 167
Sensation, 31, 70
Sense-judgment, 116, 117
Sensuous: desire, 88; feeling, 31
Serious: experience, 40, 46, 101; feelings, 25; ideas, xlvi, 24, 40; presupposition (*Ernstvoraussetzung*), 81; thought, 24
Serious-like experience, 45
Shadowiness, 165
Shadowy assumption, 43, 44
Similarity, 57, 92
Sollen, xxiv, 36
Sorrow, 111, 112, 113
Soseinsmeinen, xxxii
Spencer, H., 161
Subsistence, xxxvi, 61, 121

Thought: content, 4, 101; experience, 4, 17, 42, 74
Total: other-presentation, 46; presentation, xix, xlvii, 24, 25, 32, 40, 41, 46, 56, 57, 58, 161; presentative, 38
Transmitted reduction of content, 168
True, liv, 91, 95, 169
Truth, 118, 137, 154, 169
Truth-dignitative, 119
Truth-feelings, 117, 119

Ultimate object, xliv
Unpleasant, 103